Shotgun Summer

The Other Side of Why

Sean Mulcahy

Shotgun Summer: The Other Side of Why
Copyright © 2023 by Sean Mulcahy

Editing by Leya Booth
Cover, interior, and ebook design by Steven W. Booth
Cover photo by Tayne Smith

ISBN: 979-82-18132-57-6

230507

Table of Contents

Shotgun Summer looks at the realistic gritty world of policing in a major city. Police officers across America deal with the types of calls and people portrayed in this book every day. Sean Mulcahy brings the reader into the dirty hallways and streets where real police work happens.

— Chief of Police **John Meier**, (Ret.)

Shotgun Summer paints graphically clear details that make for a compulsively readable account of police work. I truly felt transported to the scenes described in *Shotgun Summer*.

—Deputy Chief **Cyril Ritter** (Ret.), Kansas City, Missouri Police Department

Shotgun Summer is a gritty, authentic look at policing on the streets of a major metropolitan city. It is sometimes raw in its depictions, sometimes humorous but always riveting. As a retired 40-year Law Enforcement Officer, I would highly recommend *Shotgun Summer*; Sean Mulcahy makes you feel you are there when it's happening!

—Detective **Mark Meyer** (Ret.), Overland Park, Kansas Police Department, Criminal Investigation Division

Acknowledgments

Joe Neenan
I had many long conversations with Joe over certain aspects of the book. His encouragement helped me sustain my work over three years.

Casey Mulcahy
Casey painstakingly read over each chapter for insights to help me write a better book.

John Prussing
John lent me his ear for three years while I talked about this book. A heroic feat.

Leya Booth
Nobody can write a book without a great editor. I had one in Leya.

I would like to express my deepest gratitude to my wife, Cathy. She put up with my police work for over twenty-five years without complaining too much. Through good times and bad, I had her support. She gave up so much of her life to support me in mine.

Thank You

A man once told me about his plans to sail across the Pacific Ocean. So I asked him, "Isn't that dangerous?"

He replied with a subtle grin, "You can't have an adventure without a little risk." Well, I guess if that's true, then this was the start of one hell of an adventure.

Sean Mulcahy
January 2023

Prologue

I arrived at the scene; my backup had disappeared. Then I heard the screams. I peeked around the corner of the tenement apartment building and saw two men holding down a young naked girl, viciously raping her while she screamed in absolute terror.

This is one of my stories from the first three years I worked as a patrolman for the Kansas City Missouri Police Department.

The book will let you experience the action and the darker side of police work. You'll feel the rush of adrenaline through your body as you realize the suspect in the shooting you are working is standing right behind you with a

12-gauge shotgun, and your hand, slippery from the victim's blood, can't grip your holstered weapon. You will cry, feel anger, and laugh at some of these encounters.

I want to immerse the reader in the situations I talk about in this book. How would you react? Do you find yourself becoming a little jaded about what is going on? Perhaps a lack of empathy for the officers or maybe the people they encounter? Can you understand how officers could become this way, or would you be above it all? Now, notice how your opinion of the police changes as you go through the stories. It will one way or the other, I promise.

I answer timeless questions and misconceptions about the police, like why aren't you out stopping real crime instead of writing me a ticket? Why did you have to get physical with that person? You don't even care about the people in the inner city, do you? These questions and more are addressed by using actual police experiences as examples. *Shotgun Summer* is a collection of over sixty-five stories of my first three years on patrol.

Chapter 1:
The Beginning

I grew up tough. It might have been part of my nature all along, but maybe it was a trait picked up from my environment. Attending a Catholic grade school in a different part of the city from where I lived gave me a deeper perspective on life than my neighborhood friends enjoyed. At too early of an age, I learned life was not always fair and could be cruel, dangerous, and even deadly.

In fourth grade, the boy across the aisle was in a knife fight away from school. Small penknives were used with only one-inch blades, which probably saved his life. The kid was resilient and only missed two weeks of school while he healed from his numerous cuts and stab wounds. Nonchalantly, he said the fight ended in a draw.

Then there was the time an eleven-year-old sixth-grader, Lori Sandifer, became pregnant. The nuns set an example by tutoring Lori after school and generally looked after her. They didn't judge or condemn but instead ensured Lori ate healthily and received proper medical care.

Lori's apartment building was across the street from the school. One day in the middle of class, everyone stopped and stared out the windows. We watched as two MPs removed Lori's twenty-something paramour from her apartment building in handcuffs. It turns out the soldier was AWOL, and nobody ever said who told the Army where to find him.

A few weeks later, Lori moved away and was never heard from again. I hoped she fared well.

Another time, a seventh-grader, John Diaz, was attacked by three hoodlums on the way home from school. As a result, John lost an eye when one of the assailants hit him in the face with a brick. The reason for the assault: They wanted his leather jacket, and John wouldn't give it to them.

I was in several fights in grade school. Back in those days, the teachers never said much about it, thinking that is what boys do and was a part of growing up. Then one day, fighting seemed a little bit more than one of life's learning experiences.

In my eight grade year I was forced into a fight with a classmate, Louie Martinez, a relatively thin boy and not strong. Louie thought I was making eyes at his girlfriend and wanted to fight. After one fist to my face and yelling for him to stop, he hit me a second time. That was it, I hit him twice, and he fell to the ground unconscious.

Some other kids helped Louie into the school. He slept through the first two classes until morning break when Sister Ann told two boys to take Louie to the bathroom and splash some water on his face. Sister probably thought he was hungover again.

The next day after school, three thugs, friends of Louie's from the local high school, showed up and wanted to fight. I was ready to take on all three of them and slowly started walking in their direction.

The biggest of the three must have gotten scared because he pulled out a switchblade; my guess was to even the odds. I liked to fight but wasn't stupid enough to get into a knife fight and walked back into school, figuring they wouldn't follow me in there.

Someone told Sister Ann, who went outside and threatened to call the police immediately if they didn't leave. No police were called, no parents were called, and that was the end of the matter. It was how things were handled back then; it was not considered a big event where I went to school.

Four months later, the newspaper ran a front-page story about the delinquent who pulled a knife on me. It seems he was charged with raping and then stabbing his high school teacher to death. I still wonder if he used the same knife he pulled on me.

Along with these experiences, the sisters instilled the values of helping others and being fair and honest in all aspects of life. They also stressed the greatest profession anyone could ever choose would be in the service of others. The nuns never said what that profession was, but I would know it when the time was right.

That was one side of my early development. The other side came from sports, where we were taught the value of working with others to achieve a common goal. The coaches called it teamwork.

They also explained the meaning of perseverance as the ability to stay focused on the desired outcome of events despite obstacles along the way.

The coaches talked about the value of hard work and self-discipline. If you want something, work for it; nobody will give it to you. Have enough self-discipline to do what is needed to reach that goal and avoid those things that keep you from it.

My head coach taught me the most important lesson of all, the one that sums up the rest. He said, "All personal choices can have good or bad consequences and you alone are responsible for the decisions you make."

During the next ten years, I accomplished some personal goals. I was married with children, a mortgage, a four-year college degree, and could continue on the same path through life being perfectly happy, but something was missing. I felt it deep down gnawing on the edge of my soul; whatever it was, it was a lot bigger than me.

Then one day, without any fanfare, my life changed forever. A friend who was an officer suggested applying for the police department. He said it was a lot of fun to chase bad guys all around, stick them in jail, and in the process, get into lots of fights. I thought, why the hell not, it sounded like fun.

As if to confirm my decision, I suddenly remembered what Sister Ann told me way back in grade school: "The greatest profession anyone could ever choose would be in the service of others, and I would know that profession when the time was right."

Deciding to apply for the police department was only the first step. The hiring process was a long six months, tedious and bureaucratic, but still kind of fun. They did thorough background and financial checks, physical and psychological exams, and eye and lie detector tests.

The lie detector test was a little annoying. The polygraph operator, a grizzled, old, retired detective, asked toward the end of the test, "The last time you had sex with an animal, did you like it?"

"How in the hell am I supposed to answer that question?"

The operator barked in a firm, agitated voice, "Just answer the damn question!"

Think about it. You'd be guilty of bestiality whether you answered yes or no. "No!" It must have been the correct answer because I passed the test, but strangely nobody else remembered getting that question.

After the six-month process, the police finally offered me a job. The police academy was scheduled to start in June, and I'd turn twenty-eight in August. Soon I would come to learn that surviving to thirty-one would be a challenge.

Over the next three years, I arrested murderers, rapists, armed robbers, drug dealers, prostitutes, pimps, and many others. During this time, I suffered a bruised trachea, a broken hand, heat stroke, a fence-punctured hand, two broken teeth, and a severe head injury. I was shot at, and covered with human and animal excrement, lice, fleas, and other parasites. I worked in an extremely dangerous part of the city and endured it all to protect and serve the citizens in my district.

Chapter 2:
Police Academy Training

As far as police training goes, I include here only a few parts of the academy to save time and get to this book's real purpose, working the streets. This is not to diminish the seriousness of the training, but it would take a whole book to cover all the aspects of the academy. Suffice to say, it was, for the most part, a quasi-military structure within the bounds that the recruits were still civilians.

The academy turned out to be a whole floor on the local community college campus. The uniform for the academy was plain black dress shoes, black socks, a black belt, black pants, a short-sleeve button-down white Oxford shirt with a black tie, and a shiny chrome name tag.

The first morning, the sergeant in charge walked up to the class, standing in small groups outside the classroom. Sarge looked at his watch and yelled like a military drill instructor to line up, shut up, and stand at attention. The academy had started.

Later in the day, Sarge told the class to report to the school's gymnasium in our officially issued physical-education-and-defensive-tactics clothes. These were white samurai-looking outfits called a gi (pronounced *gee*, like in *geese*.) The gi was a loose-fitting, mid-arm-length, wraparound, no-button top held in place by a sturdy cloth belt and loose-fitting pants secured by a drawstring. We could wear running shoes of our own choice.

The instructor, Tom, turned out to be a good guy who wanted us to stay alive. On the first day, Tom said two things I will never forget: "You will get cut in a knife fight, and when you are hurt, shot, or are being beaten to death, do not give up; you can survive!"

His words saved me a couple of times.

During one defensive tactics class, we practiced making a suspect go unconscious without hurting the subject or the officer. The tactic, developed by Tom, was called the lateral neck restraint and proved highly effective when used correctly.

The hold could be applied from the right or the left side and the front or back of the suspect. The crook of the elbow had to be at the center of the throat and pointed down with the forearm and biceps on either side of the neck. The officer's free hand would grip the back of the engaged wrist and push. The resulting vise-like grip would close off arterial flow to the brain, rendering the suspect unconscious within seconds. There are a lot of other fine details involved, but that was the gist of it.

During practice, a big, strong recruit named Barney did not quite get his elbow centered on my neck and about crushed my trachea. It felt like a chicken bone was lodged horizontally in my throat. The instructor sent me to the hospital for X-rays, and there, the doctor said to take it easy for a couple of days.

No one could afford an injury at this point, as you would be dropped from the class. My throat hurt swallowing or talking; my wife noticed and wanted me to quit. I learned not to speak to her about any injuries that did not show or the dangerous situations I encountered.

Tom also had us practice knife blocks and pistol retention until we could do it without even thinking about it. To do something without even thinking about it might sound like a tired cliché, but when I was in and out of consciousness in a life-and-death fight, thanks to Tom, nobody could take my gun. He also read all the injury and use-of-force reports generated in the department. Tom must have had to spend many hours reading mine but never complained.

Chapter 3:
Felony Car Stop a Major

Even training, on occasion, could be funny.

One day all the recruits went to a park with a long circular drive several miles around at the base of a tall hill. Because of the hill, you could not see around the curve in the road, and there was almost no traffic, making it a perfect area to practice radio procedures and felony car stops. The setup was for two suspects to be parked out of sight about a half a mile away in a red Chrysler four-door. The suspects in the car were reportedly bank robbers, and each cadet would take a turn engaging the suspects in their parked vehicle. Next to the car were class instructors who would grade each car check. A dispatcher would call a recruit in a real police car using a practice radio channel.

Right from the start, the very first recruit ran into trouble. Tony Jenkins received his dispatched call and headed out full of intense anticipation. When what turned out to be halfway to the suspect vehicle, Tony spotted a red four-door Chrysler with a male suspect behind the wheel.

Tony got on the radio and reported to the dispatcher that he had one suspect and the suspect vehicle parked on Penn Valley Road. Tony called for another officer, then, using the loudspeaker, ordered the driver to exit the car with his hands in the air. He then reported the second suspect, a female who poked her head over the seat.

I knew something was wrong when an instructor standing nearby said Tony was too close; the real suspect's car and actors were farther away. Before anyone could speak, Tony escalated the call, screaming into the radio that the suspects were fleeing the scene. The instructors standing around started yelling, "What the hell is going on? There's not supposed to be any car chase!"

One of the instructors finally figured out what was happening when a major and his secretary flew past him, chased by Tony, using the vehicle's red lights and siren. An instructor grabbed a mike and repeatedly yelled for the chase to end, scenario over. Since Tony was excited, he had forgotten to take his thumb off the mike button, and nobody could get on the air, consequently Tony did not hear the orders to stop. Luckily, Tony finally released the mike button and terminated the chase before entering a traffic-congested street.

As far as I know, no instructor received any disciplinary action for losing control of the situation, and no reason was ever given why a major was parked with his secretary.

Chapter 4:
On the Wall

One crucial technique we used and is mentioned numerous times in this book is putting someone on the wall. When an officer puts someone on the wall, it means the suspect has to literally put his hands on a wall or some convenient surface and take a step back.

This is a safer way for the officer to frisk, search, or handcuff someone. If the person refuses, you physically put that person on the wall by grabbing a hand, putting it on the wall, and kicking their feet away, all the while giving verbal commands.

If the suspect wants, he can of course push himself away from the wall, but it takes some effort and gives a second for the officer to react. If someone came off the wall, we were instructed the fight was on. This means the suspect has initiated an attack on the officer, who then must strike back decisively and without hesitation.

Reacting first is essential and is usually done by slamming your body into the back of the suspect, and pinning him to the wall before cuffing him. Another way to stop the suspect is to strike or kick the body or head, stunning the subject until you can get him cuffed.

The officer can also grab the suspect's arm, straighten it, push on the outside of the elbow, and force the suspect to the ground using pain compliance. This move is called an armbar takedown. If the suspect does not comply with the officer's commands at this point, the suspect's elbow can be dislocated but, usually, the initial pain is enough to gain compliance.

Grabbing the suspect's arm without some pain compliance leaves the officer open for a counterstrike to the face. I preferred to body slam the suspect back into the wall. The suspect isn't hurt and will usually comply without any more trouble. If the suspect succeeded in turning around, I used a strike to the face to disorient him, then forcibly put the suspect on the ground.

These were the standard practices taught in the academy. It might appear aggressive or violent, but if an officer does not act first and with sufficient force, he opens himself up to being assaulted and hurt by the suspect.

Something to remember if you are forced to fight, it is best to end it as quickly as possible. The longer the fight lasts, the more the suspect's chances of winning are increased. If the officer loses the fight, there is about a fifty percent chance the suspect will take his gun, then there is an eighty percent chance the officer will be shot, and if shot once, there is a ninety percent chance he will be shot more than once.

Keeping all this in mind leads to the next chapter, Fighting.

Chapter 5:
Fighting

One aspect of training I have to talk about now before continuing with the rest of this book is fighting. Imagine every time you approach someone at your job, you check if they have anything in their hands, you look at their waistline to see if there is a weapon tucked away, you observe their stance to see if they are tense, turned to one side, or leaning forward. You listen to their tone of voice, whether it is calm or angry, and look at their eyes for signs of drug usage.

If an attack comes, you will have to defend yourself, and you have on average less than a second to decide how to do it. That is why you don't stand close to anybody; the distance gives you a little more time to react. You position your body at a right angle and your gun side away from the other person. This makes it more difficult for someone to grab your gun and makes you a smaller target. You keep your hands free to defend yourself or take the offensive.

On about every call or self-initiated action, these precautions play over in your mind; you are always on the alert. It doesn't mean you are paranoid or afraid to do your job; you are simply aware of all the potential dangers present on almost any call. Even the most innocuous encounter can sometimes turn violent.

If an assault against you occurs, you should already know what to do; there is no time to think. Case in point, say you have chased someone up three flights of rickety wooden stairs on an outside fire escape, and the possibly armed subject is wanted for murder. What would you do if he suddenly turned around and charged you? Your second is up; how did you react?

What if a drug-crazed pimp comes at you wanting to pummel you with fists covered in razor-sharp rings? What would you do if a drug dealer with his hands on the wall suddenly spins around and attacks you? Say someone pulls a butcher knife on you during a traffic stop; what do you do? Most of the time, the simple answer is you fight, and when you fight, you have to win.

When you fight to win, it's vicious, and no holds barred and everything is on the table. This means you use your knowledge of specific pain compliance holds, hands, fists, elbows, slapper, feet, knees, batons, eye gouges, teeth, groin punches, even a lit cigarette to the face. You use and do anything you can to stay alive; it's desperate.

In a fight, you don't say to yourself, "Oh, I can't do this or that," you don't have time to think. You do whatever is necessary, including shooting someone.

Some of the most dangerous fights occur when you chase someone on foot. These chases are usually spontaneous and involve someone you are familiar with and know has a warrant of sufficient magnitude like murder, rape, or armed robbery for you to risk your life pursuing them in the first place.

By spontaneous, I mean you are driving down a street patrolling your district, and suddenly you see a man you know. He has a murder warrant out for his arrest, you try to stop him, and of course, he runs from you.

Now when you run after him, you are going through backyards, behind businesses, and into alleyways. You are alone, and help is miles away. You are chasing someone looking at twenty years to life behind bars; if you catch him, why would he not fight you? What does he have to lose? He has already proved himself to be a violent person by murdering someone. What are you going to do?

Some people argue you could let the suspect go, pretend you didn't see him, and catch him another time. You could wait until backup arrives, but the suspect would be long gone by then. In these scenarios, you have let a murderer go to harm citizens again. Your standard is to "protect and serve," and not just when it's convenient.

This is what it means to put your life on the line for the citizens of your district. To my way of thinking, doing nothing is just wrong.

It's not like what's on TV; at the end of the day, you don't get to take off the makeup and fake blood and go home. Think about that for a moment; if you don't win, you're probably not going home. If you lose, you will be injured or shot; there is no other outcome. This is worth repeating: You don't go home if you lose the fight. It's that simple.

I lost two fights. I went to the hospital both times and was admitted once.

Fighting to win also comes with a caveat. You may only use the force that a reasonable person would use. This means what a reasonable person would do in any of the above situations, assuming they wouldn't run away. You can only use that amount of force necessary to stop the threat; you have to stop once you achieve that outcome and render immediate aid if needed.

Well, soon enough, I graduated from the academy and would be with a field training officer or FTO for the next six weeks. Now begins a new chapter and actual work on the street.

Chapter 6:
Break-In Training

I didn't know what to expect, maybe writing some tickets and arresting a few drunks or breaking up fights, minor stuff. The things I actually did and encountered were way beyond my expectations. I was in another world, and would witness and do things few people would ever experience or even hear about during their entire lifetime.

I went to Center Zone for break-in training. It was subdivided into patrol sectors, 10-20-30-40. I was in Center Zone evenings two, sector 30, patrol district two, or radio number 232.

It's kind of confusing but necessary to understand how many officers operated on one shift. In Center Zone on any given shift, there were four sectors; each sector had a sergeant, five officers, and a wagon driver for a total of seven officers, Each sector was the same, four sectors totaled twenty officers, four sergeants, and four wagon drivers, for a total of twenty-eight police officers on the street on any shift. However, that number only existed on paper.

The count varied wildly depending on sick days, injury days, training days, vacation days, days off, and constantly being understaffed in the first place. The other zones, South, North, East, and Metro, had a similar makeup. Most of the time a sector operated with only a sergeant and four officers.

At the time, the Center Zone station building was a run-down, old, converted one-story bank building. It was small and had a mixed smell of vomit, alcohol, unwashed body odors, cigarette smoke, and old smelly clothes. Smoking was permitted anywhere in the station except the holding cell, located right in the center of the building. The holding cell was a big cage with benches for arrestees to sit on while waiting to be processed or make bail.

At the rear of the building was a small dingy locker room. Our uniforms were a WWII

Army tan shirt and dull green pants. You had to have everything perfect. You wore a hat, name tag, badge, tie, gun belt with extra ammo, and handcuffs, all in the proper place and perfectly polished or ironed. The GOs, or general orders, were in a three-ring binder that specified where everything was affixed to the uniform and a thousand other rules.

At first, I was afraid I would forget something, but after a while dressing correctly became second nature. That first day in the locker room, nobody even acknowledged my presence. The other officers did not want to bother getting to know you until you proved you had what it took to be an officer in Center Zone.

After dressing out, I headed to the roll call room, where we stood at attention while being inspected. Sometimes inspections included gun and equipment checks, which were detail-oriented and followed exact guidelines. During these special inspections, orders were given to present arms. The sergeant would walk down the row of officers grabbing each gun, unloading it, and checking it for dirt, proper department-issued ammo, and wear and tear.

Some officers were caught with larger, heavier bullets and powder charges. They believed these bullets had more stopping power, but with big loads, the bullets could pass through their intended targets and hurt innocent people. This is not to say department-issued ammo could not do the same, but uniformity among the ranks and the equipment had to be maintained.

After inspections, the desk sergeant told the officers to stand at ease and he took a verbal and visual count of all those present; this included 10, 20, 30, and 40 sectors. The sergeant would then pass on anything he felt necessary or the upper command ordered.

Special orders from command usually meant work on reducing the prostitution on Troost, Main, and adjacent streets, or whatever the command staff deemed high priority at the time. Orders flowed downhill. Someone would complain to the mayor or a council member about the prostitutes. The mayor would complain to the chief, who complained to a deputy chief, who complained to a colonel, who complained to the major running the station, who would complain to the captain, who would complain to the sergeant, who finally complained to the patrol officers who actually did the work.

The patrol officers had to produce "stats," as they were called, to be passed back up the chain of command, showing how many arrests were made. This would be good enough until the next time a politically connected person drove down the street, and a prostitute tried to solicit him from some street corner.

After roll call, my FTO, Joe Morrison, a talkative, short, gray-haired man in his mid-forties, had me inspect our car for damage. Once you drove a car off the lot, any damage was now your fault and disciplinary action could be taken. Most officers reported any damage they caused. An officer causing then not reporting damage would be ostracized by the other officers.

Also checked were radio, lights, siren, and extra trunk equipment, including crime scene tape, road flares, and anything needed during a shift. Checking your patrol car before the start of the shift felt like the films showing a fighter pilot going through a check-off list before starting up the engine.

The shotgun was unloaded, and shells counted and reloaded. The gun was locked in place, usually between the front bucket seats standing upright or on the floor between the seats. The gun fit into a heavy steel locking mount that the officer unlocked with a special key.

The weapon itself was left with an empty chamber. This had two purposes. The first was to keep from blowing off the car's roof when removing the gun under duress. The second was confronting hostile situations; the first round had to be racked into the firing chamber. This action was both loud and attention-getting. Many times just racking a shotgun calmed a situation down. The sound of officers racking their shotguns prior to the start of a shift was also a stark reminder of dangers officers faced every shift.

Finally, after all this preparation, I could start the car. Next, I would contact the dispatcher and tell her my car number, serial number, radio number, and that I was in service. There were proper radio procedures and codes used for almost every situation and type of call. And of course there were specific rules you had to follow.

You could not tie up the radio with long sentences, as no other officer could get on the air. The radio system would only let one officer talk at a time so you did not want to be on the radio when an emergency or dangerous situation developed. You also had to be listening to everybody's radio traffic to anticipate the need for you to back them up. Other officers noticed when you were there for backup when they had not called for it. Many times this anticipation and awareness of others' calls saved lives.

In my first six weeks of training on the street, Joe taught me many things about police work. I learned how to deal with prostitutes, fight pimps, and run down drug dealers, but above all else, how to survive in the toughest part of the city. The action would intensify to the point where most people would question the limits of their commitment to the job.

The following stories are divided into sections that center around one theme, like drug-related crimes or prostitution. Sometimes an exception had to be made. For example, a drug-related situation had to be moved to the dangerous section to better reflect the incident's significance. I wanted to make it easier for the reader to follow the stories without jumping from one kind of crime to another. In doing this, it was not always possible to put the stories in chronological order.

Bearing this in mind, now it begins.

Prostitution

Part of the problem with prostitution is Hollywood glorifying the act, making it seem harmless, often portraying it in movies and TV as a glamorous or even a lighthearted, comedic profession. Examples include *Pretty Woman, Night Shift, Trading Places, Risky Business,* and *Two and a Half Men,* to name a few. If prostitution is so appealing, one must wonder when Hollywood will start making comedies about rape, sex trafficking, and child pornography. The police are often thought of as the bad guys who don't understand prostitutes; after all, aren't prostitutes providing a service?

I have heard some people say there is nothing wrong with prostitution. My simple argument to that belief: the next time you and your wife, girlfriend, sister, daughter, mother, or fiance's parents are sitting around the dinner table, espouse your thoughts on prostitution to them. Make sure your daughter knows how you feel. She might think it's an excellent way to pay for college, and how proud you must be because, you were the one who encouraged her. Now think about that for a moment.

Chapter 7:
Of Prostitutes and Vampires

Center Zone evenings was the most dangerous part of the city to patrol in the early 1980s. Forty sector evenings was the most dangerous within Center Zone's four sectors. After my break-in period, I was assigned to Center Zone, forty sector evenings. The area was not big but was densely populated with prostitutes, pimps, street drug dealers, and any other criminal activity you could imagine. There were also hardworking people, simply trying to make a living and keep their children safe.

I started the academy in June, and now it was November. I was on my own in the most dangerous section of the city. Prostitution became my first target.

Officers had to interrupt the prostitutes' continuous twenty-four-seven operations and go after their pimps. There was no other way. You had to confront them and make it too expensive or otherwise impossible for them to work the streets. If you thought about it, forcing the girls off the road made them find other lines of work and maybe saved a few of their lives in the process.

One suburban housewife actually asked me why we didn't put up "No Solicitation" signs on the street poles, you know, as some people have on their front doors. That is how misunderstood prostitution was with some of the general public.

Prostitutes were a constant problem. If you drove down midtown Main Street or Troost Avenue at night, they were in the street yelling at cars to stop and even showing off their breasts to potential customers. They were like midway barkers at a carnival, all trying to out-yell each other for the chance to perform illicit sex acts.

The prostitutes dressed up in outrageous clothes. They stood out like neon lights in their colorful wigs, heavy makeup, miniskirts, and low-cut tops advertising their unique charms to eager customers, johns, or tricks, as we called them. The girls were mostly in their late teens or early twenties, although once I encountered a worn-out, toothless prostitute in her forties. She had a unique talent and was known as "The Gumer." We called the women many names: prostitutes, whores, vampires, hookers, streetwalkers, girls, and a considerable number of more descriptive names.

The hookers carried purses, which contained knives, guns, syringes with dirty, exposed needles, and various used sexual aids. The girls were often abused and had hard lives. Many were robbed and beaten regularly; some were even killed.

Unlike most movies portraying street prostitutes as pretty White girls, in Kansas City at the time, I mainly dealt with Black prostitutes and a small minority of White prostitutes. Almost all the johns I came across were middle-aged men from suburbia.

The girls were a lot like vampires: they sucked, literally. The hookers were drug-addicted and disease-ridden women, most with no hope of escaping their station in life. I doubted they took showers, judging by the heavy amounts of cheap perfume they always wore. I felt sorry for some of them, but you had to be careful; one night, they could be docile and in a drug-fueled rage the next.

The prostitutes often robbed their tricks, knowing the victims would never report the crime to the police. It was too bad because some girls stood out and could have been easily identified by their bawdy outfits. The hookers often had outstanding warrants for solicitation of sex acts, possession of drugs, carrying concealed weapons, assault, and sometimes even robbery, when a john was mad enough to report it.

On a typical night, I would stop ten to fifteen girls, other calls permitting. Usually, the stop would go something like this. I would spot a girl dressed like a typical streetwalker in a risqué outfit, lurking in the shadows of a closed business, leaning into a car, and talking to a john, walking down the street yelling at cars to stop, or sometimes in a john's car, giving a twenty-dollar blow job.

When going out of service on a pedestrian check, you always give the location and description of the person. That way, other officers knew where you were, and some would back you as these ped checks, as we called them, could turn violent in seconds. I always asked for another car when stopping more than one person at a time.

All this was done before even approaching the subject of the stop. You didn't pull up even with the prostitute you were stopping in case they started running or shooting at you, and you never let them lean into your car like in the movies. That was a good way to get shot or your throat cut.

Letting a prostitute approach your car while still seated inside was dangerous, and tough to draw your weapon quickly. If you were imprudent enough to let a hooker approach the car door while you were seated, you could never defend yourself against a sharp boning knife attack. Your face and neck would be the easiest targets to cut.

A boning knife is designed for a butcher to cut cleanly and easily remove the bones from meat. The blade is razor-sharp, six inches long, strong, thin-bladed, and with a sharp point. One slice to your throat or neck would more than likely be fatal.

Imagine one of these hookers leaning against your car door, her left arm resting on the windowsill. She's talking; her breasts are almost entirely exposed, distracting you. She slides her right hand unnoticed into her purse and grabs her boning knife. You're dead!

Chapter 8:
Dumping Purses

I always approached a prostitute wary of her hands and purse and would initially ask, "What are you doing?"

"Walking."

"I saw you waving and yelling at some cars. Were they your friends?"

"Oh yes."

"So, what's in the purse?"

"Oh, nothing."

"Mind if I take a look?"

Most of the time, the girls would let me look. Occasionally, a hooker would not let me check her purse. I did it anyway. I took so many guns, knives, drugs, and used syringes out of purses that I quit asking for them and, without any preamble, just started grabbing the purses and dumping the contents on the hood of my car.

You had to be careful about reaching into a purse because you could get cut by a knife or pierced by a bloody needle. Many of the syringes still had drugs and blood in them. The guns were always loaded and ready to fire. The girls would say the weapon was for protection, and I could believe it, as they were often assaulted. Sometimes the prostitutes would use their knives on each other, a john, or a pimp. Rarely would anybody file a complaint.

One hooker had about ten used, round silk cosmetic application pads in her purse. I removed them one by one, setting them on the hood of my car, and finally, while holding up the last between two fingers, I asked her, "Why so many of these?"

"I gots to be fresh."

I must have appeared puzzled because she added coyly, "Silly, I needs them to make me feel fresh inside for the guys."

She put her hands up to her mouth and turned her shoulders away from me as if she were embarrassed. I didn't know if she was embarrassed for telling me what she used them for or that she needed them. She was popular on the street.

I almost got sick thinking I touched them and they had been used recently. That was another reason for dumping the contents of purses onto the hood of my car. You might ask why not wear gloves. It was simple; I could not get my finger into the trigger guard to fire my weapon with gloves on. Thin gloves would not protect you from needles or sharp knives; therefore the safest alternative was to dump the contents of the purse.

Once, an old prostitute about fifty was standing in the dark, recessed doorway of a closed business. I had her move to the side of my car under a streetlight, where I noticed she was having trouble keeping her eyes open. She was wearing a see-through white lace dress with nothing on underneath, and I saw a spot of fresh blood on her skirt near her thigh. The blood had dripped from inside her elbow. I dumped her purse out, and there was a bloody syringe and needle. She had shot up with heroin. That was example of why I dumped purses out rather than sticking my hand into them.

I don't remember what I did with the hooker that night or if I did anything at all. It happened all the time; and was not an unusual occurrence. It was kind of shocking for a lot of the officers who came from the suburbs, but you'd get used to it, or you quit.

Chapter 9:
Her Last Photo

When I was with Joe my FTO, he took Instamatic photos of the prostitutes after we finished a stop and I asked him why he did it. He told me that some of these girls ended up dead, and the homicide unit would ask if anyone could identify them. Joe said none of the prostitutes carried identification, and it helped identify the hookers when you stopped them.

Later, when on my own, I started keeping records and pictures in my briefcase until I was transferred and did not have to deal with vampires anymore.

I had stopped using the old briefcase for quite some time, and it was at home collecting dust. One day my wife opened it, saw the pictures of the prostitutes in their streetwalker costumes, and got mad until I explained their purpose. I even showed her the photo of a young prostitute who hadn't yet been eaten up by her trade.

The girl, I explained, had shown up on the streets my first summer, not saying where she came from or why. The second photo of the prostitute had been taken three weeks later when I stopped her for about the fifth time. She had been severely beaten and had a fat lip, bruises on her neck, a huge, swollen black eye, and cuts to her face that probably should have been stitched because now she would be scarred for life.

Of course, she did not want to talk about it or press any charges. A john had beaten her, or maybe it was a pimp, angry she was working his turf. I told my wife the girl was found dead a month later, and I was able to identify her through the photo and the clothes she was wearing. The prostitutes rarely changed their clothes, enabling repeat customers spot them more easily.

Most of the prostitutes I stopped were not seen again after about three to six months on the street. Some were found dead. As to the rest, I didn't know if they were sold into the sex slave trade or cut up and tossed into the river. From time to time, pieces of bodies would be found in the Missouri River. Occasionally, a whole body or torso would float up, bloated, rotten, and eaten by catfish; these were never identified. Rumors circulated it could be the work of a serial killer, possibly even involving an insane cop.

These prostitutes did not marry a Prince Charming they met while working and end up on the local PTA board. They did not go back to school and get their MBA or law degree; that would be a fairy tale, and fairy tales are never real. Unlike their tricks, for these girls, there were no happy endings.

Chapter 10:
Norman and the Cowboy

Some of the vampires were men dressed as women. They were only another variation of a prostitute who worked the streets for a living, and most of the time, it was apparent they were men. Sometimes they hung out with the women prostitutes, but mostly they stayed to themselves. They seemed to prefer short shorts, tight tops, and high heels. One of these guys was Norman.

I was with my FTO Joe Morrison when I stopped Norman for the first time. From a distance, Norman was the biggest prostitute I had ever seen at about six feet two and two hundred pounds, with a lot of muscle. It was a chilly night out in late October but Norman was dressed in purple hot pants and a midriff-cut shirt tied around his stomach, high enough to show off his navel. He had on heavy makeup, including long false eyelashes, silver eye shadow, and topped off with a large black Afro wig.

Upon getting closer, I could see this was definitely a man. There was no mistaking it. When I approached Norman, he put his hands on the wall, spread his legs out, and shook his butt like a dog in heat. Norman looked back over his shoulder at me, puckered his lips, then purred like a kitten and pleaded, "Oh, officer, I wants you to search me! I'm ready, grrrr!"

Norman was playing mind games and trying to control the stop. By putting himself on the wall without being told, he could be trying to gross me out enough so I would not search him. Maybe Norman was trying to test out a rookie or find my weakness to be used against me on a later stop. You could never be sure what these night stalkers were thinking.

After frisking Norman, Joe said, "Check everywhere; you must be sure he is not carrying anything illegal."

Many suspects, not only the prostitutes, carried their dope or small guns in their crotch, thinking they would not be searched there. I sure did not want to do it, but with my training officer watching I had to. I checked Norman thoroughly by feeling his crotch and ass, finding nothing on him. When I finished the frisk, Norman just had to tell me I made him wet down there. This was the second time I felt sick stopping prostitutes but it wouldn't be the last.

I know why Joe insisted on doing the frisk thoroughly: he wanted me to get used to it without even thinking how utterly disgusting it was. I left Norman with a warning and had a strong desire to wash my hands in Clorox.

When we were back in the car, Joe laughed, "So, what did you think of Norman's performance?"

In a serious tone and deadpan expression, I replied, "Wasn't it obvious, Joe?"

Joe quit laughing, and with a puzzled look on his face, said, "Huh? What?"

"Joe, Norman was trying to make you jealous!"

I looked over at Joe with a serious expression on my face. He looked at me for a second, then we both burst out laughing.

☙

I had finished training and was out on my own the next time I saw Norman. The American Royal, a gathering of cowboys and livestock from around the country, had come to town. Norman was getting into a pickup truck parked at the side of the road. I waited a bit for things to get started, then approached the driver's side of the truck. I could see that Norman was performing his best impression of a vampire on the driver. The john's zipper was down, and Norman was feasting. I almost laughed out loud.

The driver looked like a good old country boy wearing a black Stetson and a blue jean jacket. Since the cowboy appeared to be a neophyte when it came to picking out a prostitute, I thought I would give him a few pointers and knocked on his window. In a southern country drawl, the driver angrily shouted, "Hey, can't a guy have a little fun in this here town without being hassled by the po-lice?"

In my best John Wayne impression, I answered, "Well, sure you can partner. I just wanted you to know you're not having fun with a woman… Pilgrim!" Then I quickly added, before the john processed what I said, "Hi there, Norman! Whatcha eaten?"

As I walked back to my car, I could hear the country boy screaming, "You son of a bitch!"

The cowboy kicked Norman out of the passenger side of the pickup. Norman landed, sprawled out, face down on the cold, wet street with a dull thud. The cowboy drove off a little wiser, and slowly Norman picked himself off the dirty asphalt. He stood looking at the pickup's receding taillights, brought his left hand to his mouth, licked his dirty fingers, and rubbed them on his right elbow.

Norman snatched his wig off the greasy street and, with arms at his sides, let his wig dangle precariously from two fingers. Slowly, with his head down, chin resting on his chest, he limped away into the night.

I doubted the country boy would brag to his friends about his encounter with Norman and I didn't feel like arresting Norman for prostitution and having to search him. I guess everyone was satisfied. The cowboy paid for Norman's lunch, Norman ate his lunch, and I stopped a crime in progress. After that night, I never saw Norman again; he just disappeared without a trace like so many other prostitutes... or so I thought.

Chapter 11:
Teddy the Pimp

If there were ever a recruitment ad for pimps, Teddy would be the poster boy. Teddy was a large man with a gold-capped front tooth and a relaxed Jheri curl down to his shoulders. He always wore his signature vibrant green velvet tux to match his car. Teddy drove a big 1969, Kelly-green, white-vinyl–topped, two-door Coupe Deville with a white leather interior, white, faux fur, trimmed dash, deluxe white walls, and enough chrome to blind drivers four blocks away on a sunny day.

Teddy worked a stable of women up and down Main Street. His job was making sure the girls were working and giving him his cut.

He also supplied the drugs, heroin, and crack cocaine that kept the girls working night and day. Joe told me Teddy always carried a gun under the front-seat armrest.

I found Teddy one summer evening driving east on 39th Street checking up on his hookers. I stopped him for expired plates, and sure enough, I could see what I believed was the butt of a handgun sticking out from under the armrest. Teddy did not put up a fuss or give me any grief. He knew the drill well by now. I recovered the gun, arrested him for CCW (carrying a concealed weapon), towed his car, and I also did something other officers seemed to overlook. I wrote him a ticket for no city sticker on his car.

The city sticker was a method the city used to collect more tax revenue. The sticker itself was not too expensive unless you were poor, a fact the city administrators ignored. Teddy never bought a city sticker and didn't pay the fine either, so several weeks later, a warrant for his arrest would be issued for failure to pay the fine. I would arrest him on the new warrant, and now the bail was twice the amount of the original ticket. He would have to post a bond on the new warrant, and I would tow his car again. I wrote him up every time I saw him pimping on the street.

One time I had an officer lined up each block, and if Teddy did not have a warrant or a gun, I would write him a no city sticker ticket. Teddy would drive off, and the next officer would stop him and write him the same ticket. This went on for three or four blocks. It became so expensive for Teddy that he quit the pimping game and went into narcotics full time. At least I had made a slight dent in the prostitution trade.

The last time I saw Teddy, he was parked in front of the Blue Room Lounge. Teddy had been in jail for a few months for promoting prostitution and appeared to be out of the pimping business. He had traded in his Kelly-green caddy for a four-year-old royal blue Park Avenue all shined up nicely. I cordially greeted Teddy, and after frisking him, started in on his car.

When I searched Teddy's vehicle I found roaches all over the interior, some good sized. They were not marijuana roaches but real live cockroaches. When I got out of the car I brushed two of the bugs off my pants. I wrote him tickets for an expired license plate and Teddy's favorite, no city sticker. After that night, I never saw Teddy again; he either died or moved to another city. I'd made it too expensive for him to hustle in my district.

Some people might think I was picking on or even harassing poor Teddy. On a daily basis, Teddy was actively helping enforce Black sex slavery in midtown Kansas City. He was responsible for the misery of many. I saw the violence Teddy inflicted on his hookers, their cuts, bruised lips, swollen eyes, and track marks on their arms.

What if your daughter ran away from home? Would you want Teddy to get her a job in his stable to be bought and sold at his bidding? Or your son or husband, drunk and out looking for the kind of entertainment Teddy provided, could get robbed and beaten. They would certainly bring home some debilitating social disease for unsuspecting spouses and girlfriends to endure, sometimes for a lifetime. Those diseases could even be passed on to innocent newborn babies.

There were many victims out there. Teddy was a cruel and soulless taskmaster, an enforcer of the sex trade, and a purveyor of iniquity.

Chapter 12:
Fighting the Pimps

Joe, my FTO, got me into several fights to see how I handled myself. It was essential to see if an officer could survive on the street or be counted on to help another officer in a violent situation. It was one thing to talk about violence or even train for it in the academy; it was a completely different matter when it was you against a hardened criminal.

My first fight would be with a pimp. A man bigger than me, with no qualms about fighting an officer and pounding his face with a fist, fingers covered with sharp-edged rings, meant to cut a person's face to ribbons. A pimp high on drugs, enraged because he was stopped in the middle of beating one of his whores for some unknown infraction. A dangerous man in a violent occupation and known to carry weapons.

An excited voice asked for another car at Thirtieth and Main, a man known on the street as Louis was beating a woman. I activated the car's emergency equipment, grabbed the radio mike, and listened to Joe talking over the siren while advising the dispatcher, "Two-thirty-one, I'm five blocks away en route!"

"Two-thirty-one, en route," the dispatcher calmly responded.

I executed a U-turn, spinning my tires, then pulled out of a violent oversteer, rocking the car back and forth on its loose suspension, steering with one hand until I got the heel of my right palm on the wheel while still gripping the mike in the other. I couldn't take my eyes off the traffic to put the radio mike back in its holder.

I watched every intersection looking for pedestrians crossing the street, cars pulling out from the curb, cars making left turns in front of me, gas pedal to the floor, then slamming on the brakes while going through a red light at a busy intersection. I jerked the wheel violently one way, then the other, pushing the shocks to their limit going around a stopped car, hoping the driver did not turn into me, trying to get out of my way, and counting down the blocks until my arrival. All the while, I listened to Joe's voice talking loudly over the radio traffic and a blaring siren.

"Louis is a mean pimp. He is a competitor of Teddy. He likes to carry a gun and loves to fight, so watch yourself. You handle this call; I'm not here on this one."

Training calls like this make or break a new officer. The field training officer stands back and lets the brand-new rookie officer handle the call. If a fight occurs, the FTO will not assist unless his rookie is losing, incapable of subduing the suspect. By that time, the rookie has probably sustained various injuries. If the rookie freezes and can't talk or fight if needed, he is out of a job. He would be a liability to himself and others.

I reached the scene and killed the siren but left my red lights on to help other officers locate my position from a distance, and had the dispatcher hold the air. Holding the air meant no other radio traffic was permitted until the officers at the scene cleared it, signifying all danger to the officers and victim had passed. This way, an officer could immediately access the dispatcher without waiting for someone else to finish their traffic.

I walked over and stood six feet in front of Louis. The man was a convicted felon for robbery, assault with a deadly weapon, carrying a concealed weapon, promoting prostitution, possession of drugs, and assaulting a law enforcement officer. He had been known to assault Teddy the Pimp's whores; occasionally, Louis and Teddy exchanged gunfire.

At six feet two and 230 pounds, Louis was a big man. In his mid-thirties, he enjoyed the prestige of dressing in flamboyant clothes, lots of purples and whites, wearing gold chains around his neck and large gold rings on his fingers. A T-handled steel pick stuck out of his medium-length Afro. He could stab you with the pick, something to note if he raised his hands in surrender.

The prostitute Louis had beaten was lying on the sidewalk on her side, one hand holding her face as blood seeped out between her fingers and dripped onto the concrete. She was obviously in pain and sobbing loudly. Louis was going to jail.

Joe asked the other officer, Billy Swift, a lean, strong-looking twenty-six-year-old, if he could check on the victim. Billy understood Joe did not want him to help me and went over to check on the girl. Joe took two steps back and to the right, leaving me in the center to face Louis alone. This was my test, my arrest.

Louis looked at where the other officers were and if they were paying attention. Billy was on a knee, watching Louis and the girl. Joe leaned against a parked car and casually lit a cigarette. I thought, should I order Louis up against the wall and frisk him, or make him get on the ground and cuff him?

The big pimp brought his heavily ringed right fist to his mouth and blew on it, trying to remove some flecks of drying skin hanging off one of his rings. He raised his hand from his mouth to eye level, pretending to study his cleaning efforts. He then sharply shifted his eyes to mine, his upper lip curled in a snarl for extra menace. "So, whatcha looking at, Whitey?"

He was trying to intimidate me, control me. Involuntarily, before a fight, I always cracked a closed-mouth, half-grin, with my right eye narrowing. I did it now.

I looked up at Louis and sarcastically replied, "So, Louis, after a hard day of pimping and beating up the whores, I thought you'd be home under the sheets with your butt buddy Norman."

Joe and Bill laughed. I'd taken Louis out of his game, and now whatever he was planning was lost in his rage. My grin got a whole lot wider. With a scream of hatred, Louis charged me like some wild out of control animal.

Ducking under his long arms, I sidestepped him and stuck my foot out at the last second, tripping him. Louis went down hard, face-first in the street.

I jumped on his back, pinning him to the asphalt while he yelled and screamed. I grabbed both his ears, along with hunks of his hair, and slammed his face into the dirty pavement several times, stunning him long enough to get him cuffed. I released Louis and stood. It all happened so fast.

Lying on the street, Louis turned his head toward me, his face raw from the pavement, "You mother f..ker, I'll kill you!"

Searching him, I found a loaded .32 caliber automatic in the right pocket of his purple, knee length coat, and removed the T-handled single steel pick from his hair; the end was sharpened to a deadly point. I removed two giant gold rings from his right hand, with raised initials LP for Louis Pride. The edges of the initials were sharpened like a razor, and bits of the victim's skin were still embedded in the gold letters. I let Louis stay on the ground cursing me until the wagon arrived and hauled him away.

Joe took photos of the prostitute before an ambulance took her to the hospital for multiple deep lacerations to her face caused by Louis's weaponized rings. Her face would be permanently disfigured.

Louis's car, a pimped-out purple Seville with a white interior, was parked in a no-parking zone. I had the caddy towed but not before leaving a no city sticker ticket on the windshield. I felt bad I hadn't remembered to roll up his power windows. It had started to rain.

After everything was squared away at the scene, Joe came up to me and slapped me on the back. "Good job, but next time be more careful; your knee is bleeding."

My right pant leg was cut open, and a piece of glass the size of a nickel was sticking out of my knee. I had not felt the wound at all; the adrenaline had masked the pain. Reaching down, I pulled the glass out and pretended it did not hurt. I was issued a new pair of pants and made sure my wife didn't see me limp for the next couple of days.

On this call, I was able to do several tasks at once and do them with a high level of proficiency. Driving, talking, listening, observing, planning the approach, and keeping an open mind about what to expect at the scene. I learned to control my emotions, not to get excited or overreact to a radio dispatch, and how to handle a giant rush of adrenaline. Joe was an example to me, as he dealt with every aspect of the call with complete calm.

My next fight came a few days later when another officer stopped a guy who was high on speed and loved to fight the police. This time I did not hesitate to get involved before the other officer stepped aside and let the suspect attack me. I quickly got behind the man and kicked the back of his knee as he started to swing at the other officer. When the suspect began to go to the ground, I put him into the proper neck restraint, and he was unconscious in seconds. I just forgot to let go until Joe yelled, "Let go, he's out!"

I released the guy, and he fell to the ground like a sack of potatoes. Joe said, "Good work, but next time stop once he is out and hold on to him; do not let him fall to the ground."

I was getting better and didn't get hurt this time.

Did I use too much force? I didn't think so. At the time, I knew if Louis got hold of me or hit me with one of his ring-covered fists, I would have been in a world of hurt. Could I have talked to him and convinced him to let me arrest him peacefully? Only in your dreams.

Sometimes violence is the only answer, and as a cop you better be prepared to handle it because, whether you want it to or not, violence will reach out and grab you.

Chapter 13:
Prostitute Roundup

One day, Sergeant Welsh, who looked, acted, and talked like the desk sergeant from the old TV show *Hill Street Blues*, had been yelled at by the captain about the whores on Main Street for the umpteenth time, and now he was mad.

At roll call, Sarge told the crew we were going on a prostitute roundup. The crew shouted "Yes!" in unison. Sergeant Welsh told me to get several books of general citations ready as I would get to write summons for solicitation as fast as I could.

It was an early December night and the girls were out in force. The whole crew went out and started pulling the girls off the street and bringing them in for booking, no questions asked. It was like something out of a movie; I could not believe what we were doing. Evidently, it had been done before, and everyone knew what to do.

Several cars would pull up to a bunch of vampires, check them for drugs and weapons, then quickly load them ten at a time into the wagons. The officers did this all over Center Zone until they couldn't find any more hookers.

After the initial load of prostitutes was brought in, I stayed at the station and processed the girls by the wagon load. I wrote as quickly as I could but couldn't keep up with the large volume of arrests. I wrote over fifty summonses using different court dates, locations, times, and descriptions of the girls' actions, ensuring all the hookers did not show up in the same courtroom on the same day with identical charges.

Only a few could post a bond; the rest went to the city jail awaiting bail or arraignment in court. Out of all those arrests, only one pleaded not guilty. A public school teacher with no record, dressed like a hooker, who just happened to be in a crowd of prostitutes for some unknown reason.

In court, I honestly told the judge I could not remember arresting her. The judge remarked,

"You sure have had a lot of prostitution arrests over the last three court dates."

I smiled, "Yes, judge, it's been busy out there with the holidays and all."

"Yeah, I'll bet." The judge looked at me and shook his head. The charge was dropped. I am sure he knew what was going on.

No prostitute did any time, only paid fines. The fines, fifty dollars plus court costs of another fifty dollars, were worse than jail since the pimps had to come up with the cash. Prostitutes without a pimp had to come up with their own bail money, which encouraged them to find another occupation or move out of 40 sector.

All in all, the command staff was happy all the way to the chief and the mayor.

Chapter 14:
Cruising with Howard

When there were not enough cars to go around in Center Zone, I would ride with Howard Zennie. Sometimes for a day, sometimes for a week. I thought they paired me with Howard to slow me down or to speed him up.

I was highly active every day, and I kept busy addressing the sergeant's stated goals. On the other hand, Howard was busy doing other things, and when he did do some police work, he usually had ulterior motives. By this time, I was comfortable being out on my own and did not especially like riding in a two-person car. I enjoyed setting my own pace, going where I wanted and stopping who I wanted.

Howard Zennie was the biggest officer in the department and stood six feet, five inches tall. He was large, heavy even. Howard showed no fat but no signs he hit the gym regularly either; he was just massive. He had a dark complexion with a soft, slow, laconic speech that went well with his slow-witted disposition. Unless you knew him or heard him speak, Howard could be intimidating just standing alone doing nothing.

Howard took a week to make decisions in any situation. Sometimes an officer needed to pick up the pace going to a call or deciding on a course of action. Howard would let anybody around make the decisions he should make, except with me Howard had seniority and decided what we would do each day and when we were going to do it. He drove, and I hated being the passenger.

I liked Howard. He was easy to talk to and never got excited or mad about anything. When partnered with him, I would ask leading questions and let him talk about himself. Little by little, I learned a lot about what motivated him.

Zennie liked the women and had a wife and a girlfriend. He even liked the vampires enough to spend long periods talking to them as if he were at some high school mixer. Now I had nothing against a man who liked his women, but Howard had a tough time juggling them and seemed to be in trouble with all of them at the same time. As I said, I liked Howard but didn't like working with him, especially in my car.

Howard Zennie had one personal grooming style that I'd have no problem with whatsoever, if I didn't have to ride in the same car with him. He used a hair grease that made his hair smell like chemicals and left visible oily residue all over the headrest and top of the seat. Howard used way too much grease, and it dripped off him like oil from an old Chevy motor. Sitting across from him in the summer, I could see the oily mess drip onto his face and all over his shirt collar.

During the winter, the smell of the chemicals with the heater on was nauseating and gave me headaches. I smoked cigarettes and was sure my habit annoyed other officers; consequently I never complained to anyone or to Howard. I never smoked in the car with Howard, as I'd heard the chemicals in the grease were highly flammable.

On a typical day, I would check out the car and equipment while Howard stayed in the station on the phone. When he came out to the parking lot, all the other cars were already on the street, answering calls and doing proactive work. Other officers were taking our district calls because he had been on the phone and was not listening to his radio. Sometimes Howard was oblivious to the world around him.

I remember when Howard would make a quick stop home, which would turn into forty minutes or more. It would not be bad if his house was in our district or even in Center Zone, making us available for calls in our sector and not causing others do our work. Howard's house was not even close to Center Zone; it was twenty-five blocks away. That did not seem to bother Howard or the sergeant, even though this was not police business, only personal business.

I did not like being out of my district unless it was on police matters; it made me feel uncomfortable. What if someone got hurt doing a call I should have been working but was out of my area on personal business? I decided if nobody was going to complain, I wouldn't worry about it. Anything that happened due to our absence was on Howard; he was the senior officer and the driver.

I do not know how many times my FTO Joe drilled it into my head. You never pull up even to a prostitute on the street, and you never let them approach your car while you are still seated.

A visit with the vampires was one of the few self-initiated stops Howard would make. He did not treat them as drugged-out, disease-ridden prostitutes who rob johns at knife and gun-point; no, he treated them as you would any woman at a social occasion or a bar. Howard would laugh with them and get their phone numbers.

Well, one night, he put me at risk by pulling up directly next to a vampire and a no-parking sign, pinning my door closed. Howard leaned across the front seat, his hair dripping oil on my uniform, placing me between him and the prostitute hanging on my door. Her face, close to mine, was disgusting, especially when I thought about where her mouth had been recently.

After the stop, which accomplished nothing but maybe another date for Howard, I let him know I didn't like how he approached the hookers or underestimated the danger they posed to an unwary officer. Howard seemed dumbfounded, as if it was the first time he learned prostitutes could be dangerous. I couldn't believe I had to explain it to someone who had worked at Center Zone for five years and should have known how vampires carried knives and guns and used them on johns, other whores, and pimps. He didn't get it or even care.

When an officer stops a prostitute, he does not do it to shoot the shit with them or get a date. You are supposed to check them for warrants, priors, and especially weapons. You also check them to scare off potential johns cruising the street looking for a good time.

In a quick, easy report you note so and so was stopped at such and such location on this date and time. Later if a robbery involving a hooker occurs at that location, you have a starting place to identify the suspect. Sometimes if a warrant comes out for a prostitute, you will know when and where she works. Howard was totally unproductive in his stops; they were social occasions to him.

The next time Howard pulled over to talk to some hookers, at least he did not pin me in the car. However, he did not go out on the radio and treated the stop as another episode from *The Dating Game*. I watched as Howard walked up to a couple of hookers and started talking about anything except what he should be doing. Howard had one foot up on the front bumper and his arms crossed against his chest. He looked about as relaxed as he could be.

I had seen enough. While Howard sweet-talked the prostitutes, I put us out on two female ped checks at Thirtieth and Main and gave their descriptions. I also asked for another car, believing Howard would be little or no help if things went south.

Howard did not notice my radio traffic because he didn't have his portable radio turned on; he was too focused on the vampires' bodacious charms. The girls, however, noticed my radio call and gave furtive looks around for possible escape routes.

The other car arrived, and my friend Albert Logan got out and quickly came over and positioned himself behind the hookers. I stepped in front of Howard, grabbed the girls' purses, and dumped them on the hood of the car. Howard came to the whores' defense with a "Hey, what are you—"

Howard never finished the question as an assortment of rubbers, makeup, and dental supplies landed on the hood. Then, lo and behold, out popped a six-inch boning knife and a loaded small-frame .38 caliber revolver. To make matters worse, Howard did not want to arrest the girls and wanted me to recover the gun and let the girls go free.

The girls pleaded, not to Albert and me, who were cuffing them, but to Howard. After running the girls through the computer, we learned they both had warrants for prostitution, one of them a county warrant. I never let vampires go if they were armed with a gun—it would be telling the girls it was okay to carry them. If I had allowed Howard to control the stop, he never would have even found the weapons or that the hookers had warrants.

At the station, I told my sergeant that Howard's actions were dangerous. She told me to write up my concerns, after which I never again had to ride with Howard. Within a year, he was gone because of undisclosed reasons. The obvious question here was why hadn't any supervisor addressed Howard's work habits before I arrived in forty sector?

No one ever mentioned Howard's name again. Once you are gone, it's as if you never existed.

Chapter 15:

Termites

The oldest profession in the world could also be the deadliest. Seeing the gruesome scene of a freshly murdered hooker was traumatic to most officers, though they rarely showed it. A prostitute you may have dealt with before, now naked and all cut up or worse, gets to you after a while, no matter how tough you are. If it doesn't, then something might be wrong with you.

Sometimes officers tried to relieve the stress with some gallows humor. This might be observed at a tragic death scene, and a local news channel camera catches an officer laughing or smiling with another officer. The reality can be quite different than it appears. One officer might be telling a joke to get the other officer's mind over the shock at what he witnessed.

There had been a rash of prostitutes murdered. It was the work of a serial killer, as they all were strangled, nude, and a good-sized tree branch was always shoved into the victim's vagina. The press was all over the story, and there was a lot of political pressure to catch the suspect.

At one of these murder scenes, the media and a major from the Crimes Against Persons Unit showed up. The Crimes Against Persons Unit, or CAP, consisted of Homicide, Robbery, and Sex Crimes. This was an important major, and he was full of himself. An old veteran sergeant from the Homicide unit was also on the scene.

In front of everybody assembled, the major asked loud enough for the press to hear, "Well, Sergeant, what appears to be the cause of death?"

"Well, Major…" The sergeant paused for dramatic effect and slowly looked at the body, then at the major and, like the major, said in a voice loud enough for the press to hear, "I don't know, what do you think, termites?"

The assembled newsmen, detectives, and officers howled with laughter.

I guess the sergeant had little tolerance for the major, a career bureaucrat who had probably never handled a homicide case himself. The sergeant was immediately transferred back to the field.

That one sentence by the sergeant improved the morale of the rank and file in the whole department. It was not about making fun of the murder victim but rather the narcissistic major. That was gallows humor. It helped officers get over a grisly scene, at least until their next nightmare.

Chapter 16:
FBI Stakeout

On another typical hot, muggy summer afternoon in July, my first year in Center Zone, I had left roll call, and after checking out my car, started driving a circular pattern of my district. Going north on Troost, I noticed at first one, then two, four, ten, and more unmarked police cars lining all the available parking spaces on both sides of Troost from Thirty-first north to Twenty-ninth Street.

I knew the Center Zone SWAT guys. They were the cops in uniform riding two to a car with a big antenna mounted on the center of their trunk lid. They weren't hard to miss. Then there were the half dozen or so dark four-door sedans with one White male dressed in a black suit, white shirt, and red tie behind the wheel, the FBI. Last were the cool cowboys in two-door sports cars in colors other than black or green; these were the ATF and the U.S. Customs agents.

All these law enforcement people stood out like a sore thumb. First, they were nearly all White in a predominantly Black neighborhood; second, all the cars except ATF and Customs had the big radio antennae on the trunk. Third, all their vehicles were late model and newly washed and waxed while the typical cars in the area were dirty, older models.

Anyway, I knew something big must be going down because there were so many cops on the street at one time. I thought about leaving, but not a word was mentioned at roll call about the need to avoid the area, so I continued my patrol.

One of the day crew members gave me a heads-up on a vampire named Lee Lee Brown. She was the ugliest prostitute on the street, with her bad acne and bleach-blonde hair done up in a thick lacquered row of spikes highlighted with blue tips. He said she had a county warrant for prostitution and narcotics.

I heard one of the SWAT guys on the regular Center Zone channel say, "There is Lee Lee; she has a county warrant." Because SWAT usually used their private channel to talk to each other, I figured they had seen me and threw me a bone by pointing out Lee Lee. I saw her from down the street standing in front of her apartment building, hustling tricks by yelling at passing cars and exposing herself.

She had not spotted me yet and I radioed the dispatcher on the regular Center Zone frequency to verify her warrants. Any of the SWAT cars would have heard me calling for a warrant check and could have easily stopped me if they wanted to as I drove past their positions. I figured they were staging here, and the real target was blocks away.

The dispatcher said the warrant was still good. I thought, what the hell? I told the dispatcher I would be out on a ped check on Lee Lee Brown and to send another car. Of course, Lee Lee spotted me driving up and took off running into the nearby apartment building. I told the dispatcher I was chasing Lee Lee to the second floor, apartment twenty. I knew her apartment number from previous arrests.

Lee Lee had on high heels and was not able to run fast enough to escape me. I was able to grab her shoulder as she opened her apartment door and snatch her back into the hallway. Someone inside the apartment slammed the door in her face. Desperate to stay out of jail, she pounded on the door, begging to be let into the apartment. I cuffed her and was dragging her out of the building when a dozen agents and SWAT team members came storming into the building. Wow! They came to help me. How nice. But they all ran by me like I wasn't even there. I thought, oh well, and notified the dispatcher I had Lee Lee, then headed to the station.

At the station the major immediately called me into his office. There was no "Hi" or "Have a seat." The major, an older commander close to retirement, sat with his fingers interlaced and a scowl on his face. It was obvious he was angry.

"Explain to me why you deliberately busted the FBI stakeout?"

"Major, I didn't know there was a stakeout; nobody said a word about it at roll call. I saw some support and agents lined up on the street but I didn't know where they were going or what they had planned for today."

"Well, they were after Lee Lee and were waiting to hit her apartment, where a significant gun and drug transaction was supposed to go down."

The major had probably already been called to explain my interference with the FBI's secret search warrant raid.

"Major, I was told by a day crew officer that Lee Lee had a county warrant, and I heard a support crew member say on the Center Zone radio channel, there's Lee Lee. I confirmed the warrant with the dispatcher on the air and got out on a ped check. If the FBI or SWAT wanted to stop me, all they had to do was stick their hand out the car window or tell the dispatcher to stop me… sir."

I told the truth, and the major believed me. The planners didn't tell patrol to avoid the area, and they called out "There's Lee Lee," on my channel. As for drugs and guns in the apartment, they never found any, and whoever was supposed to be inside was not Mr. Big. I heard later it was the apartment next to Lee Lee's where the drug deal went down.

A further note, I think the tipoff by an unknown SWAT member, "There's Lee Lee," was done on purpose. That officer knew I would go after her and chase her to her apartment. I wondered if the day officer who told me about Lee Lee's warrant knew about the planned raid.

It may seem a bit paranoid, but when I look back on the incident, what seemed like a series of coincidences might not have been. Someone tells the day officer to be sure to pass it along to me and no one else. I never remember getting a warrant tip from that guy before, why now? Who told him? I wondered, was it a setup? Did someone want me hurt, fired, transferred, or what?

Chapter 17:
Vice Patrol

One of the great things about working for a large police department is the chance to work at various jobs, from K-9 to helicopter pilot and everything in between. During my second summer in Center Zone, I was asked to work with the Vice Squad for a Friday night shift. The idea appealed to me, and I thought it would be fun to be out on the town in street clothes, not responsible for calls or reports.

When Friday rolled around, I met with the undercover Vice Squad at Center Zone. Vice did not operate out of Center Zone, but they came by for me that night. I had seen several of them around the station or on the street numerous times, so they were not strangers. There were four of them, a Sergeant Thomas Fisher and three detectives.

Everybody had long hair, earrings, and unshaven faces, and in general, the Vice Squad members looked like disenfranchised losers of society. These were supposed to be the people who missed their chances in life. They looked the part. They all had dirty, greasy hair, dirty clothes, bad breath, and even filthy fingernails. Sergeant Fisher explained that many prostitutes wouldn't talk to them if they were clean. He said you had to cover even the small details like dirty fingernails and bad breath.

People do not realize that to pull off the look, these guys could not go home and shampoo their hair and clean their nails. It would take days to get that dirty hair and hands look back again. A couple of the Vice officers said they would put a little cooking oil in their hair if they had showered recently and would dig in the dirt with their hands to get the right amount of that unwashed look.

Most of them wore the same dirty clothes for days on end, even weeks, to ensure nobody would mistake them for a cop. Almost all the vice squad crew members, were single or divorced. Few wives or girlfriends would put up with mates working weekends until 3:00 am and whose job was to get girls to offer them sex for a price. They did their job all over town, from strip clubs to dive bars, and drinking on the job was expected.

Can you imagine what it would be like if your spouse came home right after work, not stopping off anywhere, and smelling like cigarettes and booze with maybe a smear or two of orange lipstick on a collar from some streetwalker? Or imagine going to the local PTA meeting, soccer games, or church with a spouse that would look more at home in some skid row flophouse. It may look fun on the outside, but the price these guys paid in ruined marriages and families was too great.

There was also the danger of trying to arrest prostitutes, especially when you were out of uniform and trolling some sleazy bar. Sometimes the locals didn't want you messing with their girls and the fight would be on. Vice officers were routinely victims of assault and battery.

Still, to work Vice for a night seemed like fun. The first stop was a local twenty-four-hour diner, where over some breakfast food at 7:00 pm, Sarge explained the night's plan of action.

He said I would drive a slick car, a two-year-old two-door with absolutely no police equipment on it and only a hand radio kept under the front seat turned on but with the volume off.

If there was a solicitation with a specified price for a particular sexual act, I would key the radio twice and drive off, and none of the other prostitutes would know Vice was involved. The other squad members would hear the clicks, respond, and make the arrest. The prostitutes still on the street would think a john was simply scared off by the Vice unit. It sounds simple, but after a year of pulling every conceivable weapon you could think of off prostitutes, I was a little leery of letting a hooker approach my car while still seated in it.

I could not carry a gun along my waistband, as girls would feel for it right from the start. I could sit on it or put it under the seat. Sitting on the gun was literally a big pain in the ass, and it was hard to remove quickly from under the seat. An ankle holster would have been ideal, but I did not have one and opted for under the seat.

I drove up and down the same area I worked in every day, but due to the large numbers of prostitutes out each night, I could find plenty I hadn't already stopped. I would cruise by a girl sauntering up the street in a micro-mini skirt and platform shoes and give her the eye. Most of the time, the prostitute would look back at me, then quickly look around to see if anybody was watching. The girl then would yell something like, "Hey, honey! Are you looking for a party? I got what you need right here."

The girl would grab her crotch or breasts in a lewd manner to accentuate her meaning of *party*. I would stop and get the girl to quote me a price for a specific act. I'd say, "Hey, babe, what can I get for twenty bucks?"

If she said anything like, "Straight up or a half-and-half for twenty, or thirty for an around the world," then there was no need to go any further. She could be arrested for solicitation. Problems occurred when a girl wanted to get in the car before talking about specifics—in that case, it would force me to drive around with a hooker trying to get her to name a price for a sex act while she was putting her hands all over my body, attempting to get me excited while checking for weapons or wires. All this time, I would be trying to drive and not lose my backup in traffic.

Sometimes they would even undo my belt and put their hand inside my pants before I could get them to name a price. Then I had to stop the girl, reach under the seat, grab the radio if it had not shifted, and key the mike twice, all without the prostitute noticing my actions. Lastly, I had to get the vampire out of the car without blowing my cover or being attacked and becoming one of those johns with a knife wound.

Also, it might sound easy, but you had to keep up a steady conversation with the prostitutes while trying to get them to commit to a price. I had to act as if her advances turned me on even though you knew how truly disgusting these hookers were from stopping them on the street night and day.

It was one matter to stop the vampires on the road out in the open air, but when they got in your car up close with the cheap perfume and their tongue stuck in your ear, it was hard not to slam on the brakes and kick them the hell out of the car.

I quickly learned to always have a lit cigarette in my mouth to keep the vampires from trying to kiss me on the lips. The thought of a prostitute kissing me was worse than a shit-eating dog licking my face. I was going to need another pack of cigarettes.

After the first four or five arrests, letting the prostitutes approach the car felt a little less dangerous. I'd make a deal; the backup unit would grab the girl and stash them in a police van hidden a couple of blocks away. We would all go to the Center Zone station when the wagon was full, write up the charges, and book the girls into jail. We also made sure they could not bail out until after we went home, preventing them from warning all their sisters of the night.

After about six hours of working Main Street, Sergeant Fisher decided to take the show to another place off Twenty-seventh, an area I hadn't known was full of prostitutes. The neighborhood appeared to be a mixture of single-family homes and apartments.

Sarge wanted me to drive slowly down the street and see if I could get a particular prostitute, Latoya, dressed in a blue halter with a giant pink Afro and yelling at passing cars, to solicit me. The street was steep, and Latoya was at the bottom.

At the top of the hill, a sizable crowd gathered in front of apartment buildings on both sides of the street. Young teens and men and women in their twenties mingled under streetlights, drinking beer and smoking cigarettes and marijuana. Laughter, shouts, and insults were hurled from one side of the street to the other.

Parts of the crowd spilled into the road, so I had to drive by slowly.

Here I was, casually cruising an inner-city neighborhood at 1:30 am, listening to the FM with my windows down to talk with the hookers. It was spooky as my car drifted through the crowd and I saw their expressions as they realized I was among them. They had surprised looks at first but then ignored me and returned to their conversations. Apparently, it was not unusual for johns to drive down their street in the early morning hours, searching for a good time.

The group in the street was now maybe twenty feet behind me when a gunfight broke out. Loud bangs on one side of the road were answered by shots from the other side. Through the rearview mirror, I saw the bright muzzle flashes of the guns and heard the screams from either victims or people standing in harm's way. If I had arrived seconds later, I'd have been caught in the middle of it. It was like in some movie scene. I pulled over to the curb and watched the crowd running in all directions, fumbled for my radio, and broke radio procedure to notify Sergeant Fisher of the gunfight erupting around me.

"Sarge, there is a gunfight in the street right behind me!"

"Yeah, well, your car didn't get hit, did it?" He sounded bored.

"Well, no, not that I know of, but shouldn't we notify a district car or something?"

"It's none of our business! Now get on down the street and let me know when Latoya solicits you so we can arrest her."

Sarge sounded irritated that I would bother him with something as trivial as a gunfight. Then I realized I was in plainclothes. What the hell was I going to do about it anyway? Yell, "Stop, I'm a cop"? If I called for a district officer, he might get shot.

Well, if no one was wounded or killed and nobody in the crowd complained, why should I?

Adjusting my rearview mirror, I continued down the street to the bottom of the hill, where a small group of ten to fifteen men and women were standing at the curb smoking cigarettes. The girls were passing a quart bottle of beer around, and I wondered if they were drinking the beer to rinse their mouths out from all their work. It was a sickening thought.

I eased up alongside a group of three girls who didn't seem concerned about the gunfire up the street. The one Sarge wanted, Latoya, wasn't hard to spot in her pink Afro; she stood apart from the rest of the coven.

Latoya hustled up to my window and leaned in to check out the interior, then took a step back and said, "You want to partay baby?"

"You bet, Mom-ma! What can I get?"

She moved away from the car and pulled her top up, freeing her big 44 double Ds to sway in the breeze.

"This is what you get, honey! I'm gonna take good care of you!" She moved her shoulders back and forth, making her breasts slap against her sides with an audible smack.

"Oh, baby! How much is that going to cost me?" I smiled and licked my lips, trying to convince her my intentions were completely amoral.

"Twenty bucks for straight, thirty bucks for head, or twenty-five for a half-and-half." She smiled and grabbed her breasts, bringing them up to her mouth. "Ummm, ummm, baby, these taste so good!"

"Oh, Mama! I'll be right back!" I drove off, radioing Sarge, "Latoya offered me a *fair* price."

Sarge drove down the street, past where the shooting had occurred minutes ago, and arrested

Latoya without causing any crowd reaction. The people knew what Sarge was doing, and if you did not bother him, he would not bother you. Sergeant Fisher and his crew were something else. I can't begin to understand why someone would want to work in Vice, but they seemed to take it all in stride, another day on the job.

That was the last arrest for the night; Sarge let me off early, and after the night's disgusting work, I was ready to go home and wash off the filth I felt clinging to me. I would never again work vice. It was too dangerous, dirty, and corrosive to your soul. Someone had to do the job, but it wasn't going to be me.

Drug Dealers

There are the drug dealers, and there are the drug users. It is a symbiotic relationship. I could not affect the causes of the demand. That was somebody else's job. I went after both the street dealers and the users and went after them aggressively.

Chapter 18:
Fat Wally

It was August and I was on evenings when I first met Fat Wally standing outside the Blue Room Lounge; he was a convicted drug dealer and murderer. He stood with other dealers, killing time between deals. He was soft-spoken and not given to taunts like, "Why are you messing with me? That ain't my shit!" Fat Wally took everything in stride and never got arrested.

He was five feet ten and 280 pounds. He did not have the roly-poly, jiggly look but was solid like he lifted weights in the penitentiary.

I could never find any drugs on Wally, but a snitch told me Fat Wally carried his stash in the crack of his butt. Well, his butt was so enormous that in a frisk I could never feel the drugs in the depths of his butt cheeks, and I could not strip search him unless he was under arrest.

Wally had found a way to carry his stash and not get caught. I think that is why he was always calm and self-assured; he knew I would never find his drugs. He probably learned the technique in prison and now Fat Wally was becoming a star on the corner for surviving a month without being arrested. I wanted him out of there; he was attracting more dealers and criminals to the area.

Well, right or wrong, Fat Wally had to go and I came up with a plan I thought would work. I talked to a K-9 officer with a large German shepherd that barked on command. I told the K-9 officer about Fat Wally and how he stored his stash in the crack of his butt. Since his dog was not a drug dog, I asked if he could bring his dog and pretend to have it smell around Wally and bark to see if I could get Wally to give up his stash voluntarily. I told the K-9 officer I didn't want to have the dog touch Wally or even get too close. I did not want any so-called accidental dog bites.

On the planned day, I put Fat Wally on the wall in the search position; he knew the pose. Wally was calm as ever as he stood there waiting to be frisked. Wally didn't know it yet, but today would be different.

I explained to him, "Wally, I know you keep your drugs in your butt crack, and unless you fish them out now, I'm going to call over a K-9 officer and let his drug dog do a sniff test. Do you know what that means, Wally? If the dog smells drugs, it will probably attack the area to get at the stash. The K-9 officer will try to hold his dog back, but when Bear, a ninety-pound German shepherd, is that close to the drugs, well, Wally, I don't think anyone can hold that dog back, but he will try, I promise."

For the first time, Wally started losing his relaxed demeanor and that half-assed smirk he always wore.

"Well, Wally, what's it going to be? The easy way or the hard way?"

"I ain't got nothing, man!"

Ol' Wally was sweating bullets now. I think he was about to give up the drugs but wanted to hold out to see if I would really call a dog over. I did.

I called a K-9 for a drug search within hearing distance of Wally, building up the tension. Wally began shaking his head back and forth, denying he had the drugs. He was stressing out big time.

The K-9 officer approached and slid his car to a stop in some loose gravel to create a dramatic effect. Wally looked over his shoulder with his hands still on the wall.

"So, what have you got here, officer?" The K-9 handler, six feet two, a lean two hundred pounds, with dark aviators, looked like the epitome of a mean cop and towered over Wally.

Fat Wally took notice.

"Well, I got Fat Wally here, who everybody says carries drugs up his butt crack, but he won't cooperate and give them up. I told him your dog will find them, and you'll do your best to keep Bear off him."

The K-9 officer played up the charade. "I always try to keep Bear from biting anyone, and sometimes I'm successful. I'll give it a good try. Let me get Bear."

The K-9 officer yelled, "Here" and Bear jumped out his open window, growling. The officer attached Bear's leash, then on an unintelligible verbal signal, big Bear started barking and snapping loudly. Wally was now on the verge of giving up the drugs.

"What do you say, Wally? Are you going to give up your stash, or will you let the dog dig them out of your butt?"

"Man, I can't go back to prison. I can't do it anymore. I can't, man." Wally was looking over his shoulder and shaking his head back and forth.

Wally had given up. He might as well have said he was holding. A little bit more and he would break completely.

"Well, Wally, if you didn't want to go back to f..king jail, then why in the hell are you out here selling drugs in my district? What the f..k, Wally?" I acted as if I was mad, yelling at this murdering, drug-dealing son of a bitch. When Wally did not respond, I continued.

"Oh, okay, Bear, you ready to go to work?" On cue, the dog pulled on his leash, barking furiously. The K- 9 officer put on a good show.

Wally started to talk. "Okay, okay, I'll give it to—"

Sergeant Higgins's car slid to a stop, interrupting the pageant. She exited her vehicle quickly, not bothering to close the door.

I walked away from Wally and explained the whole situation. Sarge said I could not bring the dog up for a pretend sniff test. But for Wally's benefit, she said loudly, "I'm off the next ten days; do it then." Sarge got back in her car and drove off.

The K-9 officer said, "Give me a call. I can come back any time."

Fat Wally dropped his head against the building and gave out a loud sigh.

"Okay, Wally, get off the wall. You're free for now."

Wally pushed himself away from the side of the building and slowly walked away, hands at his sides, talking to himself while moving his head from side to side. I never saw Wally again.

Now some people might say I could not do that, as he had every right to stand on that corner even though he was a drug-dealing, convicted murderer in a high-crime location. I disagreed with them and drove him out of the area, possibly the city, and in the process, saved some people who wanted his product or wished to emulate him.

A final note: Who would buy drugs that had been stored in someone's butt crack? This is an example of how dirty and disgusting the drug trade is.

Chapter 19:
Red Beans and Rice

Another officer and I parked a block away from the Blue Room Lounge, split up, and approached the entrance from different directions on foot. The suspect we were after could not see us until we rounded the building, trapping him between us. We were trying to get a dealer that kept a small amount of speed on his person and the rest hidden nearby.

We were lucky and surprised the suspect but not before he swallowed the evidence. He was pleased with himself. I told him that, out of concern for his well-being, we would wait with him until he went into seizures. I looked at my watch, then suggested it would only take five to ten minutes before the pills dissolved. I asked the other officer, "You know how to do CPR?"

"Nah, I haven't taken that class—how about you?"

"I skipped that class, but I suppose I could fake it till the paramedics get here, but who knows when that will be." I shook my head in fake concern for the dealer.

"Yeah, this time of day, it might be a while." The other officer laughed.

The dealer watched and listened to each word. He was terrified. He started sweating profusely and looked panicked. He then stuck his fingers down his throat until he vomited. I could see half a dozen pills mixed in a lumpy pool of half-digested red beans and rice.

Sometimes I would go ahead and pick the pills out of the vomit for evidence. Today I was feeling magnanimous and said, "The next time I see you selling drugs on this corner, and you swallow them, I'll duct tape your mouth shut and let you OD."

I let him go but not before I had him stick his new Michael Jordans in the vomit and rub out the pills. I never saw him on that corner again. Sometimes a little warning is sufficient.

Chapter 20:
Chased a Guy into a Bar

It was summer, a sticky hot Saturday night, and no other officers were around, so I had to get in trouble by myself, and I did.

It was dark, getting close to the end of the shift, and I was taking one last drive by the Blue Room Lounge, the home away from jail for many drug dealers. I never encountered a single person outside of that bar who wasn't a convicted felon or drug dealer.

This time I came from out of the south on Brooklyn, and with my brights on, the dealers were blinded. They would not be able to tell the car headed toward them was a marked patrol car until the last moment. I was like a fighter pilot coming in for an attack out of the sun.

The bar was probably packed, as the parking lot was full, and in my headlights, I saw several men standing outside the lounge. A few yards from the group one man stood leaning against a wall drinking a beer out of a brown paper sack.

I put myself out on a ped check at the Blue Room Lounge. The man drinking a beer in public was in violation of a city ordinance, giving me more than enough probable cause for an arrest. Usually, I would not bust someone for drinking a beer outdoors on a warm night, but these were drug dealers in a high-crime area.

Before the subject could see it was a patrol car approaching, I slammed the car into park and jumped out. Everyone scattered. The man I was after saw me, set his beer down, and ran into the lounge. I could barely get out to the dispatcher that I was in a foot chase and entering the bar. I yelled "Stop!" for the report.

The bar was packed. The patrons wore combinations of brightly colored shirts and boot-flared pants. Even though it was summer, many patrons probably thought they looked cool with their long leather jackets and fancy hats. With a casual brush back of their jackets, everyone could see who was packing. It was a status symbol if you carried a big .45 caliber automatic or a large pearl-handled revolver. The place was loud with conversations and a jukebox that blared its soulful blues.

Nobody noticed me at first, but then the whole place fell quiet; the only sound was the throbbing music. In the still crowd, I saw one man frantically pushing his way up to the bar then look over his shoulder with panic in his eyes. I grinned. There's my man.

I shouldered my way through the crowd, pulled my gun, and put it up against the suspect's head, making it clear I was not fooling around. After a quick one-handed frisk, I grabbed the man by the back of his neck and headed for the door.

It was like Moses parting the Red Sea; a path suddenly appeared. The patrons must have figured I was crazy and left me alone. As I left, the conversations started right back up like nothing ever happened. They probably knew the guy was a dealer and was getting what he deserved.

Outside the bar, I put my arrestee against the wall, cuffed him, and was searching him as two patrol cars came to a screeching halt in front of the lounge. I continued my search of the suspect and found what appeared to be speed pills in a small baggie in his right front pants pocket.

It turns out my instincts were once again firing on all cylinders. A records check showed the man was on probation for rape in Arkansas. The drugs, resisting arrest by running after being ordered to stop, and drinking a beer in public were enough to hold him until his court date.

If it held up in court, this arrest would revoke his probation, and he would be back in prison for the remainder of his original sentence of fifteen years plus whatever they gave him for the charges that night. A wagon took him downtown.

At the scene, the last thing I did—after another officer attested it was indeed beer inside the bottle—was to recover the beer bottle in the paper sack as evidence. Other officers said there was no need to recover the beer bottle as evidence; I recovered it anyway.

I charged the guy with felony possession of a controlled substance, resisting arrest, and a city misdemeanor for drinking in public. Everybody said I was piling up charges for the stats, but I didn't care. He was a drug dealer and convicted rapist.

At the trial, his defense was no probable cause existed for the stop; if that could be proved, the dealer would walk. The drugs I found and all the other charges would be dropped, as the evidence would be tainted. This doctrine was called the Fruit of the Poisonous Tree, meaning everything found as a result of an illegal search was not admissible in court.

The defense attorney—young, with an expensive suit, fifty-dollar haircut, and manicured fingernails—asked me on the stand, "What was the basis for the stop, officer?"

"This was a known drug area, and he was drinking a beer in public," I replied.

The defense attorney then asked haughtily, "So, what proof do you have that my client was drinking a beer, and why didn't you charge him with drinking in public… officer?" He scoffed at the word *officer* and cocked his head up and to the side dramatically as if he had practiced the move in front of a mirror numerous times. Usually, on an arrest like this, drinking in public was mentioned but never charged; the alcohol was never recovered.

I replied calmly, without any emotion, "I saw him drinking from a bottle inside a brown paper sack and confirmed it was beer by the smell and personal experience. I recovered the bottle as evidence, and I did charge him with a city misdemeanor of drinking in public." I gave a barely noticeable smile to the defense attorney.

The suspect was found guilty of all charges and went back to prison. I was verbally reprimanded for going into the bar alone.

It might seem a little brash to be crashing into a bar at night by yourself, in the middle of the inner city, after a man for drinking a beer, but sometimes you have to push the envelope to get results.

I went after the dealers anytime and anywhere. I went after them with someone or by myself; either way, it didn't matter to me.

Chapter 21:
A Kilo of Jamaicans

One morning after roll call in August, Sergeant Ulnis showed me some complaints sent down from the major at the station regarding a drug house in forty sector. Sergeant Ulnis asked me to go and check out the residence and see if I could do anything about the problem. I told Sarge I would see what I could do and spend some time in the area.

This particular drug house was run by Jamaicans, who currently represented one of the city's newest and most prolific drug organizations, dealing in cocaine, marijuana, and guns. They were also known for their extreme violence against other dealers and anybody they did not like. These Jamaicans were also known as Rastafarians, the Posse, or the Rastas, among other colorful names.

A great majority were in the country illegally. As a rule, the Rastas were tall, usually over six feet, and had dark skin and hair done up in dreadlocks. A colorful wool stocking hat sometimes covered the Rastafarians' hair even in the summer. They tended to dress in bright clothes that were loose-fitting, with flowing serapes or blousy, multicolored, collarless shirts and tie-dyed T-shirts. They always wore open-toed sandals to finish off their ensemble. This seemed to be the signature dress code of the Jamaicans.

In a situation like this, if you cut off the buyers, the dealers will go elsewhere to do their business. Kind of like moving that dog that shits in your yard to your neighbor's yard. It doesn't solve the problem, only moves it from one area to the next. But at least the major would be happy and, therefore, Sergeant Ulnis. I could recognize any of the dealers by their unique dress style, and the buyers would be the ones coming off the front porch of the drug house.

This was not like the Yum Yum Club or the Blue Room Lounge areas. Dealers were not out in the open for everyone to see. Here the dealers hid from view in houses. Buyers were not allowed inside the residence, as it would be too dangerous for the dealers to open the front door to anybody. Some rival gang might force their way inside, shoot the place up, and steal all the drugs and money. It had happened before. So the Rastas came up with a solution: They reinforced the doorframe and put up thick steel doors with iron braces. Drugs and cash were exchanged via a small iron opening the size of a mail slot that could open, close, and lock.

Entry to the residence would never be gained with a hard kick, shotgun round to the doorknob, or even a small battering ram; it would take some serious hardware to breach that door. The Jamaicans were known to possess fully automatic rifles, even grenades and machine guns. They were not afraid to use that firepower against anyone, including the police.

This particular drug house was up fifteen stairs of a steep terrace and across a small weed-covered lawn, then up six more stairs to the front porch and the reinforced metal front door. The front windows were left intact but were shuttered on the inside by boards and reinforced by more metal. The house was a veritable fortress able to withstand most attacks while people inside could fire out from strategically placed slots in the outside walls.

With the new neighbors who talked with a Jamaican accent, dressed in funny clothes, fortified their residence, and dealt drugs at all hours of the night and day, it was easy to see why people in the neighborhood complained to the major.

I drove around the block several times that morning, sizing up the area, looking for possible cover, approaches, blind spots, and escape routes they might employ, or I might need. The street was one-way that went up over a hill with houses mostly made of brick or limestone on either side. Parked cars lined both sides of the road except for two or three vacant spots in front of the Rastas' fort. If any neighbors tried to park in front of the fortress, their cars would be severely abused; only the uninformed would dare park there. Those empty spots were meant for drug customers only.

I found three possible assets. The house was made of wood, the street was lined with parked cars, and there were retaining walls six feet high next to the sidewalk. Since the house was made of wood, perhaps my .38 caliber bullets would go through a wall, and of course, I do not know what would cause it, but the house could burn quickly. With only a narrow lane between the parked cars, I could completely block the one-way street by stopping my car; no vehicles could get past me. Lastly, with the retaining wall next to the sidewalk, the Jamaicans couldn't shoot me, theoretically.

Several calls took me out of the area, but I returned and got lucky. I spotted an out-of-place Johnson County Kansas license on a new, blue Camaro parked in front of the Rastafarians' home. The car stood out like a sore thumb in this distressed area. A Johnson County Kansas tag meant some rich, suburban snot had come over here to buy drugs.

As I drove by the house a second time, a kid came down the steep stairs. I parked a few houses away, jumped out, and grabbed the blond-haired, dumb-assed kid as he reached the sidewalk. Not one to waste time on pleasantries, I quickly put him on the wall to frisk him and talk to him without being shot from the house.

"So where are the drugs, kid? I know you were up there to buy drugs, so where are they?"

He was probably eighteen, from a wealthy family, and had all the advantages money could buy. I pushed his face hard against the retaining wall and bluffed him, "Go on, tell me, or I'm taking you to jail right now!"

"I didn't get any from them; the guy said they were out. They expected more real soon."

The kid was shaking, maybe because he did not get his fix, or perhaps the thought of spending some time in jail—at least until his family's lawyer could get him out—scared him. I had his name and tag if needed later, and let him go.

"Okay, get out of here, and don't let me see you around here again, or you're going to jail, got it, asshole?"

"Yes, sir, thank you, I'll never be back here again!"

The kid jumped in his car and drove off, remembering to use his blinker.

Back at my car, I noticed several neighbors looking out their windows and wondered if they thought I let the kid go because he was White or if it was the first police car they had seen here since the Jamaicans had set up shop.

I figured I might catch the delivery vehicle when it arrived with the new drug supply and made a couple of slow passes around the house. On the third pass, I fell in behind an ugly bronze-colored AMC Pacer with three Jamaicans inside. The driver had nowhere to go; they were trapped in a car in which they had no hope of outrunning me. I grabbed my mike and hit my lights at the same time. "Dispatch #141, I have three Rastafarians in the 5800 block of Kanner, and they are refusing to stop. Go ahead and send me another car."

The Jamaicans twisted their necks to continually look back at me, their long dreadlocks twirling around, sometimes hanging out the window. I hoped they were not deciding if they wanted to shoot it out with me. I thought they had to be carrying some heavy firepower since they were delivering drugs. I chased them around the block at low speed, trying not to get too close, expecting them to open up on me any second. Instead, the guy in the back seat threw a large paper sack out the window. It had to be the product. A little farther up the street, they stopped. This was it. Either they would give up or come out firing.

My backup, Lilly, arrived and racked her 12-gauge shotgun. We were able to get them out of the car and handcuffed without any problems.

I still had to be careful. There were more Rastas in the drug house. An older lady with a huge smile and outstretched hands brought me the brown paper sack that the Jamaicans had tossed out the car's window.

"Here, officer, I saw them toss this out the window as you chased them up the street! Oh lord, officer, I can't thank you enough! We have been so scared over here. We thought no one cared or would do anything to help us."

I smiled back at her. I felt good.

In their Jamaican accents, the Rastas were yelling, "Mahn, what you doing this for? We ain't done nothing, mahn; we's done nothing!"

People came out, stood on their porches, and started yelling at the Rastas, mimicking their accent, telling them, "Get the f..k out of here, mahn. Yeah, you go back to Jamaica land, mahn!" They got their neighborhood back. Some people even clapped as the handcuffed Jamaicans were loaded into a wagon. I'm sure all the other patrolmen at the scene felt the same sense of pride as I did in helping the people in the neighborhood.

Inside the sack was a clear, tightly wrapped package of compressed white powder. The wrapper was stenciled with a horse's head, identifying the product as originating from a cartel in Columbia, South America. The significance of clear wrap and the horse stencil meant the cocaine hadn't been stepped on or diluted yet. After adulteration, that one kilo could end up as five to ten kilos of product. This meant I had seized over a couple months' supply of cocaine.

I was holding the bag in my hands when Sergeant Ulnis arrived. It had only been about five hours since Sarge had asked me to investigate the problem.

Sarge was happy, and I was sure he could hardly wait to inform the major. The drug squad obtained a search warrant, and the last two Rastas voluntarily exited the house. Several handguns, rifles, drug paraphernalia, and several thousand dollars in cash were recovered, all as a result of my arrest. It turns out the cocaine was 90 percent pure and weighed in at one kilo, or a little over two-point-two pounds. I was stunned that the Jamaicans in the car were unarmed and carrying a two-month drug supply.

It turned out that the Jamaicans were in the country illegally. Eventually, they would plead guilty, serve a ten-year sentence, and then be shipped back to Jamaica. That was what I was told. However, several years later, a large Jamaican drug ring was broken up in Kansas City, Kansas, and two of the Jamaicans I had arrested were part of that gang. Funny how that works.

The Jamaicans were probably given reduced sentencing or no jail time if they cooperated and helped the Feds unravel the distribution routes, drug houses, and storage locations. No one ever told me, but I believe my arrests helped provide the Feds more leverage to crack open the Jamaican drug operations in the Kansas City area. More importantly, I freed a neighborhood from the fear they'd lived under and helped the residents see the police in a more supportive role.

Seizing one kilo of cocaine from a dealer by a patrolman was a pretty big thing at the time. However, a year later, I would be in on seizures of over twenty kilos at a time and hundreds of thousands of dollars in cash, but I still felt good about my arrest of the Jamaicans.

This was one of those rare occasions when I risked my life in a very dangerous encounter to help people in their neighborhood, and they appreciated it.

A final note: After it was stepped on, one gram of cocaine sold for $160. There are 1,000 grams in a kilo so what I recovered had a street value of around $160,000.

Routine

Routine is a funny concept. Most people think of it as doing the same thing, day in and day out, and it's boring. In police work, on the other hand, routine has an entirely different meaning. Routine means you fought robbery suspects, dealt with death and misery, chased stolen cars, etc. Contrary to popular belief, police officers do not spend all of their time in doughnut shops and writing tickets.

Here are a few incidents I considered routine calls.

Chapter 22:

There's Blood on My Taco

When I was still with Joe Morrison, my FTO, a call came out about a street robbery. The victim had suffered severe head lacerations from a probable pistol-whipping. The victim, surprisingly, was still on his feet, holding a dirty rag to a large gash on the right side of his forehead.

Blood was all over his face and hands and the front of his yellow shirt. He removed the rag to look at it for some reason; I could see the white of his exposed skull. The wound looked nasty, and as I would learn later, it hurt like hell.

By this time I was not taking other officers' reports (part of training) and was free to look for the suspect, given his description. The suspect was a male, six feet, medium build, with a waist-length brown leather jacket. There were several patrol cars in the area when the call came out, and there was a good chance the suspect was still in the vicinity.

I figured if the suspect was walking down some street by himself, he would stand out and draw an officer's eye. So I told Joe I wanted to check out the Taco Bell a block away, as it was the only open public place close by. Who knows, maybe the suspect might be trying to hide in plain sight among the customers.

I parked at the back of the restaurant. That way if the suspect was inside he would not see me arrive. The restaurant was busy with a long line of customers at the counter. Then I saw the suspect, grabbed him by his right arm, pinned him to the counter, and cuffed him. Joe asked quietly, "Why him?"

I looked the suspect over. He was dressed exactly like the description broadcast by the dispatcher, but so were half a dozen other men in the restaurant. Then I showed Joe my right-hand, wet with blood, "Look at his right coat sleeve. It's still covered in blood from the victim!"

I never found the gun.

Chapter 23:
Shots Fired

One summer night I pulled into a vacant lot made by leveling off a demolished house. A streetlight close by lit up the area. A couple of preteens were practicing their best break dancing on a piece of flat cardboard. I told them they were good. The kids smiled and nodded. I rolled up my window to keep the bugs out and started writing a report.

Out of the corner of my eye, I saw the kids stop dancing and lie flat on the cardboard, then get up and run away. It was then I noticed puffs of dust rising from the ground where the kids had been dancing. It took a few seconds before it dawned on me someone was shooting at me. I notified the dispatcher, and a voice I didn't recognize said slowly, "So why don't cha get out of there?" That was it. I moved. It was no big deal; no report was needed. I thought it was funny.

Now could you imagine being shot at and thinking it was funny? Cops don't react the way people in civilian life react, and it is a testament to the amount of actual physical violence they endure and witness that an incident like this is something to make them laugh.

I never told my wife about this story. She probably wouldn't think it was funny.

Chapter 24:
Hospital Duty

One day I was called to the station and given instructions to relieve another officer guarding a prisoner down at a local hospital. The man I was to guard supposedly shot and killed a girl and wounded her brother. The suspect himself had been seriously wounded by an unknown party. Sarge impressed upon me not to let anyone in the suspect's room except for medical personnel. Sarge said there might be an attempt on the patient's life by the deceased girl's family. I was to spend the next seven hours babysitting the patient.

I relieved the other officer at the hospital, who said it had been a quiet day. I checked out the entrances and exits to the floor and the location of the bathroom. There was a chair in front of the room, so I sat down and watched the corridor for any suspicious subjects looking to kill my prisoner. It was ironic I was protecting the prisoner from the victim's family.

A half-hour into my shift, I saw a man in his early thirties with close-cut hair wearing gray slacks badly in need of ironing and an equally wrinkled white lab coat. He started at the far end of the hallway, poking his head into every room on both sides of the corridor. I thought it was strange.

If he was a doctor making rounds, why was he not accompanied by the floor nurse in charge of the patients? I also wondered why he was dressed poorly and only popping his head into the patient rooms but never entering them. It appeared to me he was looking for someone. Something was about to happen.

The man came to my patient's room, and without introducing himself or even acknowledging my presence, he reached for the patient's door. I blocked his way and asked him for some identification. I mean, he was dressed shabbily, did not have a name tag, and was acting strangely coming up the hall. He seemed to be pretending he belonged in the area.

When Sarge told me to expect someone coming to the patient's room to kill him, I tended to notice the details. The man started yelling he was a doctor, and right then before I could say anything, a nurse came out of nowhere and joined him in yelling at me.

"This is Dr. Williams! How dare you ask him for identification!"

The "nurse" was middle-aged, overweight, and wore her dirty blonde hair in a tight bun. She had lost control and was yelling loudly.

Not yelling, I replied to her sternly, "The man has no name tag. I do not know him from Adam. How am I supposed to know he is not one of the relatives reportedly coming up here to kill the patient? It is my job to protect the patient and Dr. Williams could have introduced himself. He should know this is a highly dangerous situation for everybody on this floor! You should know better than anyone the patient's safety far exceeds that of an unidentified doctor's feelings."

"Well! I'm going right now to report you to your supervisor!" The nurse spun around and marched back down the hallway with her scrub pants struggling to contain her ample butt. Dr. Williams walked away without even checking on the patient. The nurse was like a little kid with her "I'm going to tell my mommy on you" type of threat.

Within ten minutes, another officer relieved me of guard duty. Sarge wanted to see me back at the station.

"Well, Sean, me lad, pissed off the hospital staff, did you now? In what, a half hour?" He made a show of raising his left arm and checking his watch.

I explained to the desk sergeant what had happened. He said OK, but to remind him not to send me on hospital guard duty again.

I still think it was right to stop the doctor from entering the room, under the circumstances.

Chapter 25:

The Yum Yum Club

and the Cubans

In 1980, President Jimmy Carter welcomed all the freedom-loving Cubans who wanted, come to America. It was funny; Fidel Castro took this opportunity to empty all his prisons and send the occupants along for the ride. It was Fidel's version of prison reform.

This meant all the murderers, rapists, child molesters, drug dealers, and others came to America to start a new life. It was estimated somewhere around 2,700 hardened criminals arrived this way. Upon arrival in the U.S., the criminals were separated from the freedom-loving Cubans and sent to prison to await a court decision to determine their fate.

Lawyers for these criminals were successful in getting them released from prison until their court hearings. About thirty came to Center Zone in the summer of 1984. They suddenly appeared out of nowhere. It was as if some magic bus had dropped them off in the middle of the night and with no means of support, they continued their life of crime.

The Cubans were there before I started work and were still there when I went home. The addresses they gave were usually vacant or abandoned buildings. They all smelled of unwashed bodies, dirty clothes, and cigarettes. They loved to smoke unfiltered Camels. I think it gave them something to do when they weren't stealing.

They were a rough-looking lot, with dark eyes; dirty, greasy black hair; unshaven faces; and shirts that were never tucked. Their shoes ran from cheap tennis shoes to worn out, taped-up cowboy boots. Their pants were polyester Goodwill rejects, and they had tattoos on their hands, arms, and faces. These guys were dangerous and looked the part.

One of my first calls on them was recovered property. I was sent to a vacant and falling-down building within a block of the station. Inside the building were separate rooms, each filled with piles of busted concrete, rubble, and trash. Broken rebar hung from the ceiling. The place was dark and dank; no light penetrated from the outside. I heard scurrying noises and the sharp chittering of rats running around in the dark.

From the light of my dim police-issued flashlight, I could see that people were living in this building. There were empty cans of food and burned-out fires all around. The place smelled like human excrement; piles of shit were everywhere. You would think the rooms they ate and slept in would not be used as a toilet. I found the items I was supposed to recover.

There were about twenty stolen bicycles in parts and only a few complete bikes. It seemed to me it was trash, but I was told to recover it all. The problem was the bikes were against the far wall, and I had to climb over broken slabs of uneven, slippery shit-covered concrete to get to them.

It took almost an entire shift to remove the bikes, catalog them, and transfer them to the property room. I slipped and fell in the excrement several times and smelled like crap when my shift was over.

The next day I went back and arrested several Cubans living in the filthy building for trespassing. They could never post a bond and would be out of my hair for a time. I learned to read the tattoos of the Cubans to find out what they had been in prison for in Cuba. All the ones in Center Zone were felons, mostly murderers and rapists.

Many Cubans hung out at an old run-down strip club in the 3200 block of Troost called the Yum Yum Club. The club was where female impersonators could strut their stuff back in the 1960s and '70s. By 1983, it was a falling-down relic of its former self. The entire bar was visible upon crossing the open threshold. There was no heat in the winter and no air-conditioning in the summer, so the front door was never closed.

Once entering the club, you were surprised by its small size. Immediately inside the front door were a few small wooden tables and chairs on an old dirty wood floor half-covered with cigarette butts. Across the room, opposite the front door, was a small raised wooden stage where the female impersonators had performed years ago.

On the left side of the room was a short six-foot bar, behind which stood an old sliding glass door cooler with five shelves, only two of which had any beer on them, and those were cans of

Pabst Blue Ribbon. The beer was warm because the cooler was broken. Next to the broken cooler was the only thing that worked in the place: an old Wurlitzer Jukebox. The bar had not been cleaned in over ten years and had seen better days.

Usually, a group of ten or more Cubans gathered outside the club, with another fifteen inside. The Yum Yum was their unofficial clubhouse. Every day, we would constantly get calls from there about a robbery, a stabbing, even murder. The usual suspects responsible were hookers, dealers, pimps and, for a little spice, the new element, the Cubans.

My shift started at 2:45 pm, and the Yum Yum Club had been busy since opening at ten in the morning. I decided that, instead of responding to calls at the club, I would start interrupting the cycle. Every day I went out on ped checks and soon knew all the regulars around the club. Everyone who hung out there was a felon. No exaggeration, this place was a modern-day Sodom and Gomorrah.

The convicted murderers always said it was a misunderstanding or self-defense. I was amazed some of them were out of prison in three years. To say it was a dangerous place to be patrolling is a gross understatement.

The Cubans at the club did not seem to have a leader, but rather cliques divided the group. The guys standing outside were looking out for the police, and the ones inside could afford a beer. You could be an outsider one day, then mug somebody for cash, and the next day find yourself on the inside drinking a beer.

On a typical day, another officer and I would park in the middle of Troost, then start putting people on the wall and frisking them. Usually, knives were all we found on the Cubans. Guns? I do not think they could afford them or find a place to steal them. I always arrested the knife holders.

I arrested one Cuban called Slim several times for carrying a six-inch non-folding boning knife. I hated those boning knives. Slim liked to hide his knife under his shirt at the small of his back. Some officers would miss the blade because they only patted the sides, not the front and back. Slim would get warrants after a few of these arrests, and I would start arresting him for his warrants.

Soon Slim learned not to carry a knife unless he wanted to go to jail. He finally got smart and now had a bodyguard by his side, holding the knife. Slim did not care if his underling got arrested. We always made the whole group get on the wall when we stopped Slim; we never knew who was carrying for him.

Even though Slim did not carry knives much anymore, he would frequently fight if you touched the small of his back at the beltline during a pat-down. I think he must have been raped in prison.

It might seem obsessive or overreaching to arrest these Cubans for knives, but people were getting stabbed and cut there regularly. Case in point, a popular prostitute in the area stole money from one of the Cubans. He found her in the Yum Yum Club; I saw the victim.

She was bent facedown over a table; the suspect had stuck a ten-inch-long, wide, heavy butcher knife up her ass to the handle. I imagine he did the act slowly and repeatedly to increase her suffering. She must have endured the most excruciating pain imaginable until she bled out and died.

One Cuban was always at the center of many crimes committed in and around the Yum Yum Club. He was a big guy, thickly built, with oily black hair and tattoos on his face and hands and seemed to be an unofficial leader. I saw him talking to some of his thugs and yelled at him to come over to my side of the street. He crossed the road, and I wrote him a ticket for jaywalking. He told me he would hit someone over the head the next day and get the money to pay for the ticket.

The next day he killed another Cuban for the money, and I arrested him shortly afterward. As he was being loaded into a wagon, he smiled at me and yelled, "Hey, *pinche pendejo (f..king a..hole)!* I told you I would!" I was told the man he killed was a rival gang member he would have killed anyway. I didn't feel too badly.

Another time I saw a group of three Cubans leaning against a one-story, boarded-up brick building across the street from the club. I recognized one of them wearing red polyester pants; he had a warrant, and called for another car. When my backup arrived, I told the officer, "I'm going to stop those three Cubans and arrest the tall one in the red pants. He has a current aggravated assault warrant."

The other officer, Andrew Donnegan, said, "Oh, wait a minute. I've been with you on other ped checks before. Let me get my stick."

It was not a dig at me. It was a fact. I stopped some of the most violent criminals on the street, and a lot of them had anger-issue problems. We approached the men, and I told them to get on the wall. That was all I said, and the fight was on.

These were not bad odds, three against two, but there was already a crowd outside the Yum Yum, and many of them would have liked nothing better than to join the fight. I called for assistance, and as the group across the street was coming to help their friends, several more patrol cars arrived and prevented an all-out riot.

Under these circumstances, you can't wrestle with the suspects; we were not good enough to wrestle two people at once. You had to use your nightstick to keep them at bay until help arrived. No officers were hurt, but two of the Cubans were bruised up a bit.

About this time, a new sergeant and two new officers joined the crew. My new sergeant, Beth Anderson, was a noticeably short brunette, about 170 pounds. She had bad acne and was kind of a know-it-all. Also new to the sector were Bob Wright and Carl Long. Bob was a great guy and a good officer. He was short, dark-haired, medium build, and talked with a slight Southern drawl. Bob had finished probation three months before.

Carl Long was from my academy class. Carl was of average height, thin, and had a thick brown mustache that he constantly stroked between his right index finger and thumb. Bob Wright, Carl Long, and I formed a loose-knit group who looked out for each other.

On her first day, Sergeant Anderson made a move to place all new officers with less than one year of experience back on probation because that was the way it was when she started. I did not feel it was fair as by now we had made numerous felony arrests and were seasoned officers. It was impossible to be incompetent and survive with the amount of action we had each day, and most officers who needed to be put back on probation had already quit. I complained to the desk sergeant, and he said not to worry, he would talk to Sergeant Anderson.

Back to the Yum Yum Club. There had been a problem with the spotters outside the club announcing our arrival before we even got out of our cars. I suggested a plan where several of us would sneak up on foot behind the business and through a short alley that led right up to the front of the club. The spotters almost always faced the street with their backs to the joint. If we were quiet, we could be on them before they knew we were there. Two cars at opposite ends of the street would close off any suspects trying to escape.

Sergeant Anderson supervised the operation, and the plan went off perfectly. We were able to walk right up behind the spotters without being seen. The guys outside the club jumped when we yelled, "On the wall."

I was able to rush past a spotter and into the club, ordering everyone out at gunpoint before they had a chance to drop what they were carrying. All in all, we ended up with twenty Cubans on the wall. Five had dope, four had knives, and three had warrants. All of them went to jail.

While the wagon was loading up the arrests, Slim came out of the club to see what was happening. He must have been hiding behind the bar or in the bathroom when I ordered everyone outside. I reasoned Slim was not armed or holding drugs, since he expected he would be searched. Remembering how Slim would fight if you frisked the small of his back and how Sergeant Anderson wanted to put Bob, Carl, and me back on probation, I thought a little payback was in order.

I told Sergeant Anderson that Slim had information about a stabbing the week before in front of the club and would only talk to a supervisor. I also mentioned Slim liked to carry a knife in the small of his back.

Sergeant Anderson approached Slim and had him put his hands on the wall, assuming the position. As soon as Sarge frisked the small of his back, Slim turned around and slugged Sarge in the face. Another officer and I came to her aid, returned Slim's friendly gesture, and cuffed him. Sarge thanked us for our help, and we never heard any more about being put back on probation.

A final note: The health department, liquor control, and fire department closed the club down several times for various violations. The owner always claimed ignorance about anything going on in or around the business.

Chapter 26:
Take a Seat

Sergeant West was the last sergeant I worked for in Center Zone and my third in a year and a half. I don't know if Center Zone was a punishment or a tour of duty as sergeants seemed to rotate in and out.

Sergeant Lucie West was new, recently promoted, and untested to the trials of working in Center Zone. She was a tall, pretty, and soft-spoken woman. Like a new or experienced sergeant, rookie officer, or old salt, the crew waited to see how she reacted to the constant daily battle it was to work in Center Zone. The answer came within a week of her arrival.

It was a windless, hot, sticky Saturday night in July, about nine o'clock, when the call came out. There had been a stabbing at the Yum Yum Club. No reason for the assault was given, but it was probably over drugs. The victim was at the hospital. Before going into surgery, he had provided a name and a detailed description of the suspect.

This type of call came with varying suspects, including but not limited to pimps, prostitutes, drug dealers, rapists, murderers, robbers, and drunks. When you worked in Center Zone, that was the way it was. Different weapons were used to commit the crimes, including butcher knives, switchblades, brass knuckles, handguns, sawed-off shotguns, bare fists, bricks, and bottles.

This time the suspect was described as a female prostitute with a large Afro, a white shirt, and a sparkly blue micro-mini skirt, complete with pink platform shoes. She was purportedly armed with a large knife. Bob Wright, Carl Long, and I responded. We arrived in separate cars and parked facing each other in front of the Yum Yum Club. The night was getting hotter.

A streetlight half a block away cast a dim light over the usual crowd of about twenty to thirty societal rejects outside the bar. From the club's open door, garish red light escaped, along with the blaring sound of the jukebox's deep throbbing bass. Outside, a bluish haze of cigarette smoke mixed with the pungent smell of marijuana hung over the group. The crowd was hopped up with alcohol and drugs in anticipation of a good show to break up the monotony of the steamy night.

The loud hooting and hollering of racial epithets at the presence of the police venturing into their inner sanctum added to the general mix of sound. I grabbed my nightstick in my left hand, keeping my right hand free to draw my gun if needed. The tension was palpable.

Bob, Carl, and I stood shoulder to shoulder and scanned the crowd. We looked for the suspect and watched for the bottles and rocks usually aimed our way, and any guns pointed at us. Looking back and forth, I studied the excited crowd, alert for people grabbing at their beltlines, reaching around to the small of their backs, pulling the shirts over their belts, or the most obvious, people wearing jackets. By experience or dumb luck, I spotted a large Afro bobbing up and down behind a group of several men in various stages of sobriety.

If the men were drunk, they tended to swear at you but generally would step aside. Sober men would also step aside because they did not want to be frisked. Maybe they had a weapon or did not want to have a confrontation protecting some ugly whore; that was her pimp's job. The pimp would not bother us because he was carrying a gun and did not want it taken from him; it cost too much. The drug dealer did not want his stash seized, so he would move away. That left the half-drunk or half-high men with anger-issue problems, and only a good fight would satiate them.

If a fight broke out while we arrested the prostitute, all bets were off whether the crowd would jump into the fight if they thought they could get away with it. That is what we faced as we slowly walked toward the hostile group of people, mostly men and a few barely clothed prostitutes.

I told Bob and Carl the girl was behind the group of men next to the club's front door. We had to go into that mob and make the arrest; it was our job. The three of us entered the crowd, and it parted, then closed behind us like a python wrapping its coils, preparing to devour those foolish enough to get too close.

The prostitute we were looking for was trying in vain to hide behind a skinny Cuban.

He was wearing gold-colored polyester slacks, a dirty sleeveless white undershirt, and a thin gold chain and cross around his neck. As my eyes focused on the Cuban in front of the prostitute, his two buddies quietly slipped to the sides, leaving only this one man to protect the girl. I wondered, is this her pimp? Did he have a gun? Or was he the mean half-drunk guy who wanted to fight?

"Move away from the girl!" I ordered, looking directly at the Cuban. Behind the man, the pink platform shoes and the large Afro still bobbed from side to side. The Cuban yelled something in Spanish at me, raised his arms, and came at me like Frankenstein. I blocked his outstretched arms away from my body, stepped to the side, and backhanded a baton strike against his left knee. He collapsed, screaming in pain, and was out of the picture, leaving the blue-sequined, micro-mini-skirted vampire alone.

Bob and Carl each grabbed an arm of the prostitute; she started cussing and kicking the hell out of them with her platform shoes. While they struggled with her, I quickly cuffed the Cuban I had taken down while trying to watch my back.

In this situation, a bottle to the head or a knife in the back was not unlikely. A crowd surrounds you, and nobody would see who threw the bottle or stabbed the officer. We had to get the girl in cuffs before anybody else decided to join in the fight. Also, it was possible the girl might still have the knife concealed on her someplace and would use it if she got her hands free. I called for two wagons, one for each suspect, as males and females were not allowed in the same wagon. Two additional cars showed up. We now had five officers at the scene, their vehicles blocking the street. Red emergency lights flashed eerily, illuminating the night.

Bob and Carl were able to get the prostitute cuffed, but she was still yelling, screaming, and kicking. I pulled my arrestee off the ground and, simultaneously, picked up a knife where the girl had been standing. The blade still had dried blood on it, but I shoved it in the back of my pants anyway.

I held my arrest by his handcuffs and pushed him limping and cussing towards the street. My arrestee was yelling something in Spanish, and the prostitute was screaming when a wagon pulled up. The crowd was getting agitated. We loaded my prisoner into the wagon and waited for the second wagon to arrive.

The crowd was starting to move in closer and closer, an angry wall of people tightening all around us. Several times I had to warn the group back with my raised nightstick.

The wagon for the girl arrived, and sensing her imminent transfer to jail, the lady of the night ramped up her kicking, yelling, and now spitting. Bob and Carl tried to force her into the wagon, but she would put her feet against the sides of the door and refused to get inside. They finally managed to stuff her, on her back, headfirst, partially into the wagon. In the struggle, the hooker's micro-mini skirt pushed past her butt, which was gross. She wasn't wearing any underwear.

As the officers were trying to force the rest of the prostitute's body into the back of the transport wagon, Sergeant West pulled up in her car. The crowd backed down some, as there were now seven officers at the scene, and the chance of someone getting away with throwing a bottle or doing something else had passed.

The vampire was still kicking at Bob and Carl and connecting. They had lost all their patience and were ready to get more physical. At that moment, Sergeant West approached and called for the officers to calm down; there was no need to force the girl into the wagon; she would handle it.

Bob and Carl stepped aside, breathing hard, while Sergeant West walked up to the wagon. The prostitute was still screaming when I heard Sergeant West say calmly, "Now come on, there's no need for all this."

Then, wham, the handcuffed prisoner connected with a solid kick to the Sarge's face!

Sergeant West yelled, "You bitch!" and shoved the prisoner the rest of the way into the wagon and jumped in after the hooker, smacking the hell out of her. Someone grabbed the sergeant by her gun belt and pulled her out. Sergeant West's eyes were wide open, and she was taking in big gulps of air. Sarge's cheek was cut, and her right eye was already swelling.

"You did it, Sarge. She's in the wagon now, and everything is okay." I lightly held her shoulders and used my head to block her view of the wagon. The doors had been closed, but the sound of the prostitute's yelling and kicking against the doors of the locked police van resounded into the night.

I looked at her. "You know, Sarge, when you were assigned here, I wondered how you would be."

I turned and walked away. The crowd melted into the shadows; the show was over for the night.

Sometimes when you try to be friendly and reason with someone, you get kicked in the face for your effort.

A final note: Sargent West needed three stiches to close the cut on her cheek. The victim of the knife attack died in surgery, and the prostitute was found guilty of murder.

Chapter 27:
Demon-Possessed Teen

During my first winter, when the snow was fresh and the temperature hung in the low twenties, I was dispatched to an address in the 3300 block of James with another officer, Jack Crump, an eight-year veteran. Officer Crump, dressed in his signature pressed and tailored uniform, was a strong man, about thirty years old, with an easygoing temperament.

The dispatcher said it was a domestic disturbance: parents versus a thirteen-year-old girl. My thought was, how bad can it be? It was Jack's district; he would be the one to make the decisions and be responsible for any reports.

Sean Mulcahy

I would be able to sit back and observe. This should have been an easy call. It was not.

The house was a tall, narrow two-story home, yellow with brown trim. Jack joined me, and we walked up the front stairs to the concrete porch. Approaching the front door, we heard a woman screaming in fear and what sounded like some wild thing yelling and cussing. I looked at Jack, and he raised his eyebrows and knocked on the front door.

A thin, older man, possibly in his early sixties, answered the door. He had a terrified look on his face. His plaid flannel shirt was torn, half the buttons were missing, and deep parallel scratches marked his face, with lines of blood trickling down his cheeks and neck.

"Quick, it's my daughter! Something is wrong with her. I never seen her like this. She is uncontrollable. She attacked my wife and me!"

The father was out of breath. He bent over and sank to his knees on the floor, gasping for air. A sewer gas-type smell escaped from the open front door. The father pointed a shaky finger inside the house.

On a clean but worn oak floor stood a simple dining room table that once had four high-back chairs. Three of the four were broken; chair legs and backrests splintered. On the far side of the table, centered against a wall, stood a tall, glass-front china cabinet containing the usual assortment of china and crystal glass stemware.

In the left corner of the room a few feet from the china cabinet cowered a thin, hunched-over, gray-haired woman, crying hysterically. The woman's hands enveloped her face. Her arms were covered in long, deep scratches and what appeared to be several deep, bloody bite marks.

Briefly, she lowered her trembling hands, revealing long scratches that furrowed her face from hairline to jawbone. The woman's right eye had swollen shut. With her good eye, she stared straight at me through streaming tears and implored, "Help me!"

Then I saw blood seeping from her scalp in large, uneven patches. Her hair and patches of her scalp had been yanked out with extreme violence and lay in sticky tufts on the floor and dining room table.

Standing over the mother was a thin girl, under five feet, whose face was distorted with rage. She was dressed in a filthy white nightshirt soaked in sweat and wet red splotches. The girl's eyes appeared as if every blood vessel had ruptured, and her lips were stretched tight, appearing as thin, red lines, exposing two rows of yellow teeth.

The smell of human feces and the sulfur smell of rotten eggs burned the inside of my nose. I'd never seen anything like this before. This type of call wasn't covered in any academy class. I didn't know what to do; I had no idea and was glad it was Jack's call.

Jack broke the ice, trying to take a gentle approach. "How long has she been like this, sir?"

Jack was calm but never took his eyes off the girl if you could call her that at this time.

"All last night and all day! She threatened to kill us. She hit and bit Ma! You got to take her away; we can't handle her no more!" The man was crying uncontrollably.

"Okay, don't worry, we'll take care of her, sir. Stay back."

Jack was still unbelievably calm; nothing about this scene rattled him. It was as if he had dealt with this sort of thing a hundred times. Jack was on the same side of the room as the girl and took two tentative steps toward her, still talking softly.

"All right now, calm down; we can talk about it. What is the problem?" Jack eased forward another few steps until he was a couple of feet from her.

I stepped a little closer and was across the table from Jack, focusing on the out-of-her-mind girl. Saliva was running continuously out of the corners of her mouth. Her head jerked back and forth, focusing those bloodshot eyes first on Jack, then on me. Her hair was drenched in sweat, matted on the sides of her head, framing a face that showed no trace of sanity. She was deciding who to attack first.

As Jack continued to inch closer, she backed up next to the china cabinet and dug her bloody and broken fingernails into the wall. She began ripping long streaks through the wallpaper, all the while continuing to snort and cuss at us.

"Now, let's talk about it, come on, let's...?" He never finished his sentence.

The girl howled, pushed herself off the wall, and jumped up onto Jack's chest, bending him back at the waist. She dug her nails into his cheeks and was about to bite him when his left ankle gave out with a loud snap that sounded like a big stick breaking. Jack went down hard on his back with the girl still on his chest. He screamed in pain, "Get her! The bitch broke my ankle! Get her!"

The girl popped up off Jack, sensing he was no longer a threat. She hunched her back like a damn cat and howled and cussed at me! Jack crawled backward, dragging his left leg until his back was against the wall, away from the wild girl.

I glanced down at Jack on the floor, moaning and holding his left foot, injured and unable to help. I saw the mother cowering in the corner crying in pain. Then the father, beside the front door, screamed angrily, "Do something before she kills us all!"

The girl took two steps closer to me, and then, above the crying, moaning, and screaming, she gave me an evil grin and spoke two of the most frightening words I have ever heard. "You're next!"

I didn't hesitate and took one quick step toward the girl, then hit her with a right fist to the left side of her head, lifting her off her feet. She crashed into the china cabinet, smashing the glass door and breaking several shelves along with all the crystal and china.

She was out cold, lying among the broken glass shards and dishes when I cuffed her. She awoke bleeding in several places and started her insane wailing once more. I lifted the girl out of the debris and tossed her over in the corner, away from Jack and the terrified mother.

I stared into Jack's pain-filled eyes, stunned by the violence and my part in it.

As if to assuage my thoughts, Jack spoke, "Sean, the bitch broke my ankle. You did the right thing!" Jack moaned again, slowly rocking back and forth, holding his broken ankle.

"She was going to kill us! Something got into her!" the injured father managed to say between sobs.

I informed dispatch an officer had a probable broken ankle. The parents had multiple cuts, bites, scratches, and bruises, and there was a mental suspect, all needing medical care. As an afterthought, I told the dispatcher the situation was under control.

Still spitting and cursing at me, the girl tried to get to her feet. I quickly put my foot lightly on her back, holding her down. At that moment, Sergeant West showed up along with a couple of other officers and took in the scene: four people needing medical attention, hair and pieces of bloody scalp on the dining room table, broken chairs, a smashed china cabinet, and shattered dishes and crystal. And there I stood, holding the screaming and cussing juvenile to the floor with my boot.

Jack saw Sergeant West and said in a strained voice, "Sarge, he did good!"

The father took that moment to add, "She would have killed us!"

"Okay, Sean, you better write a good report!" She smiled; it would be okay.

Whether some evil entity possessed the girl was a little out of my bailiwick, but I strongly doubted it. As often was the case, I never heard whether the girl was on drugs, had some mental condition, or how she eventually turned out. I did learn that the sulfur smell had come from a backed-up sewer line in the basement.

A final note: Later, my partner in the Sex Crimes Unit used his arcane knowledge of the occult to elicit a confession from a cannibalistic serial killer in the Jeffery Dahmer tradition. However, that is another story.

Chapter 28:
The Smell

It was my second winter as a police officer. The day had been cold and snowy, with the streets covered in a brown slush. About six in the evening, I was dispatched to an apartment building on Main Street that had a suspicious smell coming out of one of the apartments. I knew what that meant and hoped I was wrong.

The apartment building was one-story red brick and resembled a roadside motel. I hadn't noticed it before, but after tonight, I would never forget it.

I was met at the front door of the building by the apartment manager, who introduced himself as Jim. He was a polite man in his mid-forties with a slightly balding head of prematurely white hair. He had a ready smile, which bordered on a laugh when I said, "So, you have a strange smell you want to report?" He grinned. I think this was making his day.

"Yes, I noticed the smell a couple of days ago, and it has gotten worse, and some of the other residents are complaining." Yeah, he had been here before.

"So, where is the smell coming from?" I asked, not wanting to know the answer.

"Down here at the end of the hall, apartment number eight."

Jim led me along a dimly lit, pale green–painted hallway with old, worn, dark-stained hardwood floors. The awful smell grew stronger with each step I took closer to the apartment. He stopped at the end of the hall, in front of a solid, thick wooden door with the ominous brass number eight affixed at eye level.

"It's awfully warm in the hallway. Is it always this warm?" I asked Jim, thinking maybe a rat died under a heater or something that would not involve me dealing with the situation.

"Well, the residents do like it warm this time of year."

Jim gave that Cheshire Cat grin that was beginning to annoy me.

I wrinkled my nose at the nauseous odor emanating from beyond the door. I knew it. This was going to be bad. If I had to describe the aroma, it would be the foul smell from a dead mouse behind your refrigerator allowed to bloat for a day or two. You know by the scent something died but don't know where.

The smell of that dead mouse floats around the kitchen and maybe into the living room before fading. Then suppose the smell is proportional to the size of the source and imagine that smell in your kitchen was produced by a little two-ounce mouse. Then think what a two-hundred-pound dead mouse would smell like behind your refrigerator. Now I believe you can get a rough idea of what I was facing; only a dead two-ounce mouse smells pleasant compared to this absolutely horrid, gut-wrenching stench.

Unless you were there, words could not describe the smell. I walked back up the hallway to make sure the odor wasn't coming from another place and to get a breath of air. It was time to do something that was going to be awful. Slowly I walked back to apartment number eight and looked for some sort of reprieve in Jim's smiling face. No such luck.

"This is it. The tenant has not been seen in several days, maybe a week."

If I was not mistaken, Jim was pleased with himself by this point. He reveled in my obvious discomfort in dealing with this situation.

"Well, I don't suppose you have a key? I could come back tomorrow."

Then it occurred to me, why in the Sam Hell didn't he call about the smell earlier in the day? Why did he wait until the evening when it was my shift? It must be some cosmic conspiracy against me. What had I ever done to deserve this? My thoughts were interrupted by his pleasant, if not cheerful, voice. It was not right; he should at least sound sad or serious. Cheerful? Oh, come on!

"Oh yes, I have the key to all of the apartments!"

He fidgeted in his pants pocket and produced a tarnished brass key engraved with the number eight. He handed it to me like a kid handing over a red apple to a teacher.

I looked at the key in my hand, looked at the keyhole, looked at the key, then looked at Jim, who said, "It's okay. You need to do this. I'll be right here if you need me. This has happened before."

I knew it. I knew it. Jim knew all along what had caused the smell. He was not smiling now. He was showing me some compassion. He figured this was my first suspicious-smell call. I knocked, no response, then fitted the key into the lock and turned it. The lock opened with an audible clack, and I steeled myself for what awaited me behind the door. I took a deep breath of the tainted hallway air, turned the doorknob, and slowly pushed open the door.

A gush of hot, thick, foul-smelling air burst out of the apartment's interior as if under pressure to escape, and I felt my hair stir with its force. My knees bent. I could not even take a step into the apartment and had to hold on to the doorknob for support. Even though I hadn't taken in a breath yet, the horrible smell of rotting flesh entered my nose, causing an instant and violent gag reflex. I got control of my gagging and, out of breath, was forced to take in a massive amount of foul air, which in turn caused me to start retching all over again.

This cycle of breathing, gagging, breathing, then gagging went on for what seemed like forever. Finally, I got control of myself enough to take a tentative step into the apartment. At this point, the smell became a living thing, wrapping its foul presence around me and forcibly invading my body.

I still had not let go of the doorknob, maybe fearing the door would shut itself and leave me locked in this terror forever. I was looking at a simple one-room apartment with a few windows, some clean white curtains, and a clean wood floor with a small woven rug in the center. A five-drawer dresser with an old black-and-white TV perched on top was against the south wall. It was a room with no refrigerator or stove of any sort. With a slight movement of my eyes, the whole apartment became visible.

As if my mind was denying its existence, there was the bed centered against the north wall. Here was the source of the awful smell and many of my future nightmares. There was a large man, maybe two hundred pounds or more, halfway on and halfway off the bed. He had no shirt on, and his pants were around his ankles. His socks and brightly polished shoes were neatly aligned next to his feet. I could not tell if he had been getting dressed or undressed. His hands were at his sides. He was on his back, his knees bent over the edge of the bed, and his bare feet planted firmly on the floor.

It must have been eighty-five degrees inside the room and had been since the man died. There was no one to turn the heat down, and the windows were painted shut. A corpse smells worse in a warm environment; the smell is magnified by the hot temperature that slowly cooks the corpse, like meat in a crock pot. In this case, I was dealing with a big, heavy corpse in a hot room and decomposing for days—all the ingredients for the worst smell I have ever encountered in my life. There would be others, but this was the worst.

Breathing through my mouth to avoid the olfactory cells in my nose, bravely but tentatively, I approached the corpse one step at a time. He was sickly purple and white. Blood in his legs had drained to his ankles, which resembled purple grapefruits, and his toes looked like cooked sausages. Blood had settled under the skin around his back, contrasting the pale, bloodless upper body. A large purple wet spot covered the once-white sheets around his back. Blood, long since dried, had leaked out of his ears, running down the side of his head but never reaching the mattress. His eyes and mouth were closed.

Some people refer to a deceased relative as looking peaceful, but this man looked anything but peaceful. He was scary. His facial features distorted with bloat made his cheeks look like he was trying to blow up a basketball. His stomach was unnaturally huge; he appeared pregnant and ready to burst. It was not fat that made him seem so large; he was full of air to the point of exploding.

He was a fragile bubble made of skin; one careless touch or movement of the body could cause it to burst open, expelling putrid gas and rotten juices forcibly into the air. When someone dies, the bacteria in the intestines and stomach go wild, eating everything and producing gas, filling the body with awful, rotten-smelling air.

I did not disturb anything in the room. At the academy, we had been instructed never to touch or disturb anything at a possible homicide scene. There was a big wet pool of dark, purplish-colored blood on the mattress spreading out from under the corpse's back, indicating to me that he had been shot or stabbed. This meant it was a homicide. I did not have to touch the rotting body and was done with the case. The homicide unit could have it.

I left the room, going all the way down the hall, retching but happy I would be done with the case as soon as I radioed for Sergeant West to respond to confirm my analysis and call Homicide. I was bent over in the middle of a sickening retch when Sergeant West walked through the lobby door. She smiled at me as I stood up and wiped my mouth off with the sleeve of my shirt.

"So, Sean, what have you got going on here? Whew-wee, I can smell it from here!"

She waved her hand back and forth in front of her face in a futile attempt to fan the smell away. Sarge then reached inside her jacket, pulled out a jar of Mentholatum, rubbed some under her nose, and then offered it to me. I dipped my finger in the jar and put some of the savory jelly under my nose. It did not block a lot of the smell out, but it helped.

I led her to the room, and again the smell was overpowering. It was an effort to keep my gagging under control. I did not want Sarge to think I could not handle this call. I need not have worried. Soon, Sergeant West was gagging too.

I volunteered, "The man is dead, and with the blood coming out from under his back, he must have been murdered."

She looked at me and smiled. "He is dead?"

He was dead. I can't believe I said that.

"What's his name? Have you found his ID yet?"

"Ah, no."

How stupid could I be? I had not thought to check for an ID. I was too preoccupied with the smell and sight of the rotting corpse to do anything like my job. "Well, check his pants; see if he has a wallet or something with his name on it." She stood back, looked at me, then glanced around the room.

The bed and the man's pants were wet from leaked body fluids. I bent over, coming close to the dead man's putrefying legs, feeling his trousers, standing up twice and gagging, before locating the man's wallet in his back pocket. With one hand over my mouth, I slowly and carefully inched the tips of my fingers onto the wallet without popping the corpse.

Delicately, I inched the wallet out by moving it from side to side while pulling on it gently with my fingertips. My face was close enough to the gas and septic-water-filled body that I almost passed out.

After what seemed an eternity in hell, I removed the wallet without losing my balance and falling onto the corpse or puking on it. Tossing the wallet to Sarge, I ran out of the room to the lobby door and outside for some fresh, crisp winter air. I immediately bent over with another session of dry heaves. Sarge joined me in doing the same across the narrow walkway outside the front door.

Man, oh man, I did not know how much longer I could take this. The only thing saving me was I hadn't had anything to eat since breakfast over eight hours ago.

After a few minutes, the gagging stopped.

"This is your first one?" Sarge asked, still lightly gagging occasionally.

"Like this, yes." My eyes watered from gagging. I had seen a dozen dead bodies by now but no stinkers; this was my first.

"Well, we have to turn the body over and make sure there are no signs of foul play."

That was too much. The thought of touching that bloated, rotten corpse made me gag some more.

We walked back to the room and up against the bed and looked to see where we would place our hands to turn the body over without popping it. Gently I grabbed an arm, and Sarge put her hands under his shoulder, keeping her body at an angle to avoid any spray if the blood sack on his back burst open.

On the count of three, she pushed, I pulled, and I prayed his decomposing arm would not come off. Under his back, the skin had detached from the muscle, forming a large sack filled with blood, water, and decomposed chunks of flesh. If you have ever cooked a Thanksgiving turkey in a plastic cooking bag, you know the bottom of the bag becomes a brittle sack filled with water, melted fat, and bits of cooked turkey meat. That is what it looked like, only purple colored.

We had turned the body a little when I declared, "That's it, check out all of the pooled blood under him. He must have been shot in the back. We better leave!"

"Keep rolling him over. That blood sack is normal on a corpse in this condition."

We kept at it until he was on his side. The purple bag of juice on his back, of course, burst open, filling the room with even worse-smelling gas and a mist of minute particles of the toxic and lumpy fluids. A gush of fluid exploded like a water balloon, flowing onto the sheets and mattress, looking like dark purplish-red small-curd cottage cheese.

I lost it, and retched hard enough to get a hernia. I let go of the swollen arm and dashed out the door, running until I pushed through the front door and out into the cold December air. I continued to retch, throwing up some bile from my empty stomach. When I returned to the hallway, Sergeant West ran past me with her hand over her mouth. From the looks of it, I assumed Sarge ate a big lunch before coming to work.

There was no indication of foul play and, eventually, I collected the man's personal effects and bagged them for the property room. The coroner's assistants came and picked up the body and took it to the morgue, where an autopsy would be performed the next day.

It is an interesting point that as I watched the coroner's men wrangle the bloated dead man into a body bag, neither of the men showed any reaction to the gruesome task. They did it with a certain aplomb and respect toward the deceased. They say you can get used to anything if you do it enough times.

Jim, the apartment manager, smiled brightly as I thanked him. Then, as I placed the key to apartment number eight firmly in his outstretched palm, I told him with a big smile, "At least I don't have to clean the room!" Jim lost his smile instantly.

"Son of a bitch!" I heard Jim mutter under his breath as I walked out the door.

When I drove home that night, I could smell the corpse on me. It was in my hair, stuck to my uniform, my skin, and especially in my nose. This kind of smell took its time to wear off. I was never fond of turkey and gravy, cottage cheese, or even grape juice after that night.

A final note: At the time, we were not equipped with gloves or masks.

Chapter 29:

Dennis's First Felonies

One day in early fall, when the air was cool but still warm enough to wear a short-sleeved shirt, a new officer, Dennis Crowley, a recent transfer from midnights, asked me to help him find a felony arrest. He said he had not made one yet. Dennis was tall, thin, and looked young with his blond hair and lack of any facial hair. Dennis seemed like a good officer and I was flattered he asked me for some help. I was more than willing, remembering all the help Hans Storch gave me in getting acquainted with the bad guys in Metro Zone.

I told Dennis to get a pair of dark sunglasses; it would make him look older. Although he had been out on the street for at least six months, sometimes it was harder to figure out the score on the midnight shift.

I explained to Dennis, "Start stopping cars in your district. Begin with expired tags, no tags, and visible equipment violations. Gradually, you will learn which violations prove the most fruitful. For example, stopping grandma with an expired tag is a waste of your time, and while you are dealing with old grandma, several good car checks will drive right by you. Second, talk to Hans. He knows every bad guy in forty sector, and he will always let you know who is wanted and where to find them."

After roll call, I told Dennis, "Hans told me a week ago about a guy who goes by the alias June Bug and lives a couple of blocks east of Prospect and Sixty-third who needs help. I talked to June Bug several times in front of his home, and he told me a guy named Lonnie Washington wanted to kill him for messing with his girlfriend. I told June Bug I would keep an eye out for Lonnie. Lonnie also had an outstanding felony warrant for assault with a deadly weapon."

I explained to Dennis that even though June Bug is a convicted burglar and next week I might arrest him on some warrant, I will still talk to him respectfully. You never know, sometimes, a guy like that might have some information that can lead you to another arrest. I also told him, "Now I make as many as six passes on his house each day, hoping to catch Lonnie before or after he shoots June Bug."

Dennis and I went over to June Bug's "crib," as he liked to call his home, and today was Dennis's lucky day. I spotted Lonnie walking up the middle of the street toward us. I had never seen Lonnie, but I was sure this was him.

"Hey, Dennis, it's time for your first felony arrest! You ready?"

Dennis's eyes popped open wider with the surge of adrenaline running through his body.

"Ah, yeah, what's happening?"

"That guy walking in the middle of the street toward us is wearing a heavy overcoat but has shorts on and is favoring his right side. I believe that is Lonnie coming to kill June Bug."

Lonnie knew if he ran away after seeing us, we would immediately start chasing him. He continued to walk toward us, hoping we would ignore him.

Dennis did not look scared, but excited, itching to go.

"Okay, Dennis, I'm going to confront him. He will take off downhill between the houses on the west side of the street. I'll drive over to the next block and stop him if you haven't caught him, okay?" Dennis nodded. I waited until the suspect got closer, then got out of the car, gun out, and yelled for him to stop.

As I predicted, Lonnie took off running between the houses with Dennis on his tail. I yelled at Dennis, "Don't forget he's got a gun!" Then I notified the dispatcher of the foot chase.

I did not think anything of letting Dennis pursue an armed suspect by himself. My FTO, Joe Morrison, let me chase armed drug dealers, so what was the difference?

Lonnie and Dennis's path was clear of trees, shrubs, or other cover. Dennis would not lose sight of Lonnie as he chased him into the next block. Sometimes suspects get out of sight, hide behind something, wait until the officer runs by, then assault the officer.

There was one fence, but that would make it more fun for Dennis. I sped over to the next block and watched as Dennis walked a handcuffed Lonnie down a driveway toward my car. Dennis had the biggest grin I had ever seen, and he was not even breathing hard.

"I caught him in the backyard and told him I was going to shoot him. That's when he dropped a sawed-off double-barrel next to the fence! I'm going back to get it."

He started to leave when I stopped him.

"Hey, Dennis, get on your radio, clear the air, and tell dispatch you got him and are arresting him for the warrant, CCW, resisting arrest, and call for a wagon as you go get the gun and your car. I'll be here waiting with the felon you caught!"

Dennis was ecstatic he'd made his first felony arrest, and now all the other officers on the shift knew it.

"Hey, listen, Dennis, if you finish that report soon enough, Hans told me where another one is hiding out. Also, be sure to mention in your report you made the arrest based on information Hans gave you."

Sarge would give Hans some of the credit for the arrest.

"Yeah, sure, this won't take long."

I waited for the wagon while Dennis headed to the station to process Lonnie and write the report. After the wagon took off, June Bug came out of his house and nodded a thank you. Now he owed me one.

About noon, Dennis cleared, and we met up in the parking lot at East High School on Sixty-third. I told Dennis what Hans had told me a couple of days ago.

"There is a guy, Billie Cleveland, who has two felony warrants—one for assault with a gun, the other for armed robbery—staying at a house around the corner. We can park a couple of houses down and do a residence check."

The dispatcher confirmed Billie's warrants, and I asked her to hold the air. The house sat atop a steep terrace. Dennis and I struggled up the terrace on either side of the concrete stairs. Never approach a potentially armed suspect standing next to your partner; it makes you an easier target to hit.

The hill was steep and neither of us could climb it with a gun drawn. Halfway up the terrace, still not visible from the top, Billie came hurrying down the stairs, holding a gun tucked in at his waist from falling out. He was only paying attention to the steep stairs and did not see us until I yelled, "It's him!"

Dennis was ready and dove at Billie's knees, and I tackled Billie around the waist, pinning his arms to his side. We tumbled down the terrace, ending in a pile. Dennis was on the bottom, Billie in the middle, with me on top.

I reached down and felt a gun in the front waistband of Billie's pants and yelled, "He's got a gun!"

I smacked my right elbow into Billie's face, banged a knee into his side, and pulled the gun from his waist. Billie screamed in pain.

We rolled Billie onto his stomach, causing him to scream louder. I didn't hit him hard enough to cause that much screaming.

"I've been shot! I've been shot in the side!" Billie wailed. I had heard sometimes, in an incredibly stressful situation like wrestling with an armed felon, you can't hear a gunshot. We both looked down; our guns were still holstered. We looked at each other and shrugged.

I turned Billie over onto his back and checked him, looking for blood. Sure enough, there was blood soaking his shirt. I ripped it open, and there, on his left side, was a bandage seeping blood.

"I was shot yesterday, and the hospital stitched me up." Billie was now crying.

Okay, now I understood. Billie had been shot previously, patched up at the hospital, then sent home to heal. Being tackled and rolling down the front terrace had ripped the wound open.

"Okay, Dennis, you can call dispatch, clear the air, order the paramedics for Billie and notify Sergeant Ulnis. Then get some thick medical pads out of the trunk to put on Billie until the paramedics arrive."

I wanted Dennis to do the radio talk, as he would get the credit. Everyone would realize this was his second felony arrest of the day. Dennis was having a great time. The dispatcher's response to Dennis informing her of the situation was fun to hear.

"Dispatch, the suspect is in custody, but I'm going to need an ambulance; the suspect is suffering from a gunshot wound."

"Are both of you okay?"

The dispatcher had some emotion in her voice that they usually never show. As excited as he was, Dennis should have mentioned from the beginning that the shooting was from a prior incident.

"Ah, yes, dispatch, it was the suspect."

"You shot the suspect?" The dispatcher was still showing some emotion.

"I'm sorry for the confusion. We are okay, but the suspect was shot yesterday, and his wound was opened back up in the struggle to arrest him."

Sergeant Ulnis showed up and checked on everyone, including the suspect. Sergeant Ulnis told Dennis he did a good job, making Dennis even more proud. The suspect was patched up again and transported to jail for possession of a firearm and his warrants. It was a fun day for Dennis though not for Lonnie or Billie. After that day, Dennis made many more good arrests and enjoyed a long, successful career.

Chapter 30:
Popping Fresh

On a hot summer day in August, a new guy, Ken Levins, recently off break-in, joined our crew on days. He was in his early twenties, six feet, and had a thin build. As most new officers are, Ken was quiet. He handled his calls but still lacked the experience that would only come with more time on the job. He was also naive and did not always use his common sense.

Ken was only in his first month off probation when I heard him dispatched on a dead body in a nearby apartment. It was sweltering that summer, with temperatures hovering in the triple digits for the last week. I hoped for Ken's sake that the body was fresh and that the air conditioner was working. I remember thinking at the time that maybe this would be his first stinker and hoped it was not as bad as my first one.

I did not see Ken again that day and found out what happened only days later when I asked about him. Another crew member told me what had happened and that Ken had been the victim of a sick joke that had caused him to take some time off.

When Ken got to the apartment, two detectives were already at the scene. The air-conditioning was off and had been for the last week. The body was lying on a couch facing the west windows, unadorned with shades or curtains. The front door was open to let some of the hot, stagnant, foul-smelling air out of the apartment.

The detectives established that the body had been in the apartment for five days. Large blowflies circled in the air and were crawling all over the body. The smell was overwhelming, and when Ken first approached the apartment door, he started gagging and threw up in the hallway.

The homicide detectives did not mind the odor, as they were used to it from numerous calls like this one. To them, it was funny Ken was getting sick from the smell and had not even seen the body yet. The detectives calmed Ken down and brought him into the apartment to view the body, which was bloated to twice its normal size, causing the facial features to be unrecognizable as human. The face, they said, looked like a giant balloon.

Ken got sick again and had to leave the room to vomit, but by now, nothing was left in his stomach, giving him the dry heaves. This made the detectives hysterical, and they waited until Ken returned to the apartment for the third time.

One of the detectives handed Ken a ballpoint pen and told him the body had to be popped to be examined for evidence of foul play. They even told Ken to pop the stomach, as that would deflate the body the quickest and to hit it hard because the skin had toughened.

They already knew the deceased had been murdered because the victim's wife had turned herself in and confessed. It was entirely unnecessary for Ken to even be in the room; he only had to be in the hallway to secure the scene, not that anybody would want to get near that awful smell.

The detectives insisted Ken pop the body and told him all officers had done it at least once. Reluctantly, Ken took the ballpoint from one detective while the other detective encouraged Ken to go over and do it. Ken covered his mouth with one hand, trying to control his gagging, approached the rotting body, raised the pen, and brought it down hard on the corpse's stomach.

The body literally exploded. Bloody, watery fluids, mushy stomach and organ parts flew into the air. The explosion sent pieces sticking onto the walls, windows, and ceiling. Ken's face, hair, hands, and arms were covered with horrible purple fluid and bits of rotten tissue. The detectives were spared as they had stepped out the door before the pen struck the corpse. The detectives laughed out loud and thought this was the funniest thing they had ever seen in their whole lives.

Ken lost it and, violently retching, staggered out the door. He managed to get in his car and drive back to the station with his windows down. Metro had showers, and Ken walked into one with his uniform, gun belt, and shoes on and stayed there until a sergeant could coax him back out. He was finally able to change his clothes and tell the sergeant what had happened. Ken took a week off but left Metro Zone for Center Zone and a fresh start. He was a much stronger officer emotionally than I would ever be to have survived the ordeal.

The two detectives said it was a joke and never thought Ken would do it. Rumor had it they were given two weeks off without pay and transferred back to the field.

I have heard this story repeated over and over, with varying outcomes. Most of the time, it is told as a joke. This is an example of the sick humor officers use to get them through another day. It is the lack of empathy officers develop over time, a callus on their souls.

Chapter 31:

Tookie's 225

Stolen autos are a fact of life, and I chased several during my first three years in law enforcement. The one that stands out the most during that time was the "Tookie 225 Chase."

As most of these stories begin, it was a hot, muggy day with temperature and humidity in the nineties. It was a Sunday at about eleven in the morning, and I was patrolling south on Prospect, approaching Fifty-ninth Street, looking for something to do. There were no warrants to chase down, no places I needed to watch—no drug houses, chop shops, or whorehouses. I lit a cigarette.

The song "Green Onions" by Booker T. & the MG.'s was beginning on the radio and I turned the volume up. I was kind of bored; few other cars were out and looking to kick something up. I didn't know what it would be, but I would know it when I saw it…. Then there it was.

A beautiful 1972 mint-condition Buick Electra 225, four-door, white vinyl over medium blue metallic, white leather interior, and wide whitewall tires cruising east on Fifty-ninth Street. All four windows were down despite the heat. Gangs preferred the windows down with no pillars to restrict arm movement when firing guns out of the vehicle. I had never seen this car in Metro, and recognized the driver, Tookie Leeks. The car wasn't his.

Tookie shaved his head in wide strips, bald, then medium-length hair, repeated over his entire head. He was unique in that he did not braid it as most young men did at the time. Tookie passed in front of me. I saw him, but he never checked for cross traffic. That would have been uncool. Tookie could not show any concern for other drivers.

Still in his early twenties, Tookie was a versatile criminal, with felony convictions covering most of the serious crimes out there except for murder and rape. His arrest record included armed assault, armed robbery, burglary, possession of drugs, stolen auto, and theft.

It was only a month ago when I met Tookie for the first time. I had parked by the front door of a convenience store when Tookie came running out of the store practically into me with a stolen quart of Colt 45 malt liquor in his hand. Since he didn't resist, I gave him a summons for shoplifting. It was not a serious crime for a man of Tookie's stature but not below it either.

Turning left through a red light, I fell in behind the big deuce and a quarter, wondering if Tookie was packing today. He was that kind of fun guy. The dispatcher checked in the computer, and of course, the car came back stolen the day before from Center Zone.

I called for another car and followed Tookie. He was low in the front seat and only the top of his head showed. He had his right palm resting on the wheel, fingers loose, and his left hand hanging out the window by the elbow.

Gangbangers, meaning the gang members who liked to shoot guns, tried to keep their heads low in the car because they thought it made them look cool and to show the smallest profile if someone started shooting at them. There were a couple of drawbacks to keeping low in the car; the driver can barely see out the front and very little out the side or rearview mirrors.

From Tookie's position, he could barely see me. I kept a half a block away, giving time for my backup car to get closer. The rules of engagement stated on a felony car stop, which this would be, the arrest should be made with an assisting officer.

I had followed Tookie east on Fifty-ninth Street for a couple of blocks when he first saw me. He grabbed the wheel with his left hand and adjusted the rearview mirror to see me better. Tookie decided to run.

He floored the heavy Buick, and the enormous 455-cubic-inch engine responded with a cloud of black exhaust smoke. Amazingly, Tookie made a big mistake: He did not sit up straight to better his field of vision while accelerating to high speed.

I took a deep drag on my cigarette, tossed it out the window, notified the dispatcher the driver was fleeing, and floored my old worn out Chrysler four-door. My car could not keep up with the Buick, and I terminated the chase. I lost sight of the deuce and a quarter as it was topping sixty miles per hour on the narrow street. It was too dangerous to continue.

Tookie could kill somebody, but that would not be Tookie's fault; it would be my fault for chasing him, thus making him drive faster to escape. Too many times, innocent third parties were killed by fleeing suspects for minor offenses like driving stolen cars. It was not worth the risk to the general public to further pursue, especially at that speed on a residential street.

Three long blocks later, I came upon the Buick. I told the dispatcher my location and ordered the paramedics, as I did not believe anyone could survive the crash he'd had without massive injuries.

The Buick had collided full speed into the rear of a car backing out of a driveway. The front end of the stolen car was crushed; the smoking engine was knocked back into the firewall off busted motor mounts. I saw steam rising from a mangled radiator and a crumpled windshield with a big hole on the driver's side. Without a seatbelt, Tookie had been launched headfirst through the glass.

I found Tookie lying face-up about twenty-five feet away on the grass between the sidewalk and street, giving that hacking, sporadic, slight cough I always referred to as the death rattle. Each time I had heard that rattle, the person died within minutes. I took Tookie's hand in mine and said a silent prayer for him because even if it was a scumbag like Tookie, he did not have to die alone, and I thought it might make a difference in the hereafter.

The paramedics arrived; Tookie had somehow managed to keep breathing and surprisingly survived. No one in the other car was hurt.

Months later, Tookie showed up in state court with a broken leg and in a wheelchair. In his opening statement, the prosecutor asked the perfunctory question, "Officer, is the man you saw driving the stolen car in this courtroom today, and can you identify him for this court?"

"Yes, the man sitting over there with his leg in a cast is the man I saw driving the stolen car." I pointed at Tookie.

Later on, during cross-examination, the defense attorney, with a smug voice dripping with condescension, asked, "How can you be sure that my client is the same man you saw driving the stolen car?"

It did not matter that I chased Tookie and found his almost lifeless body at the scene or even that he had been in the hospital or jail since the crash and that he was in court today. Who else could it be, his identical twin who also happened to have a broken leg? The defense lawyer still wanted to know how I could be sure.

I looked at the young-faced defense attorney and answered, "Well, I recognized him when I caught him stealing from a convenience store a month before the crash. I recognized him when he drove in front of me in the stolen Buick. I recognized him when I held his hand as he was dying at the crash scene. And I recognize him now because he still has those same unique crossed eyes he's had since the first time I arrested him."

"No further questions, Your Honor, the defense rests."

That was the defense attorney's only question. Ten minutes later, Tookie was found guilty. I do not know what his sentence was; that was announced later.

Chapter 32:
A Pinto Giant

Occasionally, I would be assigned a ride-along passenger. I did not like having a ride-along for many reasons. The ride-along would want to talk, which distracted me from paying attention to my surroundings. I wasn't exactly in the safest part of town. With a passenger, I could not chase cars, curse, or even drive fast to calls; I was responsible for the safety of a civilian.

Other officers liked having a civilian passenger; it was someone they could talk to during long patrols. I had asked the sergeant not to assign me ride-alongs, but sometimes I still had to take one. Today it was serendipity. This ride-along probably saved me from great bodily harm.

My ride-along for the day was Bob Lange, a cop from Denver, Colorado, in Kansas City on vacation. He had been on the Denver PD for ten years and wanted to visit our police department.

At the beginning of the shift, I asked him, "Hey, Bob, are you carrying a gun?"

"Yes, I am. Is that okay with you?" he answered in a relaxed tone of voice.

"Oh yeah, you are a cop, so I would prefer that you did. Feel free to use it if we get in a shootout or I'm being killed in any way!" I wasn't smiling.

"Okay, I will."

Bob was large at six feet three and two hundred and fifty pounds. He looked at me, kind of unsure if I was serious or exaggerating the danger. Although Bob did not say, and I did not ask what part of town he worked in, he had that self-confidence like he had experienced a few things in his career.

It was a hot, humid day in July, and I was driving north on Garfield from Fifty-ninth around ten in the morning and came upon a bronze Ford Pinto also headed north on Garfield. The car had no rear license plate, and the fun began.

I hit my lights, and the driver pulled over slowly to the right, not quite over to the curb, as if he did not want to commit to being stopped. I radioed my location as the 5800 block of Brooklyn, which was a big mistake.

I had put the radio mike back in its holder and was getting out of the car when the driver started exiting out of the tiny Pinto. First one eighteen-inch heavy black boot hit the pavement, then the other followed; with some effort, the rest of the body emerged. I was in a state of awe. This guy was at least six feet five, maybe taller, with a barrel chest, shoulders as broad as the car, and pushing over three hundred pounds. There did not appear to be an ounce of fat on his body. He was dressed like a lumberjack with black leather boots, a red flannel shirt with the sleeves ripped at the shoulders, and blue jeans. The driver immediately started for me, raising his fists and screaming, "Why the hell did you stop me? You got no right to stop me!"

He took two more steps closer to me, his face full of rage and anger. I was not going to fight this giant. If he did not stop, I would shoot him and sort out the facts later.

"Stop right where you are, buddy! I stopped you for no license plate! Every car must have a plate; yours is no exception. Now get back in your f..king car until I tell you to get out. Now move it!"

My voice had a hard edge on it, and I put my right hand on my gun and loosened it for emphasis.

The giant grunted loudly, folding himself with some effort back into the tiny Ford, forcing the car body to tilt noticeably. With one foot in my car and one on the ground, I told the dispatcher to send me another car as the driver seemed aggressive and angry.

It has been my experience when a driver exits his car yelling and getting in your face immediately he has a reason. He is trying to intimidate the officer so they will not check the interior of his vehicle and or check him in the computer. This guy was a real danger to me, and I treated him as such. I was not going to confront him alone.

Shortly my backup car announced, "Where are you, 44? You are not on Brooklyn."

"Oh, try the next street over!" I was flustered and embarrassed by not knowing which block I was on.

"East or west?"

"Try east."

I was getting more agitated with myself with each passing second, and the giant was slamming his left hand on the door, making a booming sound. Looking at my ride-along, I asked him nicely, "Could you run down to the corner and see what street I'm on, please?"

Sometimes your mind can go blank, and mine had just left on vacation.

Bob did not answer but left the car at a good jog down the street.

"I can't find you there either, 44!" I recognized his voice—it was Sam Lyons, an intelligent officer with five years on and up for sergeant.

"Hold on a second!"

Bob returned, breathing hard, and with no wasted words, spat out, "Garfield."

"Garfield, 43, I'm on Garfield." I didn't know how much longer the giant would stay put.

Sam pulled up behind me as the giant opened his door.

"I thought I told you to stay in that damn car until I told you to get out! Now close it!"

He slammed the door shut, rocking the car. I approached the driver's door as Sam hurried to cover the passenger side.

"I need your driver's license and vehicle registration!" I stood behind his window, making it difficult for him to see me, and if he had a gun, it would slow him down trying to fire behind himself. Also, if he suddenly swung his door open, it would not hit me.

"Ah, I don't have my license with me, and this is my girlfriend's car, so I don't know about her registration."

The giant's voice had mellowed a bit.

Now I knew at least part of the reason he tried to intimidate me. I got his name, checked it through the computer, and found out his license was suspended for a DUI. Well, he had lied to me about his license, he had no tags on the car, and he was suspended. He was going to jail.

"Okay, now, sir, I want you to step out of the car with your hands up where I can see them!" I stepped back a little to give me a bit more reaction time if he tried anything when he exited the car.

"Why do you want me to step out of the car now, officer?" he asked in an innocent voice full of remorse.

Oh, brother. First he wants out, now he doesn't. What a pain in the ass. It would take a tow truck to pull him out of that car if he did not leave voluntarily.

"Okay, buddy, I'm going to issue you some tickets, and you cannot drive, so get out of the car now!"

"Okay, okay, I'm coming out. You don't have to get angry."

The guy had calmed down now.

"Put your hands on the car. I'm going to pat you down for weapons."

When he put his hands on the car he moved his feet back into the search position. Looking at his size, I knew he could easily push the Pinto over if he wanted. With the giant's hands still on the car, Sam did a cursory check of the interior and pulled out a small .38 caliber revolver from the front passenger seat. Sam did not say anything while showing it to me.

"Well, Mr. Roberts, you have to go to jail, so put your hands behind your back." I had to use two sets of cuffs because he could not touch his wrists together behind his back.

After he was safely cuffed, I asked him, "Why do you have the gun in your car, Mr. Roberts?"

"My girlfriend has a man following her around and harassing her; I thought I might need it to scare him off." He now appeared to be a big old teddy bear, a little grouchy at times but mostly pretty nice.

"With your big hands, how would you even get a finger in the trigger guard to fire the weapon?"

"Oh, I would not fire it. I meant to scare him. I don't even have bullets for the gun." Now he sounded like a poor little kid who got caught with his fingers in a pie.

"Mr. Roberts, you are a big man, I would think your size alone would scare him off. You don't need a gun."

"Yeah, I suppose you're right. I don't need the gun. You can keep it." Now his head was hanging down.

A wagon showed up and took him away. His transition from when I first stopped him until he was taken away was enormous. He'd transformed into an entirely different person. Maybe it was Sam's arrival, and he knew he would not get away with anything, or perhaps he was a nice guy who tried acting mean. I have seen other people act the opposite. They would be nice until they found out they were going to jail, and then it was Saturday night at the fights.

Not knowing my location was embarrassing in front of the Colorado officer. That was one of those times I made a serious error but was saved by unforeseen circumstances. I thanked the ride-along for his assistance and bought him lunch.

Chapter 33:
Fighting with Barry

What can start as a simple arrest sometimes will escalate in a fraction of a second. I saw it many times, and today it would happen again.

There was this guy named Bruce Williams I had stopped for an expired tag in a small strip mall. Bruce was cordial and polite; he was hard not to like. In his early twenties, Bruce had a small frame, a huge smile, and lived around the corner, a block from the strip mall. Bruce was also on probation for armed robbery.

In this small strip mall was a grocery store right next to Bruce's probation office. Bruce often shopped at the grocery store for his mother. Yet, for some reason, Bruce thought it was a good idea to rob the grocery store in broad daylight without covering his face. Several store employees identified him, and a warrant for armed robbery was issued for Bruce two days later. Bruce was likable; I didn't say he was brilliant.

I called Barry Lynch, a wagon driver, to join me on a residence check to arrest Bruce. We arrived at his house and climbed up fifteen stairs from the sidewalk, split apart in the front yard, then up another five stairs to the front porch. We were not expecting any trouble since Bruce had been calm and polite in my first encounter with him. I knocked on the door, and Bruce's mom, Mrs. Williams, an older medium-built, gray-haired woman in a shapeless cotton dress, answered the door.

"Hello, ma'am, is Bruce home?"

"I am his mother. What do you want with him?" she asked in a friendly tone.

"Well, ma'am, we need to talk to him for a moment. Would that be okay?" I smiled at her.

"I guess so. Come on in, get out of this heat. He's right in here on the couch." Mrs. Williams ushered us into her modest living room, and there was Bruce relaxing on the worn sofa, drinking some iced tea.

"Hi, Bruce!" I said with a big smile that his mom must have seen because she then offered, "Would you officers like a glass of iced tea while you talk with Bruce?"

I felt bad having to arrest Bruce in front of his mother, but hey, Bruce was an armed robber out on probation. She should be used to dealing with the legal system.

I moved closer to Bruce while Barry stepped between Bruce and his mother.

"Why, thank you Mrs. Williams, that was nice of you to ask but no, ma'am. We're here to arrest your son for armed robbery. We won't be here that long ma'am. Now Bruce, could you please stand up? I have to handcuff you. You have a robbery warrant."

Everything was going smoothly. Bruce even stood up and turned around for me to pat him down and cuff him. Then Bruce's mother started yelling, "My son is innocent. He hasn't done anything wrong!"

She made a move toward me, but Barry intercepted her. He told her calmly, "Ma'am, it is okay. Bruce only has a warrant and can post bond and be back home today no problem."

Barry had put his hands up, and the angry mom walked right into them.

I had one cuff on Bruce when he got agitated. "Don't you go putting your hands on my mama!"

Bruce tried to pull away from me and attack Barry from behind and succeeded in kicking Barry in the back of the leg. I pulled back on Bruce, but he now was enraged. Bruce was cursing at us and trying to get at Barry, and Bruce's mom was slapping Barry and throwing punches at him. At this point, Barry was trying to keep Mrs. Williams off me and avoid her fists.

Bruce was out of control, and I used an armbar hold to control him. Bruce was still jumping around despite the move. With his elbow still locked I put him down hard, but the room was small and Bruce landed on the coffee table, which splintered under his weight, stunning him momentarily. I quickly finished cuffing Bruce and pulled him to his feet.

Meanwhile, Barry was still trying to defend himself without hurting Mrs. Williams. I pushed Bruce towards the door as he cried out like a baby, "Mama, help me, help me, I didn't do anything!"

I was almost out the door with Bruce in front of me when Mrs. Williams got in behind Barry somehow and launched herself up onto Barry's back, clawing at his neck and pulling his hair. Barry reached up and grabbed Mama by the neck, then he bent over and violently threw Mama onto what remained of the smashed coffee table.

"You son of a bitch, you clawed me! If you get off that damn floor, I'm going to stick you in jail with your son. Now stay down and shut the hell up! All right, let's get the hell out of here!"

Barry was pissed, but Mama had gotten the message. She stayed on the floor among the broken pieces of her coffee table.

Bruce was furious now, kicking me and screaming.

"Shut the f..k up, Bruce, you're upsetting your mother, and if you kick me again, I will throw you head first down those stairs!" Now I was getting mad.

Out of the house, Barry grabbed Bruce's other arm, preventing him from turning and kicking me. Bruce continued to yell and pull against us with all his strength. Halfway down the stairs, Bruce lunged at me, and I almost lost my balance on the steep incline. I placed both of my hands on Bruce and started to toss him down the stairs.

"Stop, you are going to knock me down the stairs with him!" Barry almost lost his balance.

"Lift him, and we'll drag the son him the rest of the way to the wagon."

We eventually got Bruce to the wagon and loaded him up, still kicking and cussing. Mama was on the front porch looking at us but not saying anything.

"You want to go back up there and get the old lady?" I asked Barry as he leaned against the wagon, feeling the scratches on the back of his neck and looking at the blood on his fingers.

Barry took a long look up the stairs at the lady. "Hell no! I'm not fighting her again, and I don't want to write no damn report. Let's go, and I'm not going with you on another residence check. You get into too damn many fights!"

Barry had already turned and headed for the front of the wagon when I shouted after him, "Hey, I didn't start this fight. You and Mama started it!"

Barry raised his hand and gave me the finger. I didn't start the fight, and it goes to show you how quickly the dynamics of a situation can change. This is one example where talking nicely to a suspect did not help at all.

Off-Duty Work and Guns

Many officers could not make ends meet, and worked off-duty jobs up to thirty to forty hours a week in addition to their regular forty-hour workweek. Off-duty work was a fact of life if you had a wife and kids and wanted to live in a better neighborhood. As a result, you gave up almost all of your free time with your family. It was a catch-22 situation.

Some officers never carried a gun away from work, but for me, having an off-duty gun was an absolute necessity and saved me from becoming a victim several times. People asked why I carried one, and I'd reply, "It's a mean world out there." They wouldn't believe me.

Chapter 34:

The World Series

Sometimes working an off-duty job was worth more than the pay itself.

One of the officers I knew was head of security for all the KC Royals home games, and through him, I worked an entire season in 1985, the year the Royals won their first World Series title. After working the day shift in Metro Zone, I arrived at the stadium in uniform two hours before the start of the game and stayed one hour after the end of the game. I was usually assigned to walk through the crowds in either the right or left field general admission section, or GA. The GA section had the lowest-priced tickets and the rowdiest drunk fans.

If fans interfered with the game, became too big a nuisance, or fought with other fans, my job was to remove them from the event and sometimes make an arrest. I saw fans jump onto the field, reach over the wall to touch a ball in play, take their clothes off, throw beers on players and other fans, and of course, fight.

Usually, the fights were decided before I could get to them; sometimes, though, I was forced to fight to save some innocent fan with children from getting pummeled by a drunk. It was a bit intimidating fighting on the steep incline of the stadium seating or on top of the seats themselves.

One of the perks of working at the stadium was the free food. I was able to dine on hot dogs, sausages, peanuts, potato chips, and soda. I figured the pay was not as good as other jobs, but it was worth it with the free food and being able to watch the game.

Working the playoffs and the World Series that year was exciting. In the final game of the World Series, I started in the parking lot before the game, then moved inside the admission gate to stop people from jumping the turnstiles. About the third inning, I walked inside the perimeter fence, arresting fence climbers and people selling counterfeit T-shirts. One of the main bathrooms was packed with arrests and used as a temporary holding cell until a wagon was available for transport. I made numerous arrests and confiscated several hundred illegal T-shirts, and the best part was I never had to take a report.

At the start of the eighth inning, I was moved outside the Saint Louis Cardinals' dugout. I saw a pitcher taken from the game who took a baseball bat to a toilet deep inside the dugout. I could see myself laughing if some higher-up asked me to arrest the pitcher for property damage.

At the top of the ninth inning, I went on the field by the left-field seats. There were only six or seven of us to guard the whole left-field line. The idea was to keep the thousands of fans from swarming the field and interfering with the post-game festivities. I knew there were not enough officers.

Sure enough, when the last out was made, hundreds of fans jumped out of the stands onto the field. At first, we convinced the majority of the crowd to stay on their side of the fence, but it was hopeless as more fans charged onto the field. A rookie I did not know was choking out an errant fan a hundred feet from me, so I ran over to find him still struggling with his apparent arrest.

I yelled in his ear over the noise of the crowd, "Hey, we are on national TV! You do not want to be seen choking out a fan. Command staff should have hired more officers if they wanted us to stop the crowd. Let him go!"

The rookie released the fan, and we walked away, going through the motions of doing crowd control as if nothing had happened. There was nothing else we could do. I never heard anything about the incident, so I assumed we did not make the highlight films. However, I did get mentioned in an article on the second page of the paper next day. A reporter asked me if there were any arrests at the game, so I told him about the bathroom used as a holding cell and all the bootleg T-shirts confiscated. I got a whole paragraph.

Chapter 35:
Metallica

Another off-duty job I had was working plainclothes a Metallica rock concert at Arrowhead Stadium and confiscating any illegal T-shirts brought into the venue. All the off-duty officers were instructed to ignore marijuana-related offenses. That was fine. I did not want to spend hours writing arrest reports.

The knockoff T-shirts looked real, but they were cheaply made copies. The artwork was poor quality, misspelled words, and the T-shirt material was third-rate. An organization had bought a hundred thousand shirts dirt cheap and followed the concert tour from city to city, selling them. The organization could afford to lose a high percentage of them and still maintain a high profit margin.

I was with a partner from work, and we walked around the perimeter fence before the concert as the crowds arrived. Away from the gates, we grabbed boxes and boxes of T-shirts from would-be hustlers. Groups of bootleggers would gather at a section of fence and catch the boxes stuffed with shirts thrown over by accomplices. In plainclothes, we could walk right up to the sellers and take all their merchandise. We took all the confiscated shirts to a large storage room. After the concert, all the shirts we grabbed would have filled a large box truck.

The infield was crowded with people smoking joints or rolling them; marijuana was everywhere. I'm surprised I didn't get high walking around. Occasionally we would walk up on someone with a small towel spread out with bags of marijuana for sale. In those instances, we would rip open the bags and fling the contents all over the place.

We had been ordered not to make drug arrests, so getting rid of the marijuana was the best alternative. By scattering the dope to the wind, we could destroy more drugs than if we arrested people for it. It angered the dealers, but hey, what could they do? File a police report and say, "Some undercover cops threw my stash away, man."

The music at the concert was so loud that my ears hurt and rang for days. I never wanted to work another concert. The pulsing of the bass felt like someone pushing on your chest, and I kept looking at the stands to see if they were going to come crashing down. The whole stadium shook with the sound of guitars, thundering drums, and the screams of thousands of fanatical fans. Everybody was having a fantastic time; I am sure some fans even remembered it.

Chapter 36:

Defamation of Character

Sometimes working off duty was more trouble than it was worth.

I worked an off-duty job one nice summer evening and solved the business's crime problem. A new bar had opened, and the patrons were being robbed and their vehicles broken into.

In my vehicle, dressed in plainclothes, I parked a bit up the street from the bar, where I could see the parking lot entrance and surrounding area. I looked for someone who did not fit in the bar crowd and acted like he was about to commit a crime. It may sound funny: How do you know someone will commit a crime? You observe them. They practically wave a flag: I am your man, arrest me. I did not have long to wait for someone to do exactly that.

Sitting in my car I had a good view north down Main, and the comings and goings of the patrons. A subject caught my eye walking south on Main on the opposite side of the street from the bar. He was rubbernecking in all directions and acted nervous.

He appeared to be looking to see if anyone noticed him. The man was in his mid-twenties with a thin build and wearing a torn, dirty white T-shirt and black slacks. He was not dressed like any of the patrons I saw going to the bar. He was clearly not a customer.

The man continued up to the corner, where he stopped, crossed the street, and headed back toward the business. He continued looking all around as he walked past me, and I was surprised he did not notice me sitting in my car. The man walked past the front of the business, looking up the stairs to the front doors. When he reached the entrance to the parking lot, he stopped and turned halfway around, looking behind himself for a long moment, then headed into the lot.

I lost sight of him as he rounded the corner of the building. If he were planning to pull a robbery, he would be armed and hiding to catch the victim by surprise. If I rounded the corner and did not see him, I would know he had robbery on his mind, making it harder for me and a lot more dangerous.

Getting out of my car, I walked to the corner of the building and peeked into the lot. Good, I saw him with his back to me, hunched over a front passenger-side car window. He was moving a Slim Jim up and down, trying to unlock the car. I still had to be careful. He might be armed, but the odds were getting better that he wasn't.

I pulled my gun out, held it slightly in front of me belt high, pointed it at him, and quietly approached the thief from behind. He was so intent on getting the car unlocked that he didn't notice me at all. I got within a foot behind the man, watching him work on the door lock, until I heard an audible click. As he opened the door, I asked him, "Lose your key?"

Surprised, he about jumped out of his pants. I pushed him up against the car and identified myself as a police officer. He was really jittery, and I had to keep one hand on the back of his neck, pinning him to the vehicle while putting my gun away and cuffing him. I searched him and found no weapons. This whole time, he had been yelling at me, "What are you doing to me? I ain't done nothing! You can't arrest me! Why did you stop me in the first place?"

I turned him around, facing me, and showed him my badge. "You are under arrest for breaking into a vehicle, having burglary tools, and anything else I can think of!"

"You didn't see me break into this car, and I don't have no damn burglary tools!"

He was working himself up, trying to get some sympathy from the gathering crowd. It wasn't working, as several people had been victims or knew a victim.

"The Slim Jim at your feet is illegal to possess."

"That ain't my jimmie, I came into the parking lot 'cause I had to take a pee!"

"Then why were you breaking into this car? Why am I going to find your prints all over your Slim Jim? Were you breaking into the car to take a pee?"

"Man, I told you I ain't done nothing, and you didn't see me do nothing. You see a man walking down the street and immediately think he's a criminal!"

"You forget I was standing right behind you while you broke into this car."

This friendly banter went back and forth. Since I did not have a radio, someone from the crowd called the police. Within minutes, several police cars arrived and transported the suspect to the station for booking.

I did not hear any more about the arrest until a few weeks later, when summoned downtown to legal affairs. The attorney in charge made me stand and wait while she continued working with some papers on her desk, ignoring me. After a couple of minutes, I was about to ask the attorney if this was the wrong time; I could come back when hell freezes over.

The attorney, a woman in her mid-thirties with dyed blonde hair, waved her hand up with a dismissive air bordering on contempt and told me, "You and the department are being sued for defamation of character. The man you arrested for allegedly breaking into a car at a bar parking lot says you embarrassed him in front of his family and the community at large. You arrested him for no reason. Did you know this man has little if any record?"

I told the attorney what had happened, and she rolled her eyes and said, "Sure, I'm going to have to look into this." She emphasized the "sure."

Then, without another word, she looked back down at her paperwork and moved her hand quickly several times as if brushing away some lint. It was an indication the interview was over and that I should leave.

I didn't know if the attorney was rolling her eyes at me, the suspect's lawsuit, or that there was more work for her to do. In many of these cases, the department settled, making the officer look like he did something wrong. The idea is if the department goes to court and loses, the settlement will be many times higher than if the department settles out of court. This meeting was on a Friday.

On Sunday, the *Kansas City Star* did a full-page story on my arrest's whole family. It would appear they had all been involved in one serious crime or another, including a double homicide. On Monday morning, I requested a short meeting with the same department attorney regarding new information in the lawsuit. Meeting with the attorney, I laid the full-page story of the suspect's family on her desk.

"This is the story of the suspect's family I supposedly embarrassed. The family members are either dead or in jail for murder and armed robbery!"

The lawyer looked at the article. "Well, I think that takes care of that!" She gave me a fake smile, more of a smirk. At least this time, she did not wave me off.

I left her office, but I knew that somehow, without the newspaper story, I think she would have settled, leaving a shadow on the department and me.

Chapter 37:
Mowing the Lawn

You are a cop and wherever you go, you must be vigilant. Some prior arrest sees you and wants a little payback. It doesn't matter if you are away from work and with your family. People wonder why you carry a gun off duty and see you as a violent person or capable of violence without provocation.

Case in point.

I had finished cutting my lawn and was standing at the curb dressed in a pair of gym shorts and a T-shirt. I usually don't carry a gun while working around the yard, but that day for some reason, I did, and to this day, I don't know why. My off-duty weapon was a 2-inch stainless steel .357 caliber revolver with an inside-the-belt holster clipped to my gym shorts.

The gun was heavy, and I had to hook my T-shirt onto the outside of the holster clip. This held the weapon in place and kept my shorts from being dragged down by the weight. The gun was not visible, and unless you were a trained observer, most people would not notice it even if I was standing next to them. It was not a case where I wore the gun to show off in front of the neighbors; I tried to be inconspicuous and did not want anybody to know I was armed.

A big Olds four-door pulled up next to me at the curb in front of my house. The four men inside, all in their early twenties, were dressed in slacks and nice knit shirts. The front-seat passenger was smoking a cigarette and had his head back against the headrest. He flicked the ash off his cigarette out the window, then looked up at me and said sarcastically, "Hey, you need your grass cut?"

It is one matter to ask if you need your yard cut and quite another when you are standing there sweating with the lawnmower in front of you, and the grass has obviously been cut. This was no mistake. I knew it, and they knew it, and it was not about the need for my yard to be cut.

I lifted my T-shirt off my holster clip and put my hand on the butt of my gun, exposing it for them to see. The sight of the weapon did not faze the occupants. I asked them in an equally sarcastic voice, "Does it look like I need my f..king yard cut, asshole?"

These guys were not interested in cutting my grass. I believe they thought maybe I would be intimidated by their attitude and sudden appearance in the neighborhood. I do not know what exactly they had planned, but it was not looking for a lawn mowing job on a freshly mowed yard.

Maybe they planned to steal my mower or were stupid enough to think I carried a wallet on me while doing yard work, but more than likely they were one of any number of people I'd arrested who swore to get me.

The front-seat passenger raised his upper lip, gave me a sneer, then told his buddies, "This ain't gonna work, move."

They drove off without another word. I believe any other person in the neighborhood would have been oblivious to the reality of the situation and unaware of the imminent danger they faced. I could tell them, but they would never believe me. It was a mindset many people have: They live in a protected world, and nothing bad could ever happen to them. These guys meant to harm me. I did not imagine it and was not being paranoid.

If the guys wanted a job cutting grass, they would not have stopped at my house with a freshly cut yard next to me. They would have stopped at a residence where the yard needed cutting, would have a mower in the trunk, and would be dressed in work clothes. Lastly, they would not have been sarcastic and surly when asking if I needed my yard cut.

I did not let myself become a victim that day. How do you explain the experience gained by working in the inner city for over two years? Some people would say I could not be sure that anything would've happened. What they are saying is that you must become a victim rather than protect yourself. I could not, short of letting myself become a crime statistic, prove myself correct. Given the circumstances, I know I was right.

A final note: I am positive a violent crime would have occurred if I hadn't worn my gun that day.

Chapter 38:
The Beaches at Padre

I went on a vacation with my wife. It was the honeymoon we could never afford when we were first married. We flew down to South Padre Island for four days of sun and sand. For some reason, I went through the trouble of checking my handgun. I had an uneasy feeling in the back of my mind about this trip, and while not consumed by the idea of taking a gun with me on vacation, something told me... I'd need it.

We got off the plane in Harlingen, Texas, and were waiting for our luggage when several Texas Rangers ran into the baggage claim area chasing a subject for some unknown reason. The Rangers had their guns drawn, so I assumed this might be a dangerous fellow they were chasing. The man was eventually caught, and we retrieved our luggage. I noted other passengers picked up about twenty rifles in soft and hard gun cases. It seemed I would not be the only person who carried a gun in Texas.

My wife and I drove to our hotel and settled in for a nice little vacation, just the two of us. The following day I drove our rental car with a Hertz sticker on the back window down the road next to the beach.

Back then, stickers on the rear window identified the car as a rental. Would-be thieves and muggers saw the sticker and attacked the occupants, figuring they were out-of-towners. If the thieves were caught, they knew the victims would likely not return for a court date, and any charges would be dismissed. It was a low-risk crime for the suspects.

The view from the beach road was absolutely amazing, with the beautiful aqua-blue waves churning a hundred yards away. We could not drive onto the beach, as the sand was too loose, and the car would get stuck. We left the rental car parked off the asphalt and took our towels and cooler to the shore. We enjoyed a few hours, marveling at the clear blue water and deserted beach. It was like our own private paradise until I glanced up and saw a county maintenance truck pull over to the side of the road close to our car. I would not have thought anything about it, but with miles and miles of deserted beach, why did they have to stop where we were?

Five workers got out of the truck and stood by the side of the road staring at my wife and me. Two of the workers had long machetes sheathed on their hips. All of the men wore dirty uniforms of dark blue khaki pants, and white, untucked and unbuttoned shirts.

I felt these guys were intruding on our privacy and was uneasy about how they were acting. It was as if the men were trying to look nonchalant but doing a lousy job of it. One of the workers picked up a rock and tossed it to the side. The others followed the first man's pretense of enjoying throwing stones and trying hard not to seem out of place.

I thought, what the hell? They had to stop where we were because this area had the best rocks to throw?

The men would stop and talk as if unsure what they wanted to do next, then continued walking towards our spot on the beach. The workers seemed to be deliberately coming closer to us while trying to act as if they were not. It was like the cartoon where a cat had his hands behind his back, head up, whistling and pretending the bird in the cage was not right next to him.

They kept up the charade until finally stopping within fifteen yards of us, standing menacing line abreast. The two with machetes were on either end of the line, their right palms resting on the handles of their long blades. A heavyset man, probably the boss, stood in the middle, wringing his hands together with a slight grin. The two on either side of the big man seemed to be followers, constantly looking up to their boss for instructions.

That was it. I wasn't going to ask them why they picked this isolated spot to stop and admire the beach. I picked my gun up from under a magazine and stared at the workers with their open shirts flapping in the breeze. I turned with my left side toward the men and told my wife, "Put your fingers in your ears. This will be loud!" Then I raised the gun, took aim at a wave, and pulled the trigger.

With the smell of gunpowder in the air, I lowered the revolver to my side and slowly turned to face the men staring into the dark eyes of the boss. I had a dangerous presence about me; maybe it was the gun in my hand. They knew now I wouldn't be some easy out-of-town mark.

I only had four rounds left and five targets. I planned to shoot the men with the long machetes first, as they presented the most imminent danger, followed by the fat boss. Without their leader, I figured the last two workers would run away. If not, I'd shoot one and beat the other with my empty gun.

I had practiced long hours and could hit targets at twenty-five yards. I pulled the hammer back; fifteen yards wouldn't be a problem. The men lost all interest in the beach, turned around, and ran back to their truck, gears grinding as they drove away.

I am positive, beyond a shadow of a doubt, if I did not have a gun that day, a terrible crime of violence would have occurred. I'll let you speculate on what kind.

When people say, "You couldn't know what would've happened!" I reply, "Oh, but I did know… that's why nothing happened."

Stress Relief

Funny is a relative term. What some people think is funny and what police officers think is funny can be very different. Sometimes police officers will laugh at something others might think is sickening or repulsive. Officers call it gallows humor.

If you dealt with the kinds of things police officers routinely witnessed, you too might need a little stress relief sometimes.

Chapter 39:
Shooting Pigeons

With fall in the air and bird season in full swing, some guys complained their shotguns were always out of shells. No one seemed to know what was happening.

Soon an anonymous complaint came in that officers in the downtown district on nights were throwing rocks at the pigeons under the overpasses, then trying to shoot the birds on the fly. No one got in trouble. The officers were told to buy their own ammunition and to clean the guns.

I think shooting pigeons was one of the perks of working downtown on nights. I was told pigeons taste like chicken.

Next time you see a dead pigeon downtown, it might make you wonder about the midnight crew.

Chapter 40:

The Motorcycle Officer

and the Stripper

Heading for the station late one cool November night in Center Zone, minutes before the end of shift, I was stopped for the light at Thirty-ninth and Gillham Road. The light turned green, and I had started across the intersection when a white 1980 BMW ran the red light and almost took off the front of my car. This is the moment most people would complain about where is a cop when you need one. Well, I stopped this one for you.

The white BMW crossed over into oncoming lanes of traffic and came close to hitting another car head-on. I think my red lights and siren helped alert the other driver of the approaching car. The BMW lost traction, sliding sideways back into the correct lane. I called for another car on a possible drunk driver and gave my direction of travel and a description of the suspect vehicle.

We were headed westbound on Thirty-ninth Street approaching Westport High School when the driver took a hard left, striking a curb in front of the school. I called the dispatcher and again gave my direction of travel.

At this time, I had still not heard another car dispatched or any other car volunteer to back me up. The driver stopped halfway down the street, on the east side of the high school, parking at a forty-degree angle to the curb. I gave the dispatcher my location and repeated that this would probably be a DUI. I asked for an assisting car for the second time.

I approached the driver and tapped on the car window. An attractive blonde in her early twenties with shoulder-length hair looked up at me and smiled.

"Step out of the car, ma'am."

I received no response.

I tapped on her window lightly with my trusty Kel-Lite for the second time. Still no response. With a roll of my eyes and a sigh, in a louder voice, I said, "Ma'am, step out of the car."

I knocked on her window for the third time and, in a still louder voice, told her, "Get out of the vehicle!"

Always say *the vehicle* rather than *your vehicle* to stop any arguments: "This isn't my car, it's my mom's," and so on and so on.

Finally, I got through to her. She said in a slurry voice, "Huh?"

I was making progress and raised the door handle. It was locked.

"Ma'am, open the door!"

Notice the subtlety. I did not say, "Please open the door?" or ask if she would get out of the car, I commanded it. That does not mean I had to yell. I still wanted her cooperation.

She again replied, "Huh?"

The lady had a limited vocabulary up to this point. I tapped on her window with my flashlight for the fourth time and felt like the bird in Edgar Allan Poe's poem "The Raven." A light tap, tap, tapping at her windowpane.

"Exit your car now!" As soon as I said it, I knew it was a mistake.

"Huh, this isn't my car."

"Get out of the car."

"Huh, why?"

Many people would be exasperated by this point, but I was making progress. She had spoken more than one word.

In a loud, commanding voice, I said, "Get out of the car now."

I sensed victory! She unlocked the door and clumsily exited the vehicle, relying heavily on the door and doorframe for support.

She backed away from the door and said in a deep smoker's voice, "What's up?"

I could smell alcohol on her breath and the heavy, stale perfume she wore. She was dressed in a black bra and panties, loosely covered by a white faux fur coat, which she tried to close about herself, failing delightfully. I did a long visible search, ensuring she had nothing to hide. Noticing me looking her over and as if reading my mind, she said, "Look! I have nothing to hide!"

She paused, smiled widely, showing her perfect white movie-star teeth, and to my surprise, she opened her coat wide, exposing her large breasts, overflowing a skimpy brassiere. She also had a flat, muscled stomach and softly molded hips, covered only by a tiny glittering G-string.

Proving she had nothing to hide, the blonde then did a drunken pirouette and happily proclaimed, "I'm a stripper!" and raised her arms in celebration of the fact.

Joe said you always search everyone. I did not search her. A big mistake.

I got on the radio, ordered a city tow and a wagon, then told her she was under arrest. She was drunk and shouldn't be driving.

"You can't arrest me; I'm a stripper!" she said, and to confirm it, she opened her coat, showing off her charms, and staggered through another pirouette.

Out of some hiding-place—maybe she was also a magician and hid it up her sleeve—she suddenly had an eight-inch butcher knife in her right hand. She waved the knife lazily in front of her, forcing me back several steps from her.

"I'm not going to jail. I have to go somewhere."

I was not quite sure if she meant she had to be somewhere or literally had to "go" somewhere. There is a difference, as she proved a moment later. She staggered to the front of the BMW, squatted, gave an audible sigh, then released her bladder onto the street. The bottom portion of her white coat also lay in the street. Since she was on a slight incline and faced uphill, her urine rolled behind her, soaking the bottom part of her white imitation fur coat.

She stood and continued to slowly wave the knife back and forth in front of her, only now it was not as sloppy a movement. It was more deliberate. I was beginning to think she'd practiced with her knife, given her somewhat hazardous working environment. I advised the dispatcher the driver was now armed with a large butcher knife and requested another car for the third time.

The dispatcher advised it was a shift change and no cars were available. She would have an officer respond as soon as one cleared for service. I should have said I had a gorgeous, young, naked female stripper, and I bet ten cars would have come to a screeching halt at my location in the next thirty seconds.

I started taking the girl more seriously. "Drop the knife."

"This is my knife. I need it for protection. I'm a stripper."

This time she did not twirl around. She looked at me, not quite staring eye to eye but watching me closely. She was still drunk, but not as much as before, and I sensed this was all an act she had practiced many times before to protect herself. I don't think she saw me as a policeman but rather as someone who would make her do something she did not want to do. I remembered what Tom had said about knife fights back in the academy: "In a knife fight, you will always get cut."

I wasn't in a knife fight yet and thought about ways to disarm the stripper short of shooting her. Things were not so funny now. I wished another car had responded because whatever happened now would happen in the next sixty seconds, and it did.

Out of nowhere, a traffic officer on a motorcycle rode up to the scene. He parked in front of her car, nonchalantly put the kickstand down, and dismounted. He had his shiny white motorcycle helmet on, a short black leather jacket, gloves, and of all things, he had his sunglasses on at eleven o'clock at night.

He was an enigma. I could not see who it was but was glad he was here. I heard the heavy, menacing click-clack, click-clack, click-clack of the steel taps on the heels and toes of his thick black leather motorcycle boots. He walked with a deliberate stride on the wet pavement, and had not even bothered to shut his motorcycle off. I could hear the irregular lope the big Harley made at idle. "Watch out!" I called "She has a butcher knife in her hand!"

He did not acknowledge if he heard me. He just kept walking toward her, getting closer and closer with each step. The stripper was oblivious to his arrival or approach. His dark aviator sunglasses were locked on her from the moment he left his motorcycle; he gave her his full attention. There was a mean look and a dark aura surrounding him that made me glad he was on my side! I thought we would discuss strategies. I was wrong.

When he got close to her, he did not utter a word. He did not tell her to drop the knife but quickly cut to the chase and, reaching back, crushed a gloved fist to the side of her head. She dropped like a rock, her coat muffling the thump of her body hitting the pavement. Effortlessly, he rolled her limp body onto her stomach, pulled her hands behind her back with practiced ease, and without taking his eyes off her, reached back to me with a gloved hand and barked, "Give me your cuffs."

I retrieved mine from my gun belt and put them in his outstretched hand. He cuffed her with a staccato click-click, stood up, reached down, grabbed the woman under both arms, and lifted her to her feet. He leaned her back against her car, holding on to her with one hand, and lightly slapped her face until she groggily gave her go-to response: "Huh."

She continued to lean unsteadily against my car as he turned his back to me and returned to his bike. He did not give even a backward glance. Stunned by the abruptness of the encounter, I called out naively, "What is your name for my report?"

Without turning around, he waved a hand over his helmet, saying in a gruff voice, "You don't need my name; I was never here."

I watched as he lifted his right leg over the bike, mounted it, gave the throttle two quick revs, and was gone, the sound of the Harley fading into the night.

Now there I was, alone with a mostly naked stripper, a butcher knife, and a story I could not tell. I notified the dispatcher the driver was now secured. After all my reports were done, tickets issued, the knife recovered, and the prisoner housed, I arrived home after 2:00 am. My cold dinner was in the refrigerator.

This was a textbook example of why you listen to all radio traffic so you can help another officer who might need assistance with a drunk, and in this case, a nearly naked stripper with a butcher knife. The stop, I am sure, would not have ended the same without the timely help of that motorcycle officer.

As far as not getting any backup from the other officers in the crew, I think they were assholes for not assisting me. It wouldn't be the last time I couldn't get backup, and I almost learned a valuable lesson: Do not stop cars at shift change.

Blood would be drawn in my next encounter with a knife: an officer sliced in the face.

Chapter 41:
Blue-Faced Smurfs

One warm Sunday afternoon during my first summer in Center Zone, I had made a felony arrest of an ex-con with a gun and transported him downtown. To complete the arrest report and check the prisoner into the jail, a detective from the Crimes Against Persons Bureau, or CAP, had to sign what we called a May I form. The form said there was probable cause to book the prisoner in on state charges.

I took my prisoner to the detective on duty responsible for approving the booking. The detective, David Samson, asked me to watch two other prisoners while getting the necessary paperwork for my arrest. The two arrests were there for inhaling or huffing fumes from spray cans. The fumes gave the huffer a mind-altering high. Depending on the price of the spray paint, it was a cheap multidose high.

When David got back, I watched him interrogate the two huffers. He asked them if they had been huffing paint, and with their heads lolling from side to side, they spoke in slurred voices. "No, no, not us, man."

David said, "Why, then, are your faces blue?"

They felt their faces, looked at each other, and one said, "Your face is blue, dude!"

"So is yours man! This is so cool!"

Their noses, eyelids, eyebrows, and lips were covered with blue spray paint that made a circle around the center of their faces which contrasted with the rest of their pasty-white skin. They looked like the cartoon characters the Smurfs. On the desk were two nearly empty blue spray paint cans and two brown paper lunch bags, each with blue paint coating the inside. It was funny to see them deny huffing the paint with their blue faces.

Detective Samson explained the huffers spray the paint into the bag, seal the bag up against their face, and breathe in the toxic fumes.

After photographing them and recovering the paint cans, I would have loved to see the huffers deny it in front of a judge. If their faces were blue, I wonder how the lining of their throats and lungs looked.

Chapter 42:
The Bootlegger
with the Wooden Leg

On East 39th street, there once was a large three-story house with a huge gravel parking lot big enough to hold fifty cars. I always wondered why a place needed such a large parking area as only a few cars used it. I didn't pay it much attention, as there weren't any apparent crimes being committed and no calls for the police. In fact, I had never heard anyone in Center Zone mention the house. The only time I saw anything unusual was on Sundays when the lot filled up. Naively, I thought the guy who lived there was a sports fan and had a lot of friends over to watch professional sports.

On a chilly fall Sunday evening, a few hours before dark, I was called to the station and briefed on a raid about to occur at the house. Two SWAT teams were conducting the raid along with ATF and the Vice unit. I thought this would be fun, and it turned out to be an entertaining evening.

I was assigned to stage about a block away, and when the dispatcher gave the signal, I would block the large entrance/exit driveway along with several other marked cars. There was an illegal bootlegging operation going on, and we were going to shut it down, arrest everyone, and confiscate all the liquor. I thought there would be a liquor still in operation with cars loaded down full of moonshine, and that this was going to be something like the movie *White Lightning* with Burt Reynolds.

The dispatcher gave the signal—one long tone on the radio—and all hell broke loose. I had difficulty getting to my assigned position. Fed cars, unmarked SWAT cars, and numerous marked police cars competed to get to their assigned positions as well. Several other marked patrol cars were already there when I finally arrived at the exit. All the patrol cars had their red lights on, and some still coming had their sirens on. The whole situation was funny to me and looked like a modern-day Keystone cop movie.

People were trying to leave the parking lot in their cars but slammed their brakes on when they realized we were blocking the only exit. Cars were doing doughnuts in the gravel, stirring up dust clouds, trying to find a way out of the lot. The sights and sounds of cars crashing was hilarious. The whole property was four feet above street level and fronted by a stone retaining wall. Anybody trying to leave the lot and not using the driveway would have to navigate the four-foot drop to the sidewalk.

Some cars were driven over the wall, only to get hung up, the front of the vehicle on the sidewalk with the rear end up in the air, or go fast enough to fly onto the street, where they invariably crashed into parked cars or other cars trying to leave.

It was hilarious to see a large four-door Buick high-centered on the wall with the rear wheels five feet off the ground, the front end on the sidewalk, and the driver flooring the engine. Sometimes another car would crash into a car stuck on the wall and knock it the rest of the way off, and then the front of the vehicle was damaged with both front fenders bent, the bumper knocked off or pushed back into the radiator, and the car's rear end destroyed.

Wrecks were littering the street. It was getting hard to see as dust clouds turned up by spinning tires combined with the steam from busted radiators created a red haze that was lit by rotating emergency lights from the swarm of police cars.

If that wasn't enough, a horde of people poured out of windows and side doors into the arms of SWAT officers and various agents from other agencies. People were yelling and screaming in their excitement and cussing when caught. Several men ran down the driveway but turned around when some unidentified officer racked a round into his 12-gauge shotgun.

Man, I wished I had a movie camera. Nobody seemed to understand that the charge for drinking at or buying alcohol from an unlicensed establishment was just a misdemeanor and carried only a small fine. Caught up in the hysteria of the moment, people totaled their cars and resisted arrest to avoid these minor penalties.

After the tow trucks finished removing all the wrecked and abandoned cars on the street and the wagons had loaded up all the arrests, large trucks appeared, and hundreds and hundreds of cases of beer, whiskey, and any brand of alcohol you could ever want were removed from the house. Gaming tables and assorted equipment were also loaded up and hauled away. It was hours before I finished writing my last vehicle tow-in report and went back to the station. The owner of the house and man behind all the bootlegging was in the process of being booked.

The man was short, round, bald at the top of his head, and dressed in a neatly pressed white shirt with rolled-up sleeves with green garters around the biceps. He also wore bright green pants with gold-colored suspenders and black shoes adorned with silver buckles. I thought he looked like a little leprechaun.

He seemed amiable enough until the booking officer noticed the wee man had a wooden leg. The booking officer wanted someone to grab the wooden leg and pop it off, making the little man scream like a banshee. I thought, wow, this booking officer was kind of mean about removing the man's fake leg.

Finally, after three patrolmen held the man down, two others succeeded in removing the leg. One of them held it up in triumph like a prized trophy. The booking officer asked for the wooden leg while the little man begged for it to be returned; he said it was a social disgrace to be removing a man's leg in public.

The booking officer slowly put on some leather gloves, making a big show of it; then, like a magic act, he reached into the hollow leg, and removed a .38 caliber revolver, a six-inch steak knife, a bottle of bootleg whiskey, and a handcuff key. Officers gathered around "oohed" and "aahed" as each item was removed, and gave a big cheer when the last item was retrieved: a new issue of Playboy. The little man had planned on going to jail in style.

As much as I knew about Center Zone, I knew nothing about the bootlegger, and even more surprisingly, I never saw any trucks unloading alcohol at the house. I was told bootlegging in Kansas City was selling beer on Sundays, not running an illegal still.

I remember as a kid that Mr. O'Fallon up the street sold Sunday beer out of a large commercial cooler at the back of his house. When I was in grade school, my dad would give me two bucks, and I would walk up the block and buy a six-pack of PBR from O'Fallon. Sometimes he even asked if it was for my dad.

Chapter 43:
Hans and the Deer

One lovely summer day, a cool front came across the city and dropped the humidity enough you could have your windows down, breathe in the fresh air, and not sweat to death. It was a pleasant and happy day; everything seemed perfect to me. This was one of those TV moments about to happen, only this was not a made-up story for a half-hour comedy show.

Hans Storch and I received a call about a wild deer loose in the parking lot of a local hospital. The dispatcher said the deer was trapped in the lot, and people were afraid to go to their cars. There was also a danger that the deer would leave the lot, run out into traffic, and cause an injury accident. Oh, and by the way, there was no animal control available.

We arrived at the lot and found the deer, a large doe, excited and, I am sure, afraid, wandering the lot looking for a way out. The lot was surrounded on three sides by a six-foot-tall chain-link fence topped with sharp spikes, and the hospital itself formed the fourth side. The fences went up a steep hill, so the deer couldn't jump high enough to clear the fence.

Sergeant Conley arrived and consulted with Hans; I listened. We had hoped to euthanize the deer, but without animal control, it looked like we would have to shoot the doe with a service revolver since no car carried a rifle other than a shotgun.

We could not chase the deer around like a 1920s movie comedy, shooting at a moving target. We couldn't shoo it out into traffic, or let it roam the lot, either way someone could get seriously hurt. Sarge said, "If we only had a rifle or something, we could get it with one shot, drag it away, and leave it for animal control. Shit if we just had a rifle!"

Hans took that moment to address the problem. "Well, Sarge, I think I have the solution to our problem!"

Sgt. Conley looked at Hans with a slight turn of his head, puzzled.

Hans walked over to his car, popped the trunk open, and pulled out an AR-15 with a thirty-round magazine. I had worked with Storch for several months now and had never heard him mention the unauthorized rifle in the trunk of his car. Sarge looked astounded as if he had seen someone walking on water. Hans smiled like he had won the lottery.

"Ah, cheese, Hans, what the hell is that? And why is that thing in the trunk of your carrrr?"

When Sarge became frustrated, he had that whine like Archie Bunker used to say, "Jeez, meathead."

Sarge turned around in a circle and ran his hand through his thinning hair.

"That thing isn't loaded, is it, Hansss?" Sarge pleaded.

"You bet, Sarge, it wouldn't be much good if it wasn't!"

With that, Hans happily removed a loaded magazine and showed Sarge the bullets to prove it.

"You never know when you might need something like this, Sarge."

Hans smiled and ran his hand down the rifle like it was something precious.

Sarge only had a few more weeks to retirement and did not need to deal with shooting an itinerant deer with an unauthorized firearm in a public hospital parking lot at midday. Hans seemed oblivious to the trouble he was in for having the gun in his car, and now that Sarge was aware of it, he could get into trouble if he didn't report it. Hans had been on for many years. I wondered, how long had he been toting around the extra firepower?

"Oh hell, Haansss, let's get this over with!" Sarge was still running his hand over his head when the deer somehow cleared the fence and disappeared over the hill. The relief that showed on the Sarge's face was short-lived as we heard a loud screeching of tires.

"Oh damn, I bet that was that stupid deerrrr. Great, another mess. Shitttt, Hans, what are you doing to meeee?" Sarge turned and put his hand on his car, then removed it quickly. The hood was hot, burning his hand. Sarge's car was overheating again. "Shit, shit, shit, shittt!" Sarge hopped in a circle, blowing on his reddened palm.

"Well, at least we are in a hospital parking lot, Sarge!"

Hans smiled, putting the AR-15 back in the trunk.

"Okay, this is it! I never saw that gun, Hans! And nobody says anything about it! Is that clear?" Sarge pointed his finger at Hans and me, and we nodded our heads in agreement.

A final note: The deer did not cause an accident that day, Sarge made it to retirement, and nobody ever mentioned Hans's gun again.

Chapter 44:
The Hanger

It was July and I was on days and over at Gregory and Cleveland looking for a murder suspect who lived in a house around that area. I was parked close by, waiting for his car to drive up and to catch the suspect away from his home. His house was up a long flight of stairs and had no bushes, trees, or anything to hide behind if things went wrong while approaching the house. Sometimes suspects did not mind shooting at cops, especially when they had a homicide warrant outstanding.

The dispatcher interrupted my surveillance and sent me on a medical emergency only a half a block away. A mother reported her teenage daughter was in the bathroom with a hanger stuck in her. In those days, a coat hanger was the preferred method to perform a self-abortion.

I assumed the worst and imagined a young girl crying in extreme pain, lying on the bathroom floor, blood everywhere, and the hooked end of a metal coat hanger stuck in her vagina. I hoped the paramedics were close.

Between facing a murder suspect and going on an emergency call like this, I would take the murder suspect every time. As I walked up to the front door, I could not get the image of a teenager trying to give herself an abortion out of my brain. I knew this was going to be awful.

The mother opened the front door and greeted me frantically. "Hurry, hurry, officer, my daughter is in the bathroom with a hanger stuck!"

I knew it, I knew it, and the ambulance wasn't close enough.

"Okay, ma'am, what do you mean by hanger?"

I was delaying the inevitable. There wasn't anything I could do anyway.

"You know, a hanger! She's on the toilet, and her poop won't come out; it's stuck, you know, a hanger!"

It took me a moment to understand.

"You mean you called in an emergency because your daughter is constipated?"

I was starting to feel both relieved and angry.

"No, officer, she's got a hanger!"

The mother was probably in her early thirties but looked like she was in her sixties with her wrinkled mouth and no teeth. I realized she did not know what the word constipation meant; I would have to put it in terms she could understand.

"Okay, ma'am, do you mean there is no hanger like you hang clothes on stuck inside your daughter? Your daughter isn't trying to give herself an abortion? Your daughter just has some shit stuck coming out her asshole?"

"Yes, officer, that's what I've been a'saying—she's got her poop stuck and can't get it out, you know, a hanger!"

"Okay, ma'am, never, ever call the police when your daughter can't take a shit! You understand? There is nothing, I repeat nothing, I can do about it."

"Okay, but what do I do?"

I could see she was distraught and plain ignorant. I was about to tell her to put her finger in some bacon grease and dig it out, but thankfully, the paramedics arrived. As I walked out, I heard one of them yell, "It's not a hanger; it's a shit!"

Sometimes calls went like that. You never knew what to expect.

A final note: I caught the murder suspect the next day on the street in front of his house without incident.

Chapter 45:
The Talking Peacock

Now and then, something would come up like a mandatory training class, and days would cover the evenings or midnight shift. On one such night in early summer around two in the morning, Officer Lilly urgently called for backup in Swope Park on a rape in progress.

"Dispatch, I can hear a woman screaming for help in the park east of Cleveland and Meyer Boulevard!"

Lilly sounded excited. This was turning out to be the event of the night. About five minutes later, half a dozen cars, the sergeant, a K-9 car, and the helicopter were all searching the park for the woman screaming. I did not understand why we had not found the girl yet.

Lilly called out to everyone, "I'm getting closer. The screams are getting louder."

Someone asked, "Where are you, Lilly?"

The helicopter pilot added, "I haven't spotted her either!"

Lilly shouted over the radio, "I hear her! I'm close now!"

Lilly's voice showed she was under a high level of stress. Everybody waited breathlessly; the helicopter was low, its searchlight illuminating great swaths of the ground as the copter's blades chopped at the air loudly. Officers were desperately searching for Lilly, worried for her safety and the woman needing help.

Lilly suddenly broke the radio silence with an extremely low, calm voice. "Ah, dispatch, you can put all cars back in service. It was a peacock calling for his mate."

Sergeant Ulnis called Lilly, increasing her embarrassment, "Can you repeat, Lilly? You were low volume."

Lilly responded slowly and louder, "I said all cars can clear. It was a lonely peacock from the zoo!"

Her transmission was followed by multiple voices calling for her to repeat; they could not hear her, while others added strange bird calls. I think Lilly never forgot that night. I never did.

A final note: Next time you are at the zoo, close your eyes when you hear the shrill cries of the peacock. What does it sound like to you?

Chapter 46:
Buffalo Bill

One of the officers I worked with had the nickname Buffalo Bill. One day over a beer after work, I asked my sergeant how Bill got his moniker, and Sarge told me the following story, which I later confirmed with Buffalo Bill himself.

One early afternoon in July, close to shift change, a deer had been struck by a car and was lying injured in the roadway. Two officers were dispatched, Buffalo Bill and some rookie: one to direct traffic, the other to euthanize the deer since, as usual, animal control was not available. This particular area had only two traffic lanes, and cars were backed up for quite a distance.

The vehicle involved in the accident had left the scene, so no crash report was needed.

Once euthanized with a shot to the head, the deer could be left at the side of the road to be picked up later by animal control, and the officers could go home. The only problem was whenever a gun was fired, a report had to be filled out detailing the circumstances, shooting angles and, in general, a myriad of questions had to be answered.

It was right at the end of the shift, and both officers wanted to avoid a report. As the story goes, Bill came up with a solution. He would pull the deer to the side of the road to block the view of any cars. Next, instead of shooting the deer, Buffalo Bill would use his big Bowie knife he always kept in his car to dispatch the deer. Bill figured he would slit its throat, and that way, no discharge of a firearm report would be needed. It seemed like a good idea at the time.

Upon arrival, the officers found the injured deer in the roadway, repeatedly lifting his head in the air, then letting it fall back onto the pavement, a sorry sight. The other officer stopped traffic, but instead of stopping the traffic a hundred feet back to keep the drivers from witnessing the spectacle, he stopped traffic only a car length away from the deer. Now the drivers had an unobstructed view.

Well, Bill grabbed both rear legs, and the deer struggled. Bill slipped and fell on his butt in front of traffic twice before succeeding in dragging the deer to the far side of his car, out of the sight of any vehicles.

Buffalo Bill got out his big knife and proceeded to try to cut the deer's throat. The deer suddenly managed to get to its feet and struggled back in front of traffic while dragging Bill, who had his left arm around the deer's neck and his right hand holding the large Bowie knife. Bill kept trying to slice the deer's throat. He finally succeeded, but now blood sprayed all over the place, drenching Bill, and yet still the deer would not go down. Bill, exasperated and forgetting he was in full view of the stopped cars, started stabbing the poor deer multiple times while yelling, over and over, "Die, you son of a bitch, die! Die!"

Well, the deer finally bled out and dropped to the ground. Buffalo Bill stood up, a long bloody knife in his hand and copious amounts of deer blood all over his uniform and dripping from his face and arms. He wiped his blood-covered face with the back of the hand that was holding the Bowie knife, smearing the blood everywhere. Then, for the first time, Bill realized he was standing in full view of both east- and west-bound traffic.

Bill's mouth dropped open and his lips formed a perfect circle as he slowly looked around and saw the shocked look of the driver in front of him: A lady with four kids in a car who all started wailing. Bill snapped his hear around looking behind him and got the same reaction from station wagon filled with Girl Scouts who, it turns out, were on their way to visit a wild animal rescue center. Bill was so focused on the job at hand, he failed to notice the rookie officer had not stopped the cars far enough back, and many of the drivers and passengers had seen the whole gruesome spectacle.

Bill shook his head, shrugged his shoulders, and dragged the now lifeless deer back to the side of the road. Buffalo Bill and the rookie drove back to the station and spent the next three hours explaining to the major what happened and filling out reports. Bill took a couple of days off without pay to contemplate his actions as the senior officer. The rookie ended up making captain down the road.

I know people will say the whole incident was not funny, but this was funny compared to seeing someone's head blown off by a shotgun. It is called gallows humor; we used it to keep our sanity.

Chapter 47:
The Golden Mercedes

At roll call one morning, Sarge read a bulletin about a car stolen the previous day. The car was described as a late-model blue four-door Mercedes with gold trim, gold headlight covers, gold curb feelers, a large gold TV antenna mounted on the trunk, and gold wire wheels with large whitewall tires. This car would stand out a mile away.

The day was hot, and all our cars were out on reports of one sort or another. I had cleared one report and was en route to another when the stolen Mercedes passed me heading in the opposite direction. There was no other car like it in the city with all the gold accessories. I made a

U-turn, sped up, and pulled in behind the stolen auto and its two male occupants. They turned around in their seats several times, looking right at me—rubbernecking, we called it. I thought it was funny and almost waved back. They looked like someone caught red-handed doing something, then saying, "Who, me?"

I notified the dispatcher of the stolen car and asked for a backup. As a reminder, procedural instructions dictate that upon finding an occupied stolen auto, the officer must wait for backup before initiating any attempt to stop the vehicle. That does not mean if the driver speeds off, you can't chase him within certain reasonable bounds. A dozen rules and even more interpretations govern when an officer can or cannot pursue a car. Basically, the danger to the public has to be greater if you don't chase the subject than if you do chase him. This keeps officers from pursuing minor traffic offenders in stolen cars who might crash into innocent drivers and severely injure or kill them. At least that was the way I remember it back in the early 1980s, but it is probably even more restrictive now.

The suspects knew I was behind them, and I didn't know why they did not speed off and start a car chase. The dispatcher asked if any other car could clear and assist me, but as usual, nobody would clear from their calls. We were busy and I almost regretted even trying to stop the vehicle. I was about to turn around and head back to my dispatched call when our helicopter appeared overhead and told the dispatcher he would back me up. I had never heard of a helicopter as a second car, but what the heck. I was game.

I wondered what good he would be if the suspects stopped. I would not have a second officer at the scene, and the helicopter could not land. Handling two possibly armed felons by yourself was a dangerous business. No sergeant raised an objection, so I hit my lights and got ready for the chase. To my surprise, the driver pulled into a vacant lot. I pulled in behind the suspects. The dispatcher held the air, and with the helicopter hovering above, I approached the driver of the stolen Mercedes.

Both suspects appeared very calm and respectful. I had my gun out and by my side. Generally, with a second car, I would have conducted the felony car stop I practiced in the academy. Today's stop was different, unorthodox, to say the least, but I would adapt the best I could. I got both suspects' licenses, put them in my shirt pocket without looking at them, and kept my eyes on both men.

The driver, in his early twenties, was dressed in black empire-waist slacks and a white ruffled shirt. He was of thin build and had a lot of gold bling around his neck and on his fingers. He fit right in with the gold-accessorized car. Heck, he might even be the owner who forgot to notify the police the car should no longer be listed as stolen. It happened sometimes.

The passenger, also in his early twenties, appeared tall and thin, wearing a ruffled light green shirt with sparkly dark green pants. The passenger, like the driver, also wore a lot of gold bling. Together, the two looked as if they had dropped off their prom dates and were headed home after a long night out.

"Say, guys, to keep everything casual, why don't both of you lean forward and put your hands on the dash, please," I asked the driver nicely; the threat was implied. The suspects never asked why I stopped them, and I never told them but was pretty sure they knew.

"Hey, is this your car?" The driver could see my gun out and hear the helicopter overhead.

"Ah, no, officer, it is a friend's car," the driver answered casually. I figured he was innocent or had been arrested enough times he did not care anymore.

"What's your friend's name? Who owns the car?" I tried to keep my eyes on both of them.

"You know, I actually got this car when some guy came up to me on the street and asked if I wanted to drive it around while he attended to some other business."

The driver smiled, I smiled back. This was getting fun.

"So when and where are you taking it back to someone you don't know?"

"Well, now, it's such a fine ride. I was thinking I would keep it for a while."

Both occupants bobbed their heads, smiled, and "umm-hummed," confirming their statement.

"You guys have any weapons?" I still smiled at both men since they were both calm and polite.

They looked at each other, then shrugged their shoulders as if they didn't know.

"Well, gentlemen, suppose one at a time, the driver first, step out of the car and let me cuff you till we figure all this out. That way, I would be in trouble if something bad happened to either of you, okay?" I smiled.

The driver said slowly, "Sure, why not? That sounds like a plan, man." The two fist-bumped.

The driver stepped out of the car, and I cuffed him, then the passenger. Both men were getting more relaxed and sleepier as time passed, and now I believed they must have taken some downers sometime before the stop.

"Say, do you have the vehicle registration with you? That would clear up things in a hurry."

"No, but I think the registration is in the glove box," the driver replied sleepily.

"Okay, do you mind if I check quickly?"

"Sure, man, but you have to use the car key to get into it."

He nodded his head. Both men now leaned over the back of the stolen car and started to go to sleep.

Using one of the car keys, I opened the glove box. I removed the car registration and found a loaded .32 caliber automatic, safety off and fully loaded with one in the barrel; otherwise known as ready to fire. The dispatcher ran both suspects in the computer. They came back as convicted felons for armed robbery. As felons, they were not allowed to possess or even be in the presence of a firearm. It was a federal crime.

The gun was listed as stolen. The car owner confirmed he did not know the suspects and that his car had indeed been stolen the day before while he was getting gas. I called for a wagon and the owner to respond to get his car, then thanked the helicopter pilot and started my reports.

Nothing was ever said about the unusual circumstances surrounding the stop or the complete violation of procedural instructions. On this one rare occasion, talking nice to the suspects produced cooperation. Sometimes people practically arrest themselves.

Chapter 48:
The Hapless Car Prowler

One pleasantly warm early afternoon in September, I was dispatched on a car prowler in the parking lot in front of the Jacob L. Loose memorial statue in Loose Park. I remember this call because it was one of the few dispatched to the city's west side. At the time, I was on the extreme eastern boundary of the town, and with traffic, it took almost fifteen minutes to arrive at the location. The dispatcher noted the subject in question was a male, early twenties, medium build, and wearing white tennis shoes and a green army jacket.

En route to the call, I received several updates: "The suspect has now entered a green 1980 Ford four-door."

Then a few minutes later, the dispatcher updated me again: "The suspect is now up under the dash removing the radio."

"Okay, dispatch, I'm getting close. Go ahead and send me another car."

I pulled off Wornall Road into the circle drive around the Jacob L. Loose statue, looking for a green four-door Ford or a male wearing a green army jacket. It had been fifteen minutes since the call originally was dispatched, a testimony to how busy we were that day, as no other cars could clear to take or assist the call. It would be a miracle if the suspect was still in the area. Well, miracles sometimes happen.

Parked close to the statue was a green four-door Ford, and of all things, a pair of blue jean–covered legs ending in white tennis shoes were hanging out from under the dash into the parking lot. Whoever called this in must have been mistaken, as no half-decent car prowler would still be working on his target twenty minutes later. In such a nice area of the city, he must be the owner working on something. I almost felt embarrassed to talk to the guy, as he would probably think that because he was Black I would automatically think he must be stealing something. Oh well, there was no law against talking to him.

I could see he was hard at work and had most of the radio knobs off, and the radio appeared about ready to fall out of the dash. Wires and an antenna cable were hanging down. The man hadn't noticed me and kept working, loosening a radio mounting bracket. His hand patted the floorboard carpet, feeling for a small pair of pliers lying by his leg. I squatted, resting my butt on my heels, then reached in picked up the pliers and put them in his hand. He was cool as a cucumber, as if he did this sort of thing all the time, and pulled his head down from under the dash to see who had handed him the pliers. "Oh thanks, officer."

"Hi there, what's the matter? Got some radio problems?"

I smiled, my forearms resting on my knees, enjoying the day.

"Ah yeah, a friend of mine asked me to come up here and see if I could get the radio to work." He continued to fiddle, moving stuff around.

"So, this is your friend's car you are working on? Where is he? Is he going to make you do all of the work by yourself? Oh, by the way, I'm Officer Mulcahy. How are you doing today? And you are?"

I liked to ask several questions quickly, as it confused the individual, so he couldn't remember what he was going to say and would make mistakes. This guy was not working on a friend's car. He was stealing the radio and not particularly good at it.

Now the radio fell out of the dash, and he quickly pushed it back in.

"So, hey, why don't you take a break for a moment and talk to me."

He started to wiggle out from under the dash, and I stopped him, lightly putting my hand on his leg. "You know, you look so comfortable lying on your back under the dash; why don't you stay there, relaxed?"

He was no threat to run or fight while under the dash, so I had him stay where he was until my backup arrived.

"What did you say your name was again?"

"Leronge Walker, but everybody calls me Johnny."

"Yeah, like the Scotch whiskey?"

"Yeah, I think so."

"So, Johnny, what is the name of the guy who owns the car? And where is he, by the way?"

"I gotta tell you the guy's name is Larry, and he is a friend, so I don't know his last name… and he is walking around the park getting some exercise." Johnny nodded his head.

"So, Johnny, you got the ignition key to turn the car on to see if the radio works?"

"You know, my friend said the radio wasn't working, so pull it out and work on it at home. Yeah, that's what he said." Johnny was starting to sweat a little.

"Sounds good, Johnny. Say, why don't you hand me your ID? I think I'm going to need to run you through the computer. Some things don't seem to make a lot of sense right now."

I got his ID, and he came back as on probation for theft from a vehicle with a probationary officer named Mary Luwenski. I also got the registration back on the car, and the owner came back to a Mary Luwenski. Johnny was listening as I did the computer checks.

"Well, Johnny, I don't know what to say. It seems you are on probation for theft from auto, and your probationary officer is a Mary Luwenski. Is that right, Johnny?"

"Ah, yeah, but I think I am off probation now. You could call Ms. Luwenski if you want."

"Johnny, what are the odds? You are on probation for theft from a vehicle, and your probation officer is Mary Luwenski, and get this, Johnny! This is her car that you are removing the stereo from!" I smiled, holding back a laugh; this was getting to be too much to believe.

"Well, I might have made a mistake. It might not be my friend's car after all." Johnny looked bewildered at how he managed to get in the wrong car.

"Wow, imagine that!" I shook my head, bewildered.

My backup car arrived and helped me cuff Johnny.

Ms. Luwenski returned from her walk and signed a complaint against Johnny. He made an appointment to see her again in about sixty days when he got out of jail. Sometimes arrests were simple, low-key affairs. Others, not so much.

Dangerous Days

Every call a police officer responds to has the potential to escalate into something more serious than the call description would indicate. On some calls, an officer knows that it is an extremely dangerous situation from the moment he is dispatched or starts a self-initiated action. Still, I never hesitated to go into harm's way regardless of the threat.

Chapter 49:
Catch and Release

It was in mid January about 3:30 in the afternoon and just two months after my six-week probationary period ended. I was dispatched along with a backup officer to a disturbance between two apartment buildings at Linwood and Wabash. Another marked car pulled in behind me close to the scene, and I assumed it was my backup. I quickly advised the dispatcher of our arrival and exited my vehicle. But now the other patrol car behind me was nowhere to be seen. That was when I heard the high-pitched screeching screams for help coming out from between the buildings.

The rules clearly state the officer should wait until his backup arrives. To do otherwise was to risk serious injury to himself and the next officer that comes to help you, especially if you have been disarmed. I did not know where my backup went or why he left me alone.

The dispatcher held the air, and I told her screams were coming from between the buildings. I peeked around the corner of the tenement into a narrow, trash-strewn alleyway about twelve feet wide. Only thirty yards down the alley, I could see two men and a naked girl who was screaming for help. The girl was being held face down by one of the men kneeling behind her head, pinning her arms to the pavement. The other guy, his pants pulled halfway down his thighs, was on top of her between her legs, savagely raping her.

I advised the dispatcher what I saw and called for another car. I took a deep breath, pulled my gun out, rounded the corner of the building, and sprinted toward the screaming victim. Whether the two men were armed did not matter at this point. I was committed.

I yelled "Freeze!" and of course, the two guys got up and took off running, leaving me with a naked girl crying her eyes out on the dirty, wet concrete pavement. Her legs were drawn up to her chest while she rocked back and forth. I did not see any of her clothes around, so I took my jacket off and put it around her shoulders.

"Can you walk?"

She nodded.

"Go to my patrol car. It's parked back at the end of the alley, unlocked. Get inside and lock the doors. More officers are on the way."

I notified the dispatcher, "The victim's in my car. Someone needs to take care of her. I'm going after the suspects on foot!"

Between the time I started down the alley and the victim running toward my car felt like seconds. The suspects were now running across a vacant lot behind the scene and were about sixty yards away.

I ran after them and put out their descriptions.

"Suspect one, male, five-nine, black leather jacket, thin build heading due west toward Brooklyn! Suspect number two male, five-ten, 250 pounds, wearing a gray top-and-bottom rubber sweatsuit."

I will never forget the second guy's boots. They were the black multi-buckle type kids wear in grade school over their regular shoes in the snow. Galoshes, I think they called them.

I watched as the slim suspect hopped over a six-foot fence like it was not even there, through a yard, and out of sight. I told the dispatcher he was still heading west two blocks from the scene. The suspect I lost sight of was the guy I had seen between the victim's legs. These men had a big head start on me, and I had already lost sight of the slim suspect and vowed that I would get the second one.

Unless you have ever been in a situation like this, it is hard to envision how mentally and physically difficult it is to keep everything together. Once I saw the suspects climb the fence, I knew they did not have a weapon in their hands. They could have one somewhere on their person, but for now, I secured my gun.

With my hands free, I gained on the second suspect, who was across the street and climbing over another fence. The man in the gray rubber suit was slowing down and fell off a fence into another yard. Meanwhile, I was fatiguing, and my breath was shortening.

It was hard to call the dispatcher because I had to reach down, twist my radio off my belt, and bring it to my mouth to speak. Then I had to find the place on my belt where the radio hooked up without looking down and losing sight of the suspect.

Snow had come often that January, but in the last two days, the temperature had risen to the mid-thirties with sunshine, and the ground I was running over was a mixture of spots of melting snow surrounded by slippery mud. I was gaining on the suspect; he had slipped and fallen to the ground.

I was a backyard behind the suspect when I climbed over the next fence, fell, and slid face-first in a dog shit-covered yard. The dog must have had worms, as there were only creamy piles, nothing hard. Struggling to my feet, the German shepherd mix was barking and charging me when I slipped and fell again, slamming the back of my head into a soft mound of dog crap. Luckily, the dog was chained. Finally on my feet, I ran and slid with arms flailing to keep my balance. I made it to the other side of the yard and over the next fence. There I fell over, landing on my chest and face sliding in more mud. By the time I got up and approached the next street, I had lost sight of both suspects.

I pulled my muddy, shit-covered radio out and told the dispatcher I'd lost the suspects in the 3200 block of Brooklyn. I could not believe it but there were no other police cars around yet. Then, incredibly, I got a break.

I saw the first suspect dart from behind a retaining wall and run across Brooklyn into an apartment building. There were no other apartment buildings on the west side of Brooklyn, and now I only had to go half a block more to get this guy. Two other cars showed up, and as I paused in front of them, I pointed and told them one suspect had run into that apartment building.

I continued across the street and approached the rear door to the building, then realized I was alone again. Nobody had joined me as a backup. I thought, *What the hell? I'll go in alone and get him.*

I entered the building to the heavy smell of garbage and cigarette smoke. It was hot inside the building, short-sleeve T-shirt hot, when I started up a three-story staircase. I had to go slow; there were bags of trash all over the stairs, making it difficult to negotiate without stepping on some refuse. People looked out open apartment doors; some sat on the narrow stairs smoking cigarettes. I guess I was a sight. A honky pig alone in a tenement covered head to toe in mud and dog poo. I was breathing hard and my legs felt rubbery as I climbed the last dozen stairs to the top floor.

Sometimes in stressful situations like this, there is something that guides you. Some people call it instinct, others some inner voice that speaks to you if you'll listen. It is a complex concept to verbalize, let alone explain in writing. Maybe it's your guardian angel, whispering in your mind fighting to be heard; who knows, but it saved me this time and a few other times, as well.

Now, this is where the subconscious action takes over. The suspect passed me going down the stairs as I approached the top. I knew it was him, but for some reason did not react.

Somehow, some supernatural force directed me up to the top of the stairs. It was urgent. I had to get there; nothing else mattered. I couldn't concern myself with the guy passing me. I got to the top, where the door to a small, crowded apartment stood open.

There were trash bags, stacked on the floor inside and outside the apartment, the contents spilling out. A large man wearing a stained sleeveless T-shirt was smoking a cigarette and sitting in an old chair outside the apartment next to the door as if he were some sort of sentinel.

I could see several other people inside sitting around a 1960s aluminum and yellow Formica top lunch table. A heavyset woman dressed in a dirty, faded T-shirt and tight-fitting black stretch pants was standing inside, holding a baby wearing only a soiled diaper.

The stench of trash, dirty diapers, stale beer, and body odor emanated from the open doorway. So many cockroaches were running around; it was like a grade B horror movie, only this was real. The people I saw did not seem to notice the bugs.

The man sitting by the door asked me, "What you want?" in a not-too-friendly voice.

I replied, trying to catch my breath, "I am looking for a thin, medium-height male I saw run into the building."

"We not seen anybody like that here!" Contempt for me was in his voice.

"Why, what he do?" asked the woman holding the baby in her arms.

I do not know where any part of this reply came from, but it did, out of nowhere. "He just finished raping a young teenage girl who is mentally handicapped."

The man on the chair looked at the woman holding the baby, and the man said, "You passed him on the stairs." I said thanks and turned and was headed back down when the lady holding the baby implored, "Wait! He put that brown paper sack down next to where you're standing."

I reached down and picked one off the top of a pile of trash. "This one?"

"Yeah, that's it. I seen him drop it right there!"

I ran down the stairs calling on the radio to anyone that would listen, "The suspect left the apartment building on the west side of Brooklyn wearing a black leather jacket."

Once out of the apartment building, I heard on the radio they had caught the suspect. When I reached the other officers on the street, they were excited about catching the rapist and congratulating each other. I was exhausted.

A couple dozen people gathered watching the police. Then I saw the fat suspect dressed in the gray rubber sweatsuit with black multi-buckle galoshes walking up the street to join the crowd. Everybody had moved away from me but I got someone's attention. "There's the other guy!"

The suspect was grabbed and brought over for me to identify.

"Yeah, that's him. See, he has the same boots, rubber suit, with wet mud and dog shit all over him."

I asked someone to look in the backyards to match a boot print to the fat suspect.

The men were taken downtown in two separate wagons to keep them from agreeing on a story. I walked back up to the third floor of the building and told the people who had helped me that we had caught the rapist. I got their information so the detectives could contact them later.

Then I realized why nobody had talked to me. I was covered with mud and dog shit from head to toe and smelled like, well, dog shit. It was in my hair, on my face, and all over my uniform, boots, and gun belt. There was goo in my gun, stuck on my radio, and all over my hands. Nobody would come near me.

Someone had helped the girl out of my car and taken her to a hospital. Physically she would be okay, but emotionally she would be scarred forever. At least she would have the satisfaction of knowing the suspects had been caught and sent to jail. Or so you would think.

My Sergeant Jerry Stanford said, "You can't drive your car back. You are so filthy you have to ride in the back of a wagon to the station."

I didn't mind. I understood. It turned out that the paper bag I took from the apartment building contained a six-inch folding lock blade knife called a Buck Knife. One of the brass ends was deeply gouged. I logged it in at the station for chain-of-custody purposes and wrote a statement for the report. By the time my report was finished, the shift was over, and I went home with crusted-over, muddy crap everywhere. I always tried to bring street clothes to work after that night.

My wife made me undress in the cold garage and hose off. I told her I was on a routine house alarm and slipped down a muddy hill in a backyard with a big dog nobody cleaned up after. I can only imagine what she would say if she knew what really happened.

⁓

The next day, the Kansas City Evening Times reported on the rape story. Basically, it stated that, two men were arrested in connection with a rape that had occurred in an alley at Linwood Boulevard and Wabash.

One of the suspects, Ronnell B. Williams, the man I saw with his pants down raping the victim, had only recently been paroled from prison after serving 13 years of a 144-year sentence for raping a nun and shooting a priest. Mr. Williams could not post bond and stayed in jail.

The article stated Jackson County Prosecutor William George said Mr. Jones, the second suspect, had what appeared to be a credible alibi from the start and would not be surprised if the charges against him were dropped.

Mr. Jones said he was home at the stove cooking greens and left the house to buy his mother a pack of cigarettes. His mother, Georgia Thompson, grandfather, cousins, a neighbor, and others all said Jones was home. Georgia Thompson's occupation was reported as a clerk in the county legal offices. The article did not indicate specifically where she worked or who her boss was.

Detective Barry Vineyard of the Sex Crimes Unit was quoted in the paper saying he believed Jones from the beginning and was sending a report to the prosecutor that Jones's alibi had been verified. The newspaper also stated the officer who arrested Jones said he was not sweating and therefore could not have committed the rape. I would add this point it was 32 degrees out, and after chasing Jones then running up and down three flights of apartment stairs, I wasn't sweating either. The paper never mentioned that Jones was wearing a gray rubber sweatsuit, galoshes, and was covered in wet mud and dog shit.

Prosecutor William George said there was only one problem. Mr. Jones was identified by the victim, the officer chasing Jones, and a witness to the chase. The case was then passed to prosecutor Mary Bailey.

A few days later, after another newspaper article was written about Jones and his alibi, he was released and all charges dropped.

On the day of Jones's release, I was ushered into an empty room before roll call by Sergeant Stanford and Detective Vineyard, an older, overweight, gray-haired detective wearing a cheap wrinkled blue suit. Stanford closed the door.

Sarge started the meeting by asking me, "Why didn't you wait for backup?"

"There was a car right behind me, and it disappeared. I even told the dispatcher we had arrived. I didn't know who it was, or why he left." I didn't like his line of questioning.

Sarge said, "Hmm," letting the word hang in the air. I got the feeling he didn't believe me, and some threat was implied. I could be fired for not letting the rape continue until my backup officer arrived. Not only did I risk my life rescuing the girl, but I also risked my job. I still wasn't told what the meeting was about; maybe they were investigating me. If this was an investigation, I had some questions of my own.

I asked Sarge, "That was a long foot chase. Where was my backup, and why didn't anybody follow me into the apartment building after the suspect?" Sarge pushed his lower lip out and looked at the ceiling.

Stanford took in a deep breath of air and blew it out with a sigh. "Jones was home at the time of the rape, and the charges against him were dismissed. The man you saw was home watching TV and had gone outside to see what all the commotion was about when he was arrested."

I looked at him incredulously. "That's bullshit! Did you compare the mud and dog shit all over him to the backyards I chased him through? A fat guy in a gray rubber two-piece sweatsuit with kids' black buckled galoshes, how unique is that? Did they take foot imprints in the mud we ran through? Did you ask how he got covered in all that mess and why it was still wet if he was home? What about the victim's identification and the other witness?"

The detective looked at the floor and shook his head, "No, none of that was done, and you should go along. You did a good job, and leave it at that. Jones is a city councilman's secretary's son, and the councilman is favorable to police pay raises. Jones told us he just went into the alley to see what was happening and only held the girl's arms down; he didn't actually rape her. You got the other guy. He was the most important one.

"The knife you recovered was the victim's. It had been given to her for protection by her uncle. Sometime in the past, she had dropped it on a sidewalk, then slipped on it, making a deep gouge on the brass end. She picked it out in a group of ten by the gash which nailed the first suspect down with a tight case."

The Vineyard then told me something that sent a chill down my spine. "You should know the victim was a young teenager who was mentally disabled."

This was what the meeting was about: I could keep quiet or possibly be fired. I didn't know what I could do anyway, as the prosecutor and detectives had already stated publicly the victim, witness, and I were not to be believed. Slowly, I turned my head from side to side and gave a half-grin and a soft chuckle. I knew what was going on, they knew it, and I would see this again. I hated politics.

Sergeant Stanford was a good sergeant but was undoubtedly following orders from someone higher up the chain of command and could do nothing about it. Stanford was promoted to Captain a few months later.

This was the first case I have heard of, where the victim, a police officer, and a witness were not believed over the suspect's family. In a case like this, it would seem I would have been asked to give a statement or talk to the prosecutor before they dropped the case. I had only been on the street for two months, and I was already disillusioned with the notion of honesty and integrity within the department and the prosecutor's office.

I never found out who was my backup. I was afraid if I looked it up, I would be disciplined, fired, or set up for a fall in some other way for being a nonconformist.

☙

Now back to the subconscious controlling us sometimes. In this case, if I had confronted the suspect on the stairs, we would have fought. The people in the building might have joined in on his side, and it was doubtful whether help would have arrived in time to save me. It was as if I was compelled to reach the top of the stairs and subsequently directed to the knife.

If I had confronted the rapist, I would have never gotten the knife that placed him at the rape scene, and he might have walked on any charges. If another officer had aided me in the building check, the fight might still have occurred, and now two officers instead of one would have been hurt, and the knife never recovered.

The fact that I was covered with muddy dog shit was also a good thing. If I was all spit and polished, the people in the apartment building might not have been so cooperative. I think, in some way, they sympathized with me.

When I told the family at the top of the stairs the victim was a young teenager and mentally slow, I don't know where that idea came from. It just popped into my head out of absolutely nowhere. I never noticed how old the girl was or whether she had an intellectual disability. This is why when Detective Vineyard told me the victim was a mentally handicapped young teenager I realized too many things had happened that I didn't control for this whole scenario to end with the arrest of Williams.

A final note: The city councilman Emanuel Cleaver, who worked to have the charges against Jones dropped, became a two-term mayor of Kansas City and is currently a nine-term member of the US House of Representatives.

Sgt. Stanford and Detective Vineyard did not take it upon themselves to drop the case. I believe high-ranking members of the department and the prosecutor's office acquiesced to Emanuel Cleaver's request to have the charges dropped.

The associated press picked up the story, appearing in newspapers from California to Florida. After seeing my name in the paper, my wife's friends asked her what had happened. She couldn't tell them. I never told her about the incident.

Chapter 50:
The Belton Boys

Around late March or early April, Bob Wright, Carl Long, and I were all together on three ped checks at Thirty-first and Brooklyn outside the Blue Room Lounge. We had the three suspected drug dealers on the wall and were frisking them for weapons. My ped check evidently had some drugs on him, and as if on cue, all three suspects pushed off the wall, and a fight abruptly began.

Somehow I anticipated their action and slugged my guy hard in the mouth, knocking him backward. I was able to turn him around and slam him back into the wall, dazing him, then cuffed and put him on the ground out of the way. Turning around, I saw Carl was cuffing his suspect, but Bob was on his back wrestling with his guy. I kicked the guy off Bob, who then cuffed the dealer. All three suspects had drugs on them, cocaine and speed, and went to jail.

I told Bob, a former amateur boxer, "Don't wrestle with these guys. You were a boxer—knock them out!" For some reason many officers did not like to hit suspects in the face with their fists and tended to go straight for the judo holds. I preferred to stun the suspect with a punch or kick and then cuff them. I made a mistake, though, by hitting my suspect in the mouth instead of the nose or jaw and, consequently, cut two knuckles on his teeth. My wife tended to notice bruised and cut knuckles.

A few weeks later, at roll call, Carl produced a printout showing the Belton brothers were wanted on murder warrants out of Kansas City, Kansas (KCK). Carl said he knew the Belton boys sometimes hung out at the Blue Room Lounge, so Bob, Carl, and I decided to go over there and do some more ped checks and watch for the brothers at the same time. Sure enough, at about 5:00 pm, we had three suspected drug dealers on the wall when Carl yelled, "There are the Belton brothers in that car!"

The car, a newer silver 911 Porsche, was stopped right behind us, stuck in bumper-to-bumper traffic. We told our peds to run, leaving us to face the probably armed Belton Boys. Bob and Carl had their guns in the face of the driver. That left me to chase the other brother, who jumped out of the car and ran. I sprinted across the stalled traffic and over a fence, chasing Jerome Belton. Jerome ran up three stories of an apartment building's outdoor wooden fire escape and I was right on his tail; he was trapped.

At the top of the stairs, Jerome turned around and charged me. I sidestepped him at the last second, grabbed him by the arm and jacket collar, and shoved him down the stairs as hard as I could. He rolled and tumbled all the way down the three flights.

At the bottom, he was bleeding and complaining of broken bones. I cuffed him, then checked him for weapons and any injuries. Finding an unlocked fence gate, I walked Jerome back to where Bob and Carl had the other Belton brother leaning on a police car, cuffed. I called for a wagon and an ambulance to check out my arrest.

A crowd was starting to gather, and I called for another car. Two cars showed up a couple of minutes later, and the group started thinning. In the middle of the inner city, it looks bad when two gangsters are against a car cuffed, and one is bleeding. The crowd does not know we arrested two men wanted for murder and only see three cops fighting a couple of guys for no apparent reason. We were lucky that day the crowd did not attack us.

The dispatcher notified KCK PD we'd caught the Belton brothers but now KCK said they only wanted us to let them know if we saw the brothers. Now Bob and Carl were asking what to do with the Beltons. I told them Jerome, at least, was under arrest for the battery of an officer and resisting arrest. The ambulance came and patched up Jerome, who had a few lumps, minor cuts, and abrasions. A wagon took him downtown for booking.

I was pissed at KCK for hanging us out like that. I fought a murder suspect up a three-story staircase, risking my life for nothing.

I went to city court on Jerome Belton; it was only city charges since I was not hurt. My regular court judge was sick, and another judge was on that day. I did not know him and had never been in his courtroom. When my case came up, the judge read the charges and asked Jerome what he had to say.

Jerome proceeded to tell the judge a fairy tale. "I was walking down the street, minding my own business, when that police officer there started chasing me for no reason at all. Why he chase me up a three-story staircase and then, for no reason, tossed me down all those stairs. I'm still hurt!" Jerome rubbed his shoulder for emphasis.

The judge then asked my side of the story.

"Judge, at the time, Jerome here was wanted for murder and ran up a three-story fire escape in an attempt to elude me. He then tried to fight me at the top, so I tossed him back down the stairs."

The judge said, "Is that it?"

"Yes, Your Honor."

The judge then looked at the suspect, banged his gavel down, and said, "Guilty, ninety days in jail!"

Then as Jerome was being led out of the courtroom, the judge asked, "Well, how are your mom and dad, Sean?"

Jerome turned around, stunned. I didn't know it, but it seems the judge was a friend of my parents.

A judge rarely knows an officer's family, and if he does, the judge will send the case to another courtroom. That didn't happen that day. Maybe the judge didn't realize it until after the hearing was over. I didn't object.

Chapter 51:
First Day in Metro

I had been in many fights not covered in this book and injured. I was eventually transferred to Metro Zone, a place some considered a less warlike atmosphere. The idea was I would be, for the most part, less likely to come into violent confrontations. I was assigned the midnight shift with the district patrolling along State Line Road, a quiet area of the city where not too much ever happened. That was the plan; it did not quite work out that way.

When I switched to Metro I requested days, and my request was approved. However, I still had to do one week of nights, 11pm to 7am, before transferring to the day shift.

On my first night in Metro, I did not know a soul on my crew or any other crew. This would be like starting all over again; the other officers would wait to see how I handled myself before trusting me. Well, it was a two-way street as far as I was concerned. I would have to see how other officers dealt with calls before trusting them. I had done about every type of call and caught and arrested more felons than most officers in Metro. I was confident in my abilities and eager to get started.

There was a little bit of a chill at roll call, and it was not from the early March night. In Metro, each district had separate roll call rooms. I took a seat around a large white table while the Sergeant read the latest police bulletins and any messages to be passed on from the command staff. No one said hello, not even the Sergeant. It was not an auspicious start.

On nights in cold weather, most of the crime was the occasional domestic disturbance, or someone would scare up an occupied stolen auto. It would be different from evenings in Center Zone, where drug dealers and prostitutes hung out in the open, easy to find. I would have to learn the hot spots and who the bad guys were.

On my first night in Metro around midnight, I was dispatched to a residence across the city from my assigned district on a suspicious vehicle. The dispatcher said a resident in the area had seen a green Buick four-door crash through someone's front yard fence and strike a tree. The caller said the car was still running, and the driver was unconscious behind the wheel. That was all the information I had to go on. My thought was the driver was drunk or on drugs and passed out, in which case a DUI would be assured. I was the backup car; the primary officer patrolled the call area and would handle the reports.

Somehow I arrived at the scene first so I waited for the primary officer. I could see the green Buick had driven through a white picket fence across a yard before slamming into a tree in someone's front yard. There were pieces of broken fence scattered over the yard, and the heavy damage sustained to the front of the car indicated the driver was traveling fast at the time of the accident. Everyone in the cul-de-sac must have heard the sound of the crash; it was midnight, but all the houses were lit up.

Due to the cold spring night or perhaps fearing some sort of gunplay, nobody came outside and checked on the driver to see if he was injured. I could see the car exhaust turning into vapor as it hit the cold night air. It was not freezing cold but a chill that made you shiver and shake once or twice before you decided how cold it was. Only a month ago, the temperature had hovered in the mid-twenties at night.

The other officer arrived, and I could tell he must have recently finished FTO training. His eyes were wide open, and his movements were uncertain, jerky, not smooth, like he did not have complete control of his muscles. If I had to guess, he was probably only twenty-one or twenty-two and had not spent much time alone on a dark cloudy night in the inner city. It could be intimidating if you let it. He hesitated and looked at me.

I remembered when I first started, and knew everybody had their own pace getting comfortable with the situations we faced. I waited for him to say something, knowing it was important to let him take charge, but after looking at each other for what seemed like an eternity, I simply said, "Let's check out the car."

Even though I was closer to the car's driver, I walked around to the passenger side to make the other officer (I will call him Tim) take the driver's side. This way, he would be the first to make contact and control the situation.

Looking through the passenger window, I could see no blood or signs of injury, and the driver appeared to be breathing fine with a steady rise and fall of his thick, dark wool winter coat. I had heard about several instances where a driver had been shot, drove away, and crashed when he passed out from shock or loss of blood. Sometimes the shooter would follow the victim to the crash site and shoot him several more times, making sure he was dead, believing that old fable "Dead men tell no lies or testify!"

There was a small black unknown-caliber automatic on the front seat next to the driver's open-palmed right hand as if he had released the gun after the crash. I looked up at the other officer to see if he had seen the weapon. Tim was hesitantly peering around the driver but had not spotted the gun yet. I did not want Tim to wake the driver, who might reach for his gun and start shooting, maybe thinking he was under attack.

I got Tim's attention by waving my arm above my head. He looked at me, startled. I put my finger to my lips, pantomiming for quiet, then drew my gun out and showed it to him; he drew his uncertainly. I unclipped my portable radio, stepped away from the car, and called the dispatcher, "Radio 244, we have an unconscious driver behind the wheel of a locked car, engine running, with his hand next to a handgun. Could you hold the air for a moment?"

"Holding the air for radio 244; they have a party armed."

I had already put my radio back on my belt before the dispatcher could answer. Tim looked over the car at me, then at the driver, back and forth, back and forth. Tim was visibly shaking and needed to calm down. The driver was still passed out and gave no signs of waking up. I remembered when I was with Joe Morrison, my FTO, and he had me take over against Louis the pimp. Joe and the other officer were calm the way they talked and acted, and it made me feel less tense. I tried to do the same for Tim.

I signaled Tim to the back of the car, where I joined him. "What do you want to do, Tim? It is your call."

I know that was a lot to ask of him, but sooner or later, he would have to get over that first big call. He shrugged his shoulders and shook his head repeatedly, no, no, no. Okay, then I will make the decisions, right or wrong. I told Tim in a calm, low voice, "Okay, I am going over to the driver and will try to get his door open without waking him. Failing that, I'll bust his window out and pull him out of the car before he has a chance to reach for his gun. Unless you want to try to get into the car?"

Tim did not say anything and shook his head no.

"Okay, Tim, you go over to the passenger side, and if he wakes up while I'm getting the door open and he grabs the gun, shoot him!"

Tim's eyes were wide and I knew he was under a lot of stress. I was too but could control it now, and I was helping him learn to do it by talking slowly and calmly. I reached over and gave him a quick pat on the shoulder and smiled. "You'll do fine Tim. Now, remember, don't shoot him unless he grabs the gun, okay? Now go over to your side and watch, and oh, Tim, don't shoot me. Okay, bud?"

I gave a slight chuckle at that last part and got a big grin out of Tim. He was getting control of the moment, and that is what I needed him to be, in command of himself. I nodded for Tim to get in position and walked up to the driver's door.

Nothing had changed. The driver was still slouched, chin on his chest, unconscious but breathing rhythmically, his right hand still next to the automatic. To get to this point, I had already gone through several scenarios in my head, and they all wound up with me getting inside the driver's door and hopefully controlling the driver, thus preventing him from picking up the gun.

We could wait for other officers to arrive and pass the buck, but it would still be the same: Someone had to get the door open. I could have let Tim try to open the door, but if anything went wrong, the person opening the door would get shot first, and I did not want that to be Tim. We could not wait until the driver woke up; he might be shot, injured from the crash, or even dying from carbon monoxide leaking into the car from a damaged exhaust system. I could have Tim call out on the loudspeaker, but again, if he made a sudden move for his gun, I would still shoot him.

The doors were all locked. I pushed on the window, but it would not budge. I finally took out my nightstick, looked at Tim, and pantomimed hitting the window. Tim gulped but gave me an affirmative nod of his head. I reared back and hit the window with my nightstick. The window was unbroken, but my cheap nightstick shattered against the window. The driver did not stir and I worried he was hurt. Even a drunk would have heard that bang on the window.

The stick handle was still in my hand with a long, tapered section ending in a sharp, narrow wedge. I looked at the window, and part of the window had fallen inside the door. I slipped the edge of what was left of my stick into the opening and pushed the window open far enough that I was able to get my hand inside the car and unlock the doors.

I was not done yet. I still had to grab the driver, yank him out of the car, and cuff him. But if he was already hurt, that might injure him more. On the other hand, it would be safer to remove the gun first. I chose to lean over the driver and snatch the weapon carefully. The driver was asleep; the odor of alcohol was strong inside the car. Without waking the driver, I grabbed the gun. It was a loaded .32 auto ready to fire with a full magazine, one in the chamber, safety off. I made the gun safe and locked it in my car.

I had Tim come over to the driver's side and turn the car off, put it in park, and advised dispatch to clear the air, the situation was under control. Then I asked Tim, "Well, how are you doing? Having fun yet?"

He and I laughed. The hard part was over. I gave Tim an ammonia capsule, "Well, Tim, it is your arrest. You can do the honors!"

Tim smiled brightly, taking the cloth-wrapped glass capsule from my hand. He broke the ampule on the doorframe and stuck the potent ammonia-soaked cloth under the driver's nose. Slowly, the driver came alert, shaking his head to escape the awful smell. Tim asked the man if he was hurt and to exit the car. Tim handcuffed and searched him.

I ordered a tow truck and a wagon and ran the vehicle tag. The driver refused to give his name or address, and the license plate came back not on file. I would run the VIN later since our call had already used up a lot of airtime. Then it started.

Tim had to grab hold of his arrest, who tried to walk away. The man started yelling at the top of his lungs, "Let me go! I ain't done nothing wrong!"

The driver started cussing us out and repeating, "Let me go! I ain't done nothing wrong! You mother f..kers! Let me go! I ain't done nothing wrong! Mother f..kers!"

Despite the cold, people came out of their warm homes to see what was happening. Some people were in slacks and T-shirts, others in thick winter coats. I could hear the murmurings of the crowd as they got closer, and the yet-unidentified driver continued his obscene ranting.

One young lady in her early twenties with no coat on started screaming at me as I stood next to the crashed car in the front yard. "What are you doing? Why are you here? Why are you arresting that man?" She fired off the questions like she had a machine gun for a mouth. The car had gone through the fence, up an incline, and smashed into a tree. It seemed pretty apparent to me what happened.

I answered her calmly. "He crashed into this tree and destroyed someone's fence. Do you know the man? Does the car belong around here?"

"I ain't tellin' you shit. You've got no right to arrest that man. He ain't done nothing wrong!"

"Well, okay then."

"You f..king pig!"

"Okay, fine, ma'am. Please move back while we work this crash."

"I don't have to leave, you mother f..ker! You have no right to be here!"

I ignored her and started writing down the VIN for the tow-in report. She did not want information; she wanted to start something and continued to scream at me. About then, Officer Johnny Blossom showed up and acted like he was the de facto commander of the whole department. He was in his mid-forties, overweight, with pasty-white jowls that wiggled when he spoke. Officer Blossom must have heard my conversation with the irate bystander.

He started yelling at me from twenty feet away, "We don't speak to the citizens around here like you did in Center Zone!" His head shook like a chicken as he spat out his words. A couple of young officers were standing behind Blossom, maybe from the same academy class as Tim, and stared at me. I stopped what I was doing and watched as Blossom continued to waddle toward me. The foul-mouthed girl quieted momentarily.

I realized then, sight unseen, Blossom and probably many other officers had already made judgments about me as I had been involved in several major incidents in Center Zone. They didn't know what happened, only what they heard fourth and fifth hand; stories change a lot over retelling. This fat cop was starting to piss me off. If he had problems with me, he needed to pick a better time and place to address it than in front of other officers, bystanders, and a ranting drunk prisoner. Blossom was trying to make himself look important. I had the feeling he was an idiot and had some other issues.

I set my clipboard down on the car to free my hands and let out a sigh. "Well, Officer Blossom, is it?"

I reached out and flipped up his name tag, pausing to study it. He did not expect that, and it knocked him a few pegs down off his pompous attitude. He was a bully, and I would not be bullied. "Too bad you could not have arrived a little bit ago. You could have helped make the arrest, but I guess I was closer being, what, clear across the other side of the city in my district? Hey, how come you didn't call me off and make the call yourself?"

I looked at him in disgust then shook my head slowly, turning away. Then, talking over my shoulder as I walked way, I dismissively said, "Why don't you go get the name of the victim of the property damage, and any witnesses, Blossom?"

The red-faced Blossom turned on his heel, waddled over to the crowd, and tried to calm the big-mouthed girl down. I looked at Blossom's acolytes and gave them a genuine smile, and they all gave me one back. The wagon pulled up, and Tim loaded up the prisoner. Once the driver was gone, the loudmouth girl had nothing more to yell about and left the area. Blossom never got her name or any witnesses; he was useless. I went over and shook Tim's hand as he started to get in his car to go to the station and process the prisoner.

"You did good tonight, Tim. I'd be happy to go on any call with you, I mean it. You did good!"

The other guys gave Tim approving looks. As far as they would ever know, he had handled the call; after all, it was his sector, and he was the primary officer. Later I heard Blossom had a nebulous past and was probably on nights for a reason. Nobody said anything concerning the call. If Blossom complained, they blew him off. I finished my week on nights without further incidents and reported to days.

A final note: I'll talk a little later about the other major incidents I referenced that occurred in Center Zone.

Chapter 52:
Sergeant Pick

On days, I was assigned the most exclusive part of Metro, but I only had two or three calls in my area for the entire year I was there. I spent all my time with Hans Storch, a congenial twenty-year veteran, in his district and the surrounding neighborhoods. I thought since I rarely received any calls in my assigned area, why not spend my time helping the other officers in theirs?

I couldn't stay in my district anyway as I was constantly dispatched on calls in the eastern part of 40 sector. If I stayed in my assigned district, it took too long to respond to calls and back up other officers. Besides, the hunting was better in Hans's district.

There was only one drawback working on days 40 sector. I had to work for Sergeant Pick.

Pick was my first sergeant on days in Metro Zone. He was a slim six feet four with a polished bald head and droopy black eyes. I honestly believe, for some reason, the man did not like me. I didn't know why and I really didn't care. I was just thankful I only had to work for him a few months until he retired.

Across from the Swope Parkway fountains, there was a little side street lined with townhouses and two-story apartment buildings under a row of large mature oak trees. Unless a person was looking for the road, you could drive by it a hundred times and not even know it was there.

Hans told me about a guy named Cole Suitor who was wanted for murder and showed me Suitor's mug shot. Cole, twenty-six, was a small, thin man with a bald head and a black patch over one eye, wouldn't be hard to pick out in a crowd. Cole hung out in a second-floor apartment with a wooden fire escape located on the short shady street across from the fountains.

I drove over to the street and parked. Beer bottles and cans littered the area under the shade of the giant oaks. Then from half a block away, I saw Cole walking up the wooden staircase to the second-floor apartment. I asked the dispatcher to check Cole's murder warrant in the computer, and she confirmed it was still good. I gave my location and asked for another car.

Then I noticed a car listed on the daily hot sheet, occupied times two. I ran the tag for that car and confirmed the vehicle was stolen. I told the dispatcher that the vehicle was parked and occupied at the same location and needed another officer.

Finally, I recognized a robbery suspect I had been looking for the past month, walking down the sidewalk, not paying any attention to his surroundings. I ran him through dispatch to make sure his warrant was still active. The dispatcher answered that the warrant was good and sent me another car for that subject.

Now I thought, I have a killer in an upstairs apartment, an occupied stolen car parked a couple of cars in front of me, and an armed robbery suspect walking toward me all at the same time. What were the odds?

I figured the murder suspect could wait; he was inside. That left me with the occupied stolen auto and the robbery suspect. The robbery suspect was a higher priority, and the occupied stolen would stay put, thinking if they drove off, I might notice them.

The armed robbery suspect got closer and I did not want to be sitting in my car when he noticed me. Ideally, I should wait for backup, but that wasn't to happen this time.

I looked at the robbery subject's hands and how he let his arms swing while walking. Someone not accustomed to carrying a gun all of the time or a firearm without a properly fitting holster will constantly check if the weapon is still secure and is not slipping. This guy walked without ever checking his belt line. He was wearing cutoff sweatpants and a white T-shirt, no place to carry a gun.

I figured that when he got closer I would exit my car and grab him before he could run. For the moment I watched his eyes, checking to see if he had even noticed me yet. Maybe he was high or having one of those days where everything was good. He still was not aware of my presence. I had the dispatch hold the air, advising her the robbery suspect was approaching me.

As impossible as it seems, the suspect came closer and was still unaware of my presence until I grabbed him, laid him across the hood of my car, and put him in cuffs. Two officers arrived, and one took custody of the robbery suspect. I had the second officer block the stolen auto while I held the occupants at gunpoint until they were cuffed. A third officer arrived, and he accompanied me up the outside wooden staircase to the murder suspect's apartment.

I pulled my gun out and knocked at the door. An unknown woman in her mid-twenties let us in without even asking why we were there. Cole was sitting on the couch, and I simply raised my gun and told him, "Raise your hands, Cole. You're under arrest for murder. Now stand up and turn around!"

Evidently, Cole had never told this woman he was a killer, as that could be a relationship changer. She took this opportunity to voice her opinion of him.

"Cole, I knew you were a no-good, two-timing son of a bitch! I don't never want to see your raggedy-ass around here again!"

"Ma'am, I don't think you will have to worry about that for at least fifteen years."

The other officer cuffed him, as I did not have any left. When I got back to my car, a wagon arrived and loaded up all the prisoners. That is when Sergeant Pick approached me.

In front of everyone, he barked, pointing a bony finger at me, "What is going on here? Why are you not in your district?"

"Well, I had information that a murder suspect would be here, and when I arrived, I saw the occupied stolen auto and a robbery suspect walking up the street, I called for a couple of cars and arrested everyone without incident, Sergeant."

I thought, what the hell is his problem? I arrested four felons and recovered a stolen auto.

"You should be in your district!"

Sarge was angry, but more than that, he wanted to get something on me.

Hans tried to cool the Sergeant down by offering, "Sarge, I asked Sean to come over here and keep an eye out for Cole while I was at the station cleaning up the squad room as you ordered!"

"Okay, but do not let it happen again!" Sarge turned around while five other officers watched him walk away, stunned by his outburst.

I thought, what a son of a bitch. Next time I see four felony arrests walking down the street, I'll let them go if they aren't in my district. In fact, I would stay on State Line Road on the days he worked. When dispatched to the other side of town, I would make sure Sarge knew I was as far away as possible from the call. I hated not being close when other crew members needed quick assistance.

Oh, and by the way, making three unrelated felony arrests simultaneously is equivalent to making an unassisted triple play in baseball.

Another day I was in the drive-through line at a fast-food restaurant when I observed a man acting like he was high on drugs. He was whipping his arms up in the air, yelling and ranting at invisible people. I was blocked with a car in front and behind me and could not open my car door because of a high curb. That's when the crazy guy realized I was watching him.

The man came over to my car in a half run and a half walk. My car window was down. I drew my gun out of its holster and held it in my lap with the muzzle against the door. Several years before I started, a man with severe mental issues and without any provocation shot and killed an officer writing a report in his car. The rule was never to let people approach you while seated in your car; always get out. I was taught this in the academy, and my FTO reinforced it.

The crazy started talking gibberish, then suddenly stuck his head in the car and spotted my gun. I did not stick it up his nose but would have shot him through the door if he had turned violent.

"Oh, is that for me?" he asked, looking at the gun.

I did not say anything but knew I had that half-grin with one raised eyebrow expression on my face and he could clearly see that I did not appreciate his head in my car. He abruptly pulled his head out and ran off, and I got my food. Ten minutes later, Sergeant Pick got on the air.

"Would the officer who bought lunch at the fast-food restaurant at Fifty-ninth and Troost please identify yourself and report to me at the station immediately!"

There was no mistaking his tone, and whoever admitted being there was in trouble for something. The fact that it could not wait and had to be addressed immediately ensured the proper measure of threat was involved. The matter was of grave importance, and Sergeant Pick was going to nail someone. Since the car number was also given every day when going in service, Sergeant Pick probably already knew who was involved. If that officer did not identify himself publicly to be humiliated, it would be evidence the officer knew he had committed some major violation of the rules of conduct or procedures.

"Yeah, that was me, Sarge. What's up?"

A reasonable response to an unreasonable request and the fact that I sounded unfazed by his orders made him angrier.

"Respond immediately to the station!" His voice was louder and more irate. I was getting to him.

"En route." I made it simple. No use in making him any madder than he already was.

At the station, Sergeant Pick met me at the door and, with other officers around, said loud enough to be heard by everyone, "Into the squad room!"

Although he was starting to piss me off, I did not respond to him, took a seat, put my arms on the table in front of me, and interlaced my fingers. Interlacing your fingers prevents you from tapping on the table, flipping the other person off, or even making a fist. If done correctly it gives an impression of calmness. I waited for him to be seated and fill me in on the emergency.

Sergeant Pick asked, "Were you in the McDonald's drive-through line when a man approached you?"

He already knew the answer: "Yes."

I would make him explain what this was all about before volunteering anything.

"Well, a man reported you for pulling a gun and threatening him!"

Pick smiled for the first time ever; I was glad he finally found something that made him happy.

I believe Sergeant Pick was trying to bring me up on some kind of charge and was getting all his ducks in a row before heading to the major's office.

"And?" I looked at him as if to say, "So?" trying to get him to lay all his cards on the table.

"Well, did you pull a gun on him when he came up to you or not?"

I could see Sergeant Pick was getting frustrated. He was developing an eye tic.

"Well, Sarge, I saw what appeared to be a crazy man ranting and raving while I was in the drive-through line. I was blocked in and could not open my door. The man saw me and came at me quickly. Before he even got close, I drew my gun to defend myself if need be." I explained how the gun was in my lap and pointed at the door.

"Well, every citizen has the right to approach an officer, doesn't he?"

"That's true. However, I was trapped in my car, and as you well know, several years ago, a mentally unbalanced man shot and killed an officer sitting in his car. Furthermore, I was taught never to let anyone approach your car while sitting in it. Is that all, sir?"

"Ah, ah, ah, yes, but remember we have to be approachable by the public."

The wind had left his sails by then. I could hear him sigh.

"Of course, sir. Anything else?"

"No, you are dismissed." He waved his hand at nothing, and I left the room.

I do not know what he was thinking, possibly that I pulled my gun randomly at people for fun or to see their reaction. He had to make a big show of it. Now everyone wanted to know what had happened, what was the big emergency. If he trusted his officers, Pick would have asked to meet me in a low, non-emergency voice and then asked in a normal tone about the incident. Now everyone could see what an asshole he was.

A few weeks later, on his last day before retirement, I met him in a parking lot and turned in a report. He checked the report, then looked up at me and said, "You're glad I am retiring, aren't you? You don't like me."

He said it without malice, a matter of fact.

I looked him in the eye and said, "You know, Sergeant, any person that can take thirty years of this job and come out alive and emotionally whole deserves everyone's respect. I think you deserve that respect for making it, and I sincerely hope you enjoy your retirement, and yes, I don't like you at all. Will that be all, sir?"

I also said it without any malice.

"Yes, that will be all."

I never heard how his retirement turned out but honestly hope he enjoyed it.

Chapter 53:

Catching the Grant Brothers

In July, six months after arriving in Metro, I rode two-man for a day with Petey Wilson, a quiet guy in his mid-thirties. The day was hot but not unbearable; a rain the night before had preceded a small cold front, providing a short respite from the ninety-eight-degree temperatures. I was the passenger as we headed north on Prospect, approaching Fifty-fifth Street.

I saw a short male in his early twenties walking north on Prospect on the opposite side of the street. The guy kept tugging at something heavy at his belt line, causing his loose-fitting jeans to sag badly on the right side, and watched as he used one hand to hold his jeans while his other hand tugged at something on his side. I have seen people do that tug and constant checking before; the weight of a concealed handgun always caused it. The man was approaching a small grocery store on the northwest side of Fifty-fifth.

I pointed to the guy. "Look at him! He's got a gun under his T-shirt! Quick, stop the car! I'll chase him from this side; you get ahead of him. If he continues north, you cut him off!"

The man took a quick look over his shoulder, saw the police car, and took off running.

I was out of the car before finishing my sentence. I was only twenty feet behind the guy and crossing Fifty-fifth when he bolted into the small mom-and-pop store. I charged through the door only seconds behind him.

I slipped on the tile floor as I entered the store, almost falling. Leaving the bright sunlight, it took me a couple of seconds to adjust to the artificial light. When my vision cleared, I did a visual search for the man but could not see him anywhere. I had pulled my gun out before entering and kept it pointed in front of me. There were customers in the store and not a sound from anybody; the two cash registers abruptly fell silent. The checkers and several customers in line were frozen in place. All eyes were on me.

I slowly walked forward, looking down each aisle. He had to be up here in the front somewhere; I would have heard him running down an aisle if he had gone that way. There were only six aisles, and now I approached the last row. Up ahead, on the floor behind a candy rack, I spotted someone kneeling wearing blue jeans. I made a last fast look around, making sure no one was behind me, and noted the positions of all the people I could see.

Three things I observed: there were no men in the store, everyone was old, and nobody else wore blue jeans. I was betting the jeans I was looking at belonged to the guy who ran into the store. Was he aiming his gun at me, because I was aiming at the spot about a foot above those knees. The cock of my pistol back to the firing position was loud in the silent store. In deference to the ladies, I did not use profanity or yell out commands. In a controlled tone, I told him, "Okay, buddy, I see you behind the candy rack. My gun is pointed right at you. Slide your gun across the floor, and come out on your knees, hands up, now, or I'll shoot you!"

"Hold it, officer, I'm coming out now! My hands are up, but I ain't got no gun! Don't shoot!"

I moved two steps to my right so I would not be where he heard my voice. It was not a lot, but he would have had to adjust his aim while I had him in my sights. He shuffled out from behind the candy rack on his knees and twisted his head quickly right by me, looking at the spot where my voice had been seconds ago.

"I ain't got nothing, officer, and I ain't done nothing wrong!"

"Keep coming with those hands in the air." He was getting closer. "Okay, now lie down on your stomach, hands out, fingers spread."

He complied but still protested his innocence, hoping to sway the ladies. They were not buying it. This was the only grocery store these women could walk to, and they protected it. If they saw a man run into their store with a gun being chased by the police, they were not going to interfere at all. In fact, they would help the police. They did this time.

"I ain't got no gun, man. You can't arrest me!"

I cuffed him despite his protests.

Petey came in and took the suspect outside so I could talk to the ladies out of sight of the suspect. The second he was gone, a woman in the checkout line cleared her throat loudly then spoke when I looked at her. "There it is, the gun," she said, pointing. "We saw him try to hide it in the candy rack!"

The lady was upset and would not be bullied by a gun-toting thug. The other women around her moved closer to her, giving her support, nodding in agreement.

"We don't need this in our neighborhood, no, no!"

"That's right, you tell him, Sadie!" They all gathered closer.

"Mmm-hmm! That's right!"

I picked up the gun. "Thank you, ma'am."

I talked with the ladies until the wagon arrived for the suspect. It felt good to know that sometimes people in this neighborhood liked you and appreciated your presence.

The gun was a long-barreled, fully loaded .357 caliber Smith & Wesson revolver. The man was a convicted robber and had an outstanding robbery warrant. It turns out he lived a few short blocks from the store. His name was George Grant. I pulled George's record and found out he had an identical twin brother, Leon, who was wanted for murder. Now that I knew what Leon looked like, I would find him.

On Sunday, a few days later, I was looking for something to do and took a drive around Swope Park. South of Sixty-third Street on Lewis Road was an old training facility that the KC Chiefs football team had once used. A little south of the training center was a one-way circle drive, maybe half a mile long.

On Sundays, the half-circle drive became the site of large crowds of people socializing and partying. The road was almost impassable, with cars parked on both sides, leaving only a narrow path to navigate around the circle. As far as I know, no police officer willingly drove through the jammed street unless it was absolutely necessary. I believed the road and the park were both public and should be enjoyed by all, so I drove the gauntlet.

Cars were backed up before I could even enter the road, and the crowd probably numbered close to a thousand. Slowly, I inched my car around the circle. There was music pouring from dozens of giant portable radios, and people were enjoying the day talking, singing, and laughing. It was loud, almost too loud to be heard.

Every conceivable color, make, and model of car was parked on either side of the road, waxed and shined to perfection. People were dressed up in a multitude of colors, fabrics, and styles, from hot pink pants to yellow suede cowboy hats. There were men with beards, bald men, those with long braided hair, and others with short to enormous Afros. It was like one giant fashion and car show put together; it was a pretty awesome scene. Some folks stared at me, but other than that, they continued their fun as if I was not there. Then there he was.

Leon Grant, the spitting image of his brother, was making his way across the road between two cars in front of me just yards away. I notified the dispatcher I was halfway along the circle on Lewis Road and could she check Leon Grant to see if he still had the homicide warrant. Leon had not seen me or even noticed the police car creeping up the street

"Yes, Leon Grant still has an active homicide warrant out of Jackson County. Do you have him?"

"Not yet. Put me out on a ped check in the circle at 63rd and Lewis, —no, make that a foot chase!"

Leon spotted me and took off running as I finished my transmission. I knew he would run and wasted no time getting out of the car after him. Leon ran into the crowd, but being as he was small, he could not force his way through. He was blocked in by a tight group of partiers and looked like a kid trying to climb a wall: His arms and legs were moving, but he wasn't getting anywhere. After a short ten-yard foot chase, I grabbed him and was surprisingly able to get him cuffed without any interference from the crowd. He was a weak man without his brother's gun.

Nobody in the crowd seemed to notice, or if they did, they were not going to let the action ruin their fun. I took my gun out, pressed it against his side, and told him that if he started yelling or caused any sort of commotion, he was going to be the first one shot, and we walked quietly back through the boisterous crowd.

On the way, I saw one of the officers from my crew in the crowd smoking a hand-rolled cigarette that sure looked like marijuana to me. Neither of us acknowledged the other. He might have been working, and I did not want to blow his cover, but I had an uneasy feeling he would not help me if things went south. He had the expression on his face usually associated with a deer caught in the headlights. I moved on past him, getting closer to my car. It was the same as working at the Metallica concert: Nobody noticed me until I walked by them.

I unlocked the car, put Leon in the front seat, then notified the dispatcher Leon was secured and that we were headed out to Lewis Road. Since no vehicles could get around me when I left my car to grab Leon, the half-circle was clear for me back to the main road. There were two cars and Sergeant Ulnis waiting for me. They couldn't have gotten into the blocked half circle to help me if something had gone wrong.

Lilly was the first officer I saw back on Lewis Road.

"What the hell do you think you are doing? You could have gotten yourself killed!" I could see she was genuinely concerned but happy I came out alive.

"Don't worry, now that Leon is in custody, I'm not going back for the other guy." I smiled at her.

She let out a soft curse under her breath, then walked off a few steps, turned partially around, and gave me a half-smile. I liked Lilly; she had moxie.

Sergeant Ulnis, unlike Sergeant Pick, said, "Good job. Maybe we should see about posting no-parking signs on one side of the drive to allow emergency vehicles to get through if needed." He smiled, and that was it.

I had arrested two felons that week, one for homicide and one for robbery, and helped some lovely ladies keep their grocery store safe.

The officer in the park smoking dope let a suspect I was trying to serve a warrant on escape out the back door of a house. I never told anyone about him in the park or letting the suspect escape but should have. He quit a short time later; nobody asked why. The last time I saw him, he was working as a security guard.

A month later, no-parking signs were erected on one side of the half-circle drive, alleviating much of the traffic congestion on Sundays.

Chapter 54:
Guess Who

One day in late summer, before the heat of the day, I saw Chester Loom, who had an armed robbery warrant, walking down the street. "Hold the air dispatch, and send me another car."

I gave my location and subject description then Chester saw me and sprinted between some houses. He was too fast. I couldn't catch him, but if I could keep him in sight, someone else might be able to cut him off.

At the first fence, a six-foot chain-link with spikes at the top, I tried to grab the top rail between the points, but a tip stuck me in the center of my left palm. Still, somehow I managed to top the fence, but now my right boot was caught on the spikes, and I ended up hanging upside down on the fence by one foot, my back to Chester.

I turned, jerking my shoulders halfway around to try to make sure Chester wasn't going to shoot me in the back. Chester glanced back at me and stopped running. He bent over, hands on his knees, and caught his breath while I struggled to free myself. Chester straightened up, pointed at me, laughed, and sprinted away. A few seconds later, I fell free of the fence, gave Chester's last direction of travel, then headed for the station.

Sergeant Ulnis met me in the parking lot and joked, "So why did you let him go? Are you getting old or something?"

"Yeah, you know, I think I am. I'm going to have to stop chasing these young guys."

"So, what did you do to your hand?"

By now, the blood from my hand was dripping on my pants, and it kind of hurt.

"I got stuck on one of those chain-link fences." I was embarrassed about getting stuck, but it was bound to happen sooner or later.

"Go wash it off, and I'll get you a Band-Aid." He laughed.

It was not too bad, but the bleeding was hard to stop, and the puncture was jagged and torn. I cleaned it up, but after looking at it, Sarge decided my hand needed a couple of stitches. I went back to the same hospital for the second time in two years and saw the same people again. They tended to remember cops in uniform.

With five stitches, Sarge let me off early. I bought some beer and headed home. This was on a Tuesday. By Sunday, I knew where Chester lived and had driven by his house several times. I talked to Sergeant Ulnis before roll call.

"Hey, Sarge, since Chester has a felony warrant, it's within policy to kick his front door in if, and that is a big if, we know he is inside the house."

"So, how are you going to know if he is in the house?" Sarge asked, intrigued.

"We'll have Latica call over to his house and ask for him. If he answers, we kick the door in and arrest him. I'll hide by the back door, and some other guys can hide by the front; we all bust in when Latica confirms he is there."

I thought it was a pretty clever plan until Sarge added, "Okay, but you go in the back door, then come to the front door and let us inside."

This was going to be a little bit dicey. Kicking in the back door would make a lot of noise and alert an armed Chester before I could get the front door opened. However, if everyone came in simultaneously, it might reduce the risk of Chester shooting one of us. If he thought it was only me, Chester might be tempted to shoot me and claim he thought it was an intruder. I would have to see how it played out.

We all got in position, and at the station Latica made the call. Some girl answered the phone, and Latica asked for Chez, Chester's street name. Latica said she wanted to come over and see him. Chez got on the phone and asked if this was Roly. Latica said she was and wanted to come over. He said, "Sure, okay."

Another officer listening to the conversation notified us that Chester was in the house.

I pulled my gun out and went up to the old dried-out wooden back door. I was about to kick it in when the door suddenly opened, and a girl in her early twenties came out, looked at me, and said, "You looking for Chester? Go on in, be my guest. That asshole is in there!" She pointed inside, then angrily stomped off down the back porch stairs.

She left the door wide open for me. I thought, What the hell? She invited me in, so I walked inside. The house was one of those they called a shotgun bungalow because you could see the back door from the front door. Quietly, I crept from the back door kitchen area through the house to the front door. There were two open bedroom doors on my way to the front, and I hoped Chester wouldn't shoot me. I unlocked the front door and let Sarge and two other officers inside. So far, so good. Luck was going my way. I hadn't been shot yet.

I yelled, "Police, Chester, come out with your hands up, or I'll drag your ass out!"

Chester deigned not to answer. I think he figured we would leave.

There was nothing to the house: the kitchen, the dining room with no furniture, and two bedrooms separated by a bathroom. I covered one bedroom with Sarge, and the other officers checked the second bedroom. The bathroom was open, and it appeared nobody was in there. There was nobody visible in either of the bedrooms.

I yelled again for Chester to come out but received no answer. Sarge covered me as I entered the small bedroom. It was empty of furniture except for a box spring on the floor with a dirty, sheetless mattress half pulled off the bed. I figured Chester was hiding under the mattress but didn't want to get shot pulling it off him. I yelled again, "Chester, I know you are hiding under that dirty mattress. Get your ass out from under it, or I am going to start shooting holes in it 'cause I think you got a gun under there!"

Sarge looked at me, raised his eyebrows, and smiled while pointing his gun at the mattress.

"Okay, man, don't shoot. I'm coming out. My hands are up." Chester managed to wiggle out from under the mattress with his hands exposed.

I cuffed him and was leading him out the door when he said, "Hey, you that fat cop that was chasing me and got stuck on the fence?"

I didn't reply, but Sarge laughed. Chester pissed me off, so I wrote him a city charge for resisting arrest by running from me the other day. It was funny because a couple of months later, Chez was out on bond for the robbery charge but had missed his court date on my city charge and got a warrant for that.

Later when I caught Chester getting out of a car in front of his house, he didn't know about the new city warrant, and didn't run this time. I arrested him again, which violated his robbery bond, and now Chester had to stay in jail until the trial, about eight months.

To add insult to injury, when Latica called Chester, it was his girlfriend who answered the phone. She got angry, and that was her who let me in the house. Lastly, Chester was not such a bad guy after all: He didn't shoot me in the back when I was hanging upside down on the fence.

Chapter 55:
All in a Day's Work

One fall day in early October while in Metro, the report load became overwhelming. Right out of roll call, I would be dispatched on a report. Then the report calls came one after another nonstop. Invariably an irate citizen would demand a car be sent on some inane problem during a busy day. Most of the time, the dispatcher would handle the call herself over the phone, keeping officers free to take more serious reports. But occasionally some stupid call would make it through the cracks in the system. When an officer was sent on one of these calls, it was essential for the officer to show respect for the citizen if for no other reason than to keep from getting a complaint. I tried to handle these ridiculous calls with concern, empathy and, a lot of times, controlled laughter.

On one of these calls the dispatcher announced over the radio someone had teepeed the caller's front yard and home. The dispatcher added the caller was livid and was on a first-name basis with a city councilman, hence the call. Immediately other officers made comments over the radio asking if the toilet paper was double-ply, already used, or extra absorbent until the sergeant got on the radio and said, "The next officer who comments will take the report!" With one brief sentence, Sarge had restored the proper decorum every call deserved. It was my call.

I arrived at the caller's address to find a large three-story residence with a white-pillared front porch that extended the width of the house. The home was reminiscent of a Southern plantation mansion, complete with a red-and-white black-faced lawn jockey adjacent to the front porch steps. My guess was the jockey was for anyone arriving at the house on a jackass.

The home reeked of old money, holiday parties attended by the social elite used to having their way, and the kind of people who knew all the city's most influential leaders. The type you did not trifle with if you like your job. The only thing missing was sizable weeping willow trees swaying in the breeze, draped with long strands of Spanish moss and cotton fields waiting to be picked.

I could see white toilet paper hanging over the lower limbs on a tall Douglas fir at the side of the home. The neatly trimmed bushes that outlined the stately veranda were covered with toilet paper, allowing only small patches of evergreen to show. The tall, round Roman columns that supported an upper balcony were looped with paper from pillar to pillar. Half-used rolls of paper littered the grounds. It was a scene right out of the movie *Animal House*. I would imagine the home was also the residence of a high school teenager who may or may not be popular.

I radioed the dispatcher that I had arrived and began my tortuous journey through the piles of wasted toilet paper. I had to break through a barrier of paper looped around the porch railings blocking my path to the front door. I took a deep breath and told myself, do not smart off, and pretend to take this seriously. No matter what the caller says, above all else, do not laugh.

As if the lawn jockey wasn't enough, I did not need to look for the doorbell. A black-painted ornamental figure of a man dressed in a tuxedo, complete with a black face, a top hat, tails, and a cane, pointed to the button. I groaned. Some people go too far. I pressed the button, heard a slight buzz, then a resounding gong sounded somewhere far inside the house. A low-pitched sound carried farther and was easier to hear, especially in such a large home.

The door opened, and an older female, mildly overweight, dressed in a light blue maid's uniform complete with a white apron and matching head cover, answered the door with one hand, a white feather duster in the other. She smiled brightly, showing perfect white teeth contrasting beautifully with her ebony skin.

"My, am I glad to see you, officer. Come right inside!"

She held the door open and stepped aside, making no noise in her white tennis shoes.

"Mrs. C. has been so upset since she got up this morning and saw the mess on the front lawn, and Mr. Charles has Mondays off, you know."

I had not even glanced around at the inside of the house before I heard a harsh voice growl, "Clorita! Now, that is enough information. Get back to your work. I'll handle this!"

"Yes, ma'am."

Clorita quickly backed up and disappeared into some other room out of sight.

Mrs. C., I observed, was a nice-looking woman past her prime but still holding on to every bit of youth she could. At one time, she was probably incredibly beautiful, but now her age was taking hold in its relentless grip. Her hands gave her away, age spots and blue veins noticeably swelling. Dressed in a dark blue knee-length skirt, she looked like she was in her late fifties. She did not introduce herself and only managed a curt "Outside."

Moving her hand back and forth like shooing flies from a picnic lunch, she ushered me out of the house. I wondered how I'd get her personal information if she demanded a report be taken.

"Well, you can see the damage. What are you going to do about it?"

She had her hands on her hips and a stern look on her face. Her head was cocked to the side, and her hair did not move even in the slight breeze. Hair spray or wig, I ventured to guess.

I took a long moment to survey the scene, knowing that before I could say anything, she would tell me what to do. Sure enough, Mrs. C. started barking out orders like she was my commander at the scene of some heinous crime.

"I want you to take this disgusting mess away and check each roll for fingerprints. I want you to take pictures, interview all the neighbors, especially those!" She pointed her finger across the street at an equally large house.

"They have teenagers who park their used cars on the street instead of the drive behind their house. It lowers the home values. I also want all the grocery stores in a twenty-mile radius checked for any large sales of toilet paper to anyone, and have Larry, your chief, call me posthaste! Who would have the audacity to commit such a blatant act of disrespect?"

She folded her arms across her chest and stopped talking for a moment. I did not know if she was winded or out of commands. I reminded myself not to laugh, but it was getting harder.

I waited a moment, and apparently, she wanted me to talk. I ventured a few exploratory questions. "Well, ma'am, let me inquire, do you have children living at home?"

"Well, yes, I have a son who is a senior at Mason, a private school. What does he have to do with any of this?" she answered somewhat haughtily.

"Is he popular with the other students and especially girls?" I continued, formulating a plan as I talked.

"Why, yes, he is. Again, why do you ask?"

She had a hard edge to her voice; she was at her limit at this line of questioning. It was now or never.

"Well, ma'am, the most popular boys and sometimes girls are the ones most targeted by friends and admirers to have some connection with them. They want to say, 'I know Stan or Bob, he is a good friend. We teepeed his house, and he laughed so hard, he's such a great guy. Do friends ask him constantly to go places? Does he get multiple invitations to every school dance or party? I do not want to seem impertinent, but it is hard not to notice. Did he get his good looks from you? Because that would explain a lot."

I gambled everything on that last statement.

"Why, yes, I mean, I, ah, well, he, ah, yes! He is very handsome." For the first time, she was at a loss for words and appeared to soften her hard veneer and take notice of me as a human being. She continued, "I see what you are saying. This is actually a sign of popularity and looks. All the girls want to be noticed by him, and this is one way they do it." Mrs. C. touched her hair lightly and smiled at me.

I had gotten to her vanity and stroked her ego. All I had to do now was get Mrs. C. to do something without seeming to tell her to do anything.

"Now, ma'am, it is going to rain the next couple of days, and most of this mess will be gone. For now, maybe your landscape company could come by and quickly get rid of all this mess. What do you think, ma'am? You would not want to embarrass your son or the girls who did this. It's because he is so popular he garners all of this attention. You know how it is, ma'am."

I smiled my best and, facing the sun, my eyes twinkled.

"Why, I am sure you are right. It would be best not to make a big deal about it." She returned my smile, then utterly shocked me by reaching out and touching my sleeve. "Thank you," she said sincerely.

Without another word, she turned around and went back into her world.

Fifteen minutes after clearing the call, Sarge asked me to meet him. There was no hint in his voice to reveal whether I was in trouble or not. Well, I'd find out soon enough when I connected with Sarge behind a drugstore.

"What the hell, did you kiss the Blarney Stone or something? I got a call from no less than the major himself. He wanted me to tell you thanks for handling that last call with such professionalism and that it was a reflection on all of the department." Sometimes it's how thick you spread it.

⁊

The same day I handled the call with Mrs. C., I initiated this final stop of the day. The contrast from the morning call to this afternoon's self-initiated stop was extreme.

This stop was another of those moments. I don't know what to call intuition or some unknown force directing you to a particular course of action. Why did I check one area rather than another, and why at that time of the shift? It wasn't a coincidence.

At roll call on the same morning of the Mrs. C. complaint, Sarge had read a bulletin regarding an aggravated armed robbery at Sixty-third and Troost. The suspect was listed as a male in his mid-twenties, six feet, 160 pounds, with short hair and a mustache, wearing green army camouflage pants, white high-top tennis shoes, a white T-shirt, and a tan leather jacket. A gold ring with a dark blue stone, a leather wallet with the victim's identification, a gold-colored wristwatch with a green dial and a broken second hand were taken in the robbery.

The suspect was reportedly armed with a long-barreled chrome revolver, and the victim could identify the suspect. This was an unbelievably good, detailed description of the suspect. He might even get caught if there was any time to look for him. Lately, though, only reports were taken, leaving little or no time for proactive patrolling.

I spent the day, as usual, taking report after report and keeping an eye out for the earlier reported robbery suspect. About twenty minutes from the end of my shift, and after writing eight reports, I could have easily sat back in some hideaway until shift change. For some unknown reason I couldn't get the robbery suspect out of my mind and decided to spend the last part of my day looking for him. I was on some back streets off Cleveland and Gregory, a long way from my district and by myself as usual. I do not know why I chose this area to look for the robbery suspect, as it was miles from the scene, and the crime had occurred at least eight hours earlier but I did. Then I turned a corner, and there he was.

Thirty feet away, walking down the middle of a residential street shaded by mature oak trees, was a male, six feet and 160 pounds, with camouflage pants, white high-tops, and a tan leather jacket. It was him! It had to be. I knew it. He fit the description of the robbery suspect perfectly. He was wearing a jacket on a warm day in the low eighties; he had to be hiding the gun. The suspect had not noticed me yet. I got on the radio and told the dispatcher, "Radio 241, hold the air dispatch. I have the robbery suspect from morning roll call on Sixty-seventh west of Cleveland, and I need a second car!"

As usual, nobody was available. For the most part, officers were out writing reports, but no one cleared to back me up. Maybe they thought there was no way I could have the robbery suspect so far away from the scene and hours after it occurred. When nobody else volunteered Sergeant Ulnis told the dispatcher he would head to my location from the station. Sarge was not close. I would be handling this armed robbery suspect by myself.

I fully expected a foot chase between the houses where I could easily be ambushed and killed or a good old-fashioned shootout in the middle of the street. I put my car in park, stepped out behind my car door, pulled my gun out, and took careful aim at the suspect's back. I would shoot him if he pulled his gun or turned facing me with his gun out. I had no choice. Maybe he felt my eyes boring into his back because he stopped then slowly turned his head to look over his left shoulder.

I yelled as loud as I could, "Police! Freeze! Put your hands above your head. Don't turn around!"

I was not nervous at this point. I knew what I would do. I just did not know what he was going to do. Slowly, the man put his hands in the air about shoulder high, but I wanted his hands higher because it would take him longer to go for his gun.

"Get your hands up higher, fully extended! Now!"

He complied slowly, inch by inch, all the while trying to crane his neck around to see me.

"I've done nothing wrong, have I, officer? I'm walking over to my cousin's house. Can I help you with something? I want to help. I like the police."

He started lowering his hands again and trying to move his shoulders around to see me. I thought he was trying to distract me. His hands kept inching down.

"You lower your hands again, I'll shoot you where you stand! Now get those damn hands up as high as they can go. Now!"

"What can I help you with, officer? I want to help you."

"Keep your hands up high, and slowly walk backwards to the sound of my voice."

I guided him towards me, intermittently reminding him to keep his hands up.

He was now even with the driver-side front fender of my car with his back toward me, only two feet away, and I was still behind my door, pointing my gun at him. I was getting a funny feeling about this guy. His voice was that of a slightly dim-witted individual who could not understand why his friend the policeman was angry with him. His voice was almost childlike. He was starting to make me wonder, could I possibly have the wrong guy?

"Keep your hands up! Turn toward the car. Now place your hands on the car. With your hands still on the car, step back from the car and spread your legs. Do it now!"

He complied. I left my position behind the car door, got behind him, and kicked his legs back further.

"I am going to check you for weapons."

Now he started moving around, lifting one hand off the car, then putting it back down. I started to squeeze the trigger.

"Yeah. I got a gun. Let me show it to you." He pulled his right hand off the car and started to turn toward me. I moved quickly and bent him over the side of my car. His hands spread out on the hood.

"Stop! Do not move! Feel that knock on your head? That is my gun! I am going to shoot you if you move again! This is your last warning!"

I should have shot him by now, but he put doubts in my head.

He kept moving his hips and telling me he had a gun he wanted to show me. The way he sounded, I was beginning to think he was mentally slow. Or maybe he was faking it. Either way, he was about to get shot. I finally got him frozen against the side of my car, and with my hammer still back, I felt around his waist and yanked a chrome .357 caliber Smith & Wesson revolver from the front of his pants then stepped back and tossed the gun onto the seat of my car.

I took my gun off full cock, replaced it in my holster, and with all my weight pushed the suspect against the car, slamming his head on the hood as hard as I could. The violent move stunned him a little, and I was able to cuff him without further incident. I cleared the air and notified the dispatcher I had the suspect under arrest and had recovered a gun.

With the suspect under control, I started looking for the victim's property. I removed a gold ring with a blue stone from the suspect's right-hand ring finger and a gold-colored watch with a green dial and a broken second hand from his left wrist. Even the victim's wallet with his ID still inside was in the suspect's jacket pocket. I read him his Miranda rights, and he chose to talk.

"Where did you get the gun?"

The man leaned his chin on his shoulder, rubbing his sore jaw, and answered almost shyly. "Oh, it is not mine. I got it from my cousin. He lets me carry it around sometimes. I was taking it back to him."

"Where does your cousin live?"

"I don't know, somewhere around here."

His voice was starting to lose that bewildered innocent sound as the evidence piled up against him. He kept looking away from me before answering my questions, an indication he was lying.

"Okay, where did you get the wallet, ring, and watch?"

Still across the fender of my car, his head cocked at an angle looking up at me, he answered with an innocent smile. "Oh, I found those on the street, and I was going to look for the owner. You can have them and give them back if you want."

"Oh, sure, that sounds reasonable. Where did you say you found them? I didn't hear you."

I knew this guy was lying through his teeth, but I let him continue. It would make for a good report.

"Oh, over around Sixty-third and Troost. I was surprised they were lying on the sidewalk. Can you imagine that?"

He smiled. He said it with such a straight face, as easy as ordering a hamburger at a drive-through.

Sergeant Ulnis arrived and bagged up the victim's stolen property and got hold of the victim, who responded to the scene. The victim, a short man in his late thirties, identified the suspect by pointing at him and yelling, "That's the son of a bitch that stuck a gun in my face!"

The handcuffed suspect said to the victim, "Hi, I found your stuff. I was bringing it back to you."

I pulled the victim over to the side and asked him, "Did the suspect sound slow when he robbed you this morning?"

"Hell no, man, he's playing with you all. He's not slow, he's as smart as I am!"

The victim was pissed off and made several threatening gestures toward the suspect. The suspect heard everything the victim said.

"So, buddy, you still going to act like a dim-witted fool?" I asked, laughing at him.

"Go f..k yourself!"

The suspect climbed into the back of the wagon, no longer sounding like an innocent man who liked the police.

Looking back at the incident, I should have shot the suspect, especially after he said he had a gun and was trying to pull it out. However, if there was a chance he was mentally challenged, I wanted to find another way, but trying to save his life about cost me mine.

Chapter 56:
The Knife Fight

The term knife fight conjures up images of TV shows and movies where two guys face one another several feet apart, one or both armed with a knife. Predictably, one party is disarmed or stabbed, and the fight is over. It has been my experience and way of thinking that I am not going to try to disarm someone threatening me with a knife, especially if I have a gun.

If you go around trying to be a hero or nice guy by using some sort of judo move to take the knife away, you are going to get cut and possibly killed. If a person pulls a knife on me, he must be crazy, knowing I have a gun. I may back up a few steps and try to talk to the guy, but I will shoot him if he makes a move at me. At the end of my shift, I am going home. That's the way I felt.

I have learned how to block knife thrusts and disarm a suspect, but only as a last resort. The best defense against a knife-wielding criminal is to shoot him. Even if you have several other officers to help you and are skilled, trying to overpower the guy will result in someone getting cut or stabbed. Nowhere does it say an officer must attempt to physically disarm a suspect armed with a knife before turning to lethal force. If someone wants to use a knife to fight an officer with a gun, the assailant deserves what he gets.

You must remember that no matter how much training a boxer has, he will still get hit. No matter how much training the officer has, he will still get cut. The difference is that a fighter rarely dies, and a referee stops the match, but nobody is going to stop the knife fight.

One night I was dispatched over into East Zone on a drug-crazed man armed with a knife at the back door of a residence trying to get inside. I arrived at the scene with an officer I did not know. We went to the back of the house and took a position about thirty feet behind the suspect. The man was in his early twenties, with dirty blond shoulder-length hair, about 150 pounds, dressed in blue jeans, a white T-shirt, and barefoot. He was yelling, screaming profanities and waving a five-inch knife in the air.

It was a chilly fall night, cold enough to wear a jacket and a long-sleeve shirt. With the way the man was acting, and with his hair and T-shirt wet with sweat, he was probably high on PCP. People on PCP overheat and, consequently, take their clothes off.

I had the dispatcher call the reporting person and find out if they knew the subject and ask them to move to another room in the house in case we had to shoot the suspect. The resident did not know the man.

The other officer had not spoken a word since we got there. Whether he was the quiet type or possibly scared, I had to know that we were on the same page.

"Look, if this guy comes charging off the porch, shoot him. We can step back a little if he steps off the porch but we are not going to back up all the way across the yard. If you trip, he could be on you in a second. Okay? You got anything to say?" If he answered, I didn't hear him.

The other officer and I stood about ten feet apart. The dispatcher held the air, and I ordered the crazy man to drop the knife and get on the ground. The man was drugged out and probably could not understand what I was saying, and started pacing back and forth across the porch. I was in no hurry, and as long as the man did not come running off the porch towards me, I would keep trying to talk to him.

Another officer arrived. Stan Kennedy, a tall man with dark curly hair and a thick mustache, took charge of the call, as this was his area, and he had several years' seniority on me. I had no problem with Stan calling the shots. That is, until he spoke. This time he was wrong, and he paid the price.

"Okay, guys, put your guns away and stay back. Sean, give me your nightstick. I'm going to get up close to him, distract him, then hit him upside the head and disarm him."

"No," I said. "I don't think that would be a good idea. You'll get yourself cut and maybe us trying to save your ass!" I knew this was going to go badly.

"No, I've done this before. I know what I'm doing." I gave Stan my stick. He held it against the side of his leg, trying to hide it.

I gave an uneasy chuckle as Officer Kennedy approached the drug user who was still yelling nonsense, waving the knife, and pacing back and forth furiously across the back porch. As soon as Stan got within ten feet of the drugged-out man, the guy jumped off the porch and attacked him.

Stan was able to get the nightstick up and strike a blow to the suspect's head, but not before the addict slashed his face. The two went to the ground fighting. The suspect was now on his back but still had the knife in his hand. Stan was twice the size of his attacker but could not hold the man's knife hand down. It seems the little skinny shit was on PCP, felt no pain, and had unlimited strength. The officer I was with grabbed the suspect's free hand and struggled to hold it down.

I kicked the suspect as hard as I could in the side, figuring I might knock the wind out of him or break one of his ribs, preventing him from breathing well enough to fight. The guy almost succeeded in knocking Stan off his chest and freeing his hand that held the knife. I stomped down on the hand holding the blade, grinding my boot back and forth, trying to break his fingers. I don't know if I broke any of his fingers, but he let go of the knife, and I was able to grab it and toss it away.

It was all the three of us could do to try to hold this guy down. Together, we weighed over six hundred pounds, and still, the suspect was almost impossible to control. We were in real danger of him grabbing one of our guns. This guy had tremendous strength. It felt like we were fighting Superman. If we got an arm pinned, he would hit us with the other or kick his legs up, trying to catch us in the groin. It took two officers to hold down one arm, and one officer could not hold the other by himself.

I was able to apply an arm bar, hyper-extending his right elbow, and with enough pressure, I could then dislocate his elbow, making his arm useless. An average person would be screaming in excruciating pain with the amount of force I applied, but it did not faze him at all.

I decided to dislocate his elbow before one of us got killed, but even with leverage, I could not bend his arm back far enough to do the job. He simply grunted and lifted his arm against all my body weight. The situation was getting worse. Blood was running down Stan's face, and I did not know how badly he was cut; the other officer was breathing hard. We had to get this guy under control and fast.

Another officer arrived and joined the melee. Even with the four of us, we could not get him under control. Since this was a no-holds-barred fight, I slugged the addict in the groin several times, hoping to slow him down, but to no effect. Finally, I got one cuff on him and, using it as leverage, was able to extend his arm out, locking his elbow. Then all together, we forced him onto his side, and after a concerted effort we managed to twist his other arm around and finish cuffing him.

Stan's left nostril was sliced open and bled profusely. A paramedic responded and patched Kennedy's face until they could get him to the hospital. The other officers were exhausted and sat in the grass catching their breath. Another officer and a wagon driver responded and hauled the kicking and screaming suspect away. I could only imagine the pain that guy would be in tomorrow or the day after when he finally came down off the PCP.

Now, if the other officer and I had tried to pull a Stan on that guy, we probably would have lost the fight. One or both of us would have been killed or severely cut up. This is why you do not give up your advantage to your opponent. If Stan had been there with the other officer, or even worse alone, he probably would have tried to do exactly what he did and would have lost the fight. If someone wants to have a knife fight and you have a gun, shoot him. I do not care how big or good you are at martial arts; shoot them or go to Hollywood, where the good guy always wins.

Sometimes people say a taser would have worked, but it does not always work, especially on people high on drugs. While an officer is deploying the taser, the suspect is still coming at him. Studies have shown a man armed with a knife can cover twenty-five feet before the officer can pull and fire his weapon. The officer could die if the taser misses, gets caught up in some clothing, or does not have the desired effect on the target. We did not have tasers back then, but if we did, I would let another officer try his taser. I'd still use my gun. It would be safer for me.

Some people argue the officer could shoot the suspect in the leg or arm. If an officer misses the arm or leg by a little bit, the suspect is still coming at him armed with a knife. The officer will not get a second shot off before the suspect makes contact.

Officers are taught to shoot at center mass to increase the chances of hitting the suspect and stopping him. With the .38 caliber, the bullet we used, a single shot would not stop a man on PCP. We were taught to shoot to stop the actions of the suspect. An officer does not shoot once, stop, and look to see if the suspect is still coming at him with a weapon. I was taught to always shoot twice. It was called a double tap.

Another misconception people have is firing a warning shot. Where would you fire the shot? The bullet has to come down somewhere. It might kill some innocent person when it lands. What if you shoot into the ground if you happen to be close to some dirt? On concrete, the bullet will definitely ricochet, and if it's fired into the dirt, what if the bullet strikes a buried rock and ricochets? There are no warning shots. You only get those in the movies.

The .38 doesn't always stop someone, and people have difficulty understanding that concept. Remember the stories of some combatants in different wars not going down when shot with a rifle even at close range? If they didn't go down back then, why would you believe a pistol will always stop the suspect?

If Stan's wound were a little bit higher, he would have lost an eye; or a little bit lower on his neck, he could have lost his life. Stan was putting his life at risk to save a suspect's life.

Officers put their lives on the line like this many times, but nobody ever hears about it.

Life and Death

Some situations are so dangerous death becomes a real possibility.

Chapter 57:

The Burning House

As many of my stories start, it was summer late in my shift, and I was about ready to call it a night. I was making one last run down Troost to make sure the vampires had not come back since I last chased them away. The street was deserted when the pungent odor of wood smoke entered my car. It was not a trash fire smell but something a lot larger. There it was: a three-story boarded-up house ablaze on the west side of Troost.

The home was perched atop a steep terrace. Yellow light pulsed in and out as the house appeared to be breathing, gasping for air. The plywood sheets nailed across the front windows bent in and bulged out as the fire tried to suck in air to feed itself. The boarded-up windows on the second and third floors were glowing bright yellow around the plywood edges.

The house was fully engulfed and within minutes of blowing out one of the cheap wood panels. If the plywood blew off a window, the house would explode from the air intake, turning the fire into a blast furnace, and blowing open all the remaining windows and doors.

I'd learned about this type of fire in the academy and remembered that when fire moves the doors in and out like this one, stay back: It is about to explode. All this was in the back of my mind when I notified the dispatcher of the fire. I moved my car into the middle of the street to block the road but out of the way of the fire trucks when they arrived. That is when Sergeant Sims arrived at the scene.

Sims was a twenty-five-year veteran with a large build and gray hair. I liked him and thought he was a good sergeant. I had worked for him on several occasions, and he always looked out for his crew. I had no problems with him at all until that night.

Sims pulled up alongside my car. "Hey, Sean, have you checked to make sure nobody is inside the house?"

He was looking past me at the home. I wondered if he was blind.

"The house is abandoned, boarded up, and about to explode. Sarge, it's vacant. No one lives there."

"Well, go up there and check inside anyway to make sure before the fire department gets here."

"Okay, Sarge."

Maybe Sarge didn't get the same class I was taught at the academy about fires. This fire was too far gone to approach safely from any direction. Not wanting to argue or appear to disobey an order, I exited my vehicle, crossed the street, and started up the front steps of the burning house.

The sounds of the fire sucking in and blowing out air were getting louder, and flames darted around the edges of the plywood-covered windows. I turned around and headed back down the steps into the street. Sims, who had started to drive off as I approached the fire, returned and, with some anger in his voice, said, "I thought I told you to go up there and check for anybody inside!"

"Oh, yeah. Forgot my flashlight."

Sergeant Sims drove off as I headed back up the stairs toward the fire. He did not even stick around to see if I found anybody inside. I thought, why would he not join me if he thought there was the possibility of someone trapped in the house? Why did he not stay until the fire department arrived? Nope, something was not quite right here. I did not know what it was, but something was wrong. The sound of the fire breathing in and out was becoming faster and faster like an old locomotive steam engine. I could feel the heat from the fire on my face and arms.

I shook my head no way, left the stairs, and returned to my car. Sims was nowhere to be seen. Then the house exploded, and twisting, snapping, screeching wood was torn from the home and hurled across the street. Flames shot out all of the doors and windows for thirty feet. Now I knew what was not right. If I had done what Sergeant Sims had ordered, I probably would have died in the fire as the house blew up.

Was it coincidental that Sergeant Sims never went out on the radio when he stopped by the scene? There would be no record of him ever being at the fire. If I died, no one would know why I was close to such a dangerous fire. If I reported Sims, he would deny ever being at the blaze, and nobody could prove otherwise.

As Sims was a sergeant and had a lot of time on with the department, he would be believed, and I would probably be fired for accusing Sims of trying to kill me. If I ever had to work with him again, I wouldn't trust him and would never come to his aid. At the time of the incident, I didn't know why Sims ordered me into the fire.

I never spoke to Sergeant Sims about that night, but when I look back on it, I should have told Sims to go screw himself or something more descriptive. Let him try to defend his order to send me into a bordered-up, abandoned residence fully engulfed in flames, ready to explode.

Not too long after this incident, Sergeant Sims retired.

Decades later, I talked to a friend who told me that, at the time of the fire, Sims was living with or in a serious relationship with one of the prostitutes I dealt with on several occasions. If I had to guess why Sims tried to kill me, I would say it was in retaliation for something related to his prostitute lover, Norman. Sims is dead now, or else I would ask him.

Chapter 58:
Heatstroke

My first summer on my own, the temperature hit 101 degrees with 90 percent humidity, a typical July day in Kansas City. I left the air conditioning in the car off so I would be acclimated to the heat when leaving the vehicle. Without ever having air-conditioning growing up, I learned to live without it. Another officer suddenly broke the quiet, sweltering, sun-soaked afternoon. "I've got an occupied stolen auto heading west on Thirty-ninth Street, two male occupants," Will Jennings said.

The sudden excitement of chasing an occupied stolen auto gives you an instant dump of pure adrenaline throughout your body. I tried to anticipate where Will would be heading next, and be close, as most occupants abandon the vehicle or crash it and try to escape on foot. I was betting on a crash.

The suspects do not care what happens to the car; they don't own it. Jennings continued to give out his location, speed, and the car description while other officers moved into the area. I was a block away when I heard the chase headed in my direction. Back then, we did not have stop sticks, so there was no way to stop the fleeing car short of ramming the suspect vehicle.

I watched as Will drove by me at over sixty miles an hour. Sixty miles an hour may not be fast in the movies, but in city residential driving, in real life, it is extremely dangerous.

By the time I got my car up to sixty miles an hour, the suspect had already reversed course. A few more turns and I was able to get in behind Will. The suspect was headed down a dead-end street; the chase would end in a crash or a foot chase. From start to finish, the pursuit had taken less than four minutes but covered twenty blocks of turns and straightaways.

Sure enough, the driver crashed the car into some thick shrubs, left the car running, and bolted into the tall, overgrown bushes.

Will said he was after the passenger; I took the driver and ran into the bushes, got stuck, and had to bull my way through. I came out of the shrubs and saw the driver leap a fence into a backyard. I followed the suspect as he sprinted into another overgrown patch of tangled shrubs and disappeared, and hoped the suspect was not waiting inside the brush to ambush me.

I hit the overgrown thorny shrubs at full speed, crashing through them and unable to slow down, went off a twelve-foot drop-off over an abandoned driveway left behind when a house was torn down for urban renewal. Landing on the old concrete, I did a tuck and roll, then sprang to my feet. The suspect had made it across four lanes of traffic and was too far ahead, so I gave up and called in his last location and description.

It was then I noticed the abandoned drive was covered in broken beer, whiskey, and wine bottles. I started checking myself for cuts, but somehow, with all the glass on the ground, I had managed to miss it all. I climbed back up the steep drop-off and pushed my way through the two sets of almost impenetrable bushes and over two chain-link fences to reach my car.

Will was back by the suspect's car and limping, unable to put much weight on his left foot. He looked at me kind of funny and asked, "You all right? You don't look so good."

I was bleeding from dozens of scratches on my arms, neck, and face from the brush. I looked at my blood-smeared arms then at Will. Suddenly I couldn't focus; the world started to spin around me. "You have pieces of glass sticking out of your back! I'm getting you an ambulance."

Will got behind me and started picking glass out of my shirt. My vest had absorbed the big pieces but I still had sharp slivers stuck in me everywhere. I had a lot of pain in my hand and was sure I'd broken it in the fall. I was nauseated and almost puked.

An ambulance arrived, and the paramedics helped Will and me inside. The air-conditioning felt great. The next thing I knew, I was in the hospital emergency room nauseated and dizzy. I told a doctor my hand felt like it was broken.

The same nurse on duty from when I hurt my throat and had my hand stitched before laughed. "You again." She helped me get my shirt and vest off then stared as small pieces of glass fell and bounced off the clean hospital floor.

I spent the next half hour grunting while a first year resident used tweezers to pull and tease the tiny slivers of glass from my arms and the back of my neck.

Another doctor came back into the room with the X-ray results. I was relieved to learn my hand was not broken, though I did have a temperature of 103 degrees and had heatstroke. I had to stay for another three hours with an IV and ice packs. It turned out Will only had a bad sprain. He stayed with me until I was released with orders from the doctor not to return to work that day.

Sergeant Liam, the big desk sergeant, must have called the hospital because he asked for my car keys and had someone drive me home. I was done for the day. At home, when taking off my boots, on one of them, I found a long slash through the leather, my sock, and a small cut on my ankle. I probably would have been cut to the bone if I had worn regular shoes instead of boots.

I told my wife I fell into some thorny bushes looking for a snake that terrified a little old lady in her backyard. I was covered in scabs for a week.

I didn't go to work the next day. Despite saving me from the glass, I never wore my bulletproof vest again. It was old, mildewy, too small, hot, and it was not mandatory to wear them back then. My uniform pants and shirt were so torn up from glass and thornbushes that I was issued another set.

It might be interesting to note I was not the only person injured in Center Zone on our shift. During my first year, one officer was shot and killed, and in a separate incident another officer was shot. It was nothing to see officers working with swollen black eyes, stitches, and bruises on their faces. I broke my hand, another officer broke his hand, and I almost forgot—Jack suffered a broken ankle.

Several officers limped around the station for days at a time from injuries, and these were from the evening shift in Center Zone. In a few weeks, five officers would be sent to the hospital during one incident. With two other shifts, quite a few police officers were injured on duty in Center Zone. It wasn't a matter of if you were going to be hurt; it was just a matter of when.

It was not unusual to see an officer cleaning his fingernails with a switchblade at roll call. Most officers carried an extra gun for backup and an assortment of knives, slappers, or lead-lined gloves in addition to the department-issued revolver.

After so many fights, I began carrying a boot knife, a small .25 caliber automatic in my pocket, a lead-filled slapper, and extra ammo. I got rid of the unreliable, cheap plastic police-issued flashlight and, against regulations, bought a heavy-duty metal Kel-Lite flashlight. Center Zone was a tough place to work.

Chapter 59:
12 Gauge

On one hot, steamy August night during my first summer on the police force, Carl Long and I were dispatched to the 2900 block of Troost on a shooting. The victim was still at the scene, and an ambulance was en route. Upon arrival, we walked up concrete stairs from the sidewalk to a large courtyard surrounded on three sides by 3-story red brick apartment buildings. Just a few feet from the top of the stairs, a small crowd was gathered around the victim.

Nobody was helping the seriously injured man lying on the ground writhing in pain. Mostly they stood around pointing at the man's wounds, speculating on how soon he would die.

I tried to scan the crowd for any hostile people, recognizable threats, or even a suspect for whom we did not yet have a description. To the group, this was another break in the long, hot summer, something to talk about over a cold beer later. Carl and I had to push our way through the crowd to get to the victim.

The man was young, in his early twenties, and dressed in dark slacks and a blood-soaked sleeveless T-shirt. He was on his side, holding his stomach, trying to keep his intestines from spilling out any further onto the concrete. A large pool of dark red blood spread from underneath his side.

Wrapped around the fingers of one hand was a plastic bag. The bag was ripped open, with a new jigsaw inside, that had a big piece of the orange plastic casing missing. I guessed the victim was shot at close range by the size of the hole in his stomach; looking at how the jigsaw was blown apart, I would say the gun used was a shotgun.

I knelt next to the man, gently moving his hand to inspect the damage, and could see a piece of orange plastic casing from the jigsaw sticking out of a huge, gaping hole in the victim's left side. There were bloody, dark, purplish intestines moving out of the wound; with each quick breath, he gasped.

Quickly, I placed his hands back over the wound and put both of mine over his for added pressure. I pleaded to the crowd for a cloth or rag, anything to stem the blood flow, but only received insults from the spectators. "Get the f..k out of here, you mother f..ker! We don't need the f..king police here! Get out of here, you pig!"

Ignoring the crowd, I looked back at the man and told him, "You are doing fine. You're going to be all right. Who shot you? Give me a name."

Feebly, the man said, "I'll take care of it."

Blood was still leaking out between his fingers and all over mine at a steady rate. Carl, who had been trying to keep the gawking bystanders back, heard the victim's response and bent down close to his face, then shouted over the noisy crowd. "Hey, buddy, you won't be able to take care of shit. You are going to be dead in a few minutes! So who shot you?"

The crowd quieted, straining to hear the victim's answer. The wounded man slowly turned his head around and fixed his eyes on a man standing a few feet behind me. "He shot me."

Carl and I looked up simultaneously and saw a man with shorts, white socks, black open-toed sandals, and a long, dark trench coat. The white socks had a lot of blood spatter on them, and the wide barrel of a shotgun poked out from the open coat. "F..k!"

I spun around, still on my knees, trying to draw my gun with blood-slick fingers. The crowd shrieked and split apart, giving me a clear shot at the suspect. My fingers slipped off my weapon on the first attempt to draw; I screamed at the suspect to freeze. Carl was faster and had his gun out, inches from the suspect's face.

The suspect had crazy eyes. You could see he had a moment of hesitation while he considered shooting us, running away, or surrendering. My fingers finally took hold, and I brought my gun up, touching the man's balls. With an audible click, I pulled the hammer back to full cock. It got the suspect's attention. The man, eyes bugged wide open, pupils dilated, shifted his stare from Carl's gun to mine.

I stood up as the gunman slowly lifted his empty hands over his head. With Carl's gun still inches from the suspect's face, I holstered my revolver and pulled the suspect's overcoat open wider. There was a single shot bolt action 12-gauge shotgun loosely held to his waist by a piece of a black extension cord. Both barrel and stock were cut down, resembling a huge pistol. The smell of gun powder indicated the gun had been recently fired.

I grabbed the forestock with one hand, and used my boot knife to cut the cord, freeing the weapon. I pulled the bolt back and ejected an empty 12-gauge round; we were lucky that the gun needed to be reloaded to fire. I think the man was high enough on drugs that he would have shot me in the back if he had remembered to reload.

Carl kept his gun leveled at the suspect's head as I cuffed him and ordered a wagon. The paramedics arrived a minute later and transported the victim to the hospital, where he was pronounced dead on arrival. We secured the crime scene and tried to identify any witnesses, but nobody would admit to seeing anything or answer any questions.

At the station, I washed the blood off my hands and from under my nails, as well as on the butt of my gun and the inside and outside of the holster. I ignored the big dark wet spots on my pant legs where I'd knelt in the pooled blood. Other officers would notice the dark spots on your uniform, but no one would ever comment on it; they knew what it was.

I think the part about trying to save a man's life while putting my life on the line and that nobody was willing to give up even a dirty rag to keep a man from bleeding to death caused me to question, why the hell was I doing this job?

Tomorrow. Today would be counted as another learning experience, a story I kept to myself.

Chapter 60:
Willy Licks

No matter how many felony arrests, drug arrests, or DUIs you made, the upper staff always wanted to see more traffic tickets. I said it was for the revenue, but command always said it improved traffic safety. My new sergeant, Mary Collins, told me I needed more traffic tickets. I did not argue. That was the way it was.

That same day I was behind a car, a mid-seventies four-door sedan that was approaching a stop sign, and the driver turned right without stopping. He didn't even slow up. The driver did it two more times, so I pulled him over about a block behind the station on a fairly busy street. The dispatcher ran the license plate, and nothing returned, meaning no warrants or felonies were associated with the tag. I learned too late that the driver was Willy Licks.

I had stepped out and walked to the front of my car when Willy exploded out of his vehicle and ran straight at me. I had a second to order another officer when the driver tackled me chest high, knocking me down in front of my vehicle.

I was on my back with a drug-enraged man weighing over two hundred pounds on my chest, straddling me. He punched me with his right fist repeatedly while trying to pull my gun out with his left hand. I was in an unbelievably bad position and held my right hand over my gun to keep him from pulling it and killing me. Using my left arm, I tried to block his right fist and occasionally get jabs into his face and throat.

A glancing blow removed my glasses, and I was lucky it was only a glancing blow, or I would be blind now. A woman came out of Willy's car, screaming for him to stop. A city bus and several cars slowed down, then drove away. Willy was screaming unintelligible gibberish all the while, slathering my face with his rabid drool.

I thought this was it. This is how my life ends. Loose bits of asphalt rock dug into the back of my head as I violently jerked it from side to side, trying desperately to avoid the blows. The sound of his fist hitting the pavement was like a tenderizing mallet smacking a piece of raw meat.

It was frightening, knowing it could be my face at any second. If one of those heavy blows landed solidly, I would likely lose the fight and my life, shot with my own gun. He grunted with each strike, throwing his whole body into the effort. A fist brushed the left side of my face. I'd survived for another second.

I remembered what Tom said back in the academy about the odds of being killed if I lost this fight. They weren't good odds, especially with the guy I was fighting. Tom also said: "You will always get cut in a knife fight, and when you are being beaten or injured don't give up. You can survive."

All these thoughts and observations seem to take mere microseconds to process. Time slowed way down, and I could see Willy's fist coming toward me in slow motion. I would turn my head, and the blows would only graze my face, striking full force against the pavement. It had to hurt, but Willy showed no signs of pain. It seemed surreal, as if I was watching myself fighting. It is hard to explain. I couldn't understand it myself.

A person on PCP has incredible strength and does not feel pain. They have unbelievable endurance. Broken bones will not stop them, and I didn't know how much longer I would last.

Well, I thought, this is how it ends, beaten to death by a crazed felon high on PCP. Another officer had been killed within blocks of here only six months ago. I thought about my wife and family and what would happen to them, then made the decision I was not going to give up. I wasn't going to die on this dirty, greasy street in the inner city while the people I was here to protect drove by unconcerned.

Slowly, I dug in my heels and, with all of my strength, pushed my body and his dead weight closer to the front of my car, giving my head some protection under the front bumper. I used my left arm to try to push him off me, but I could not budge him. He was too strong. He was forcing my right hand off my gun and I could barely hold it in the holster. If I could hold on a little longer, maybe some help would arrive.

Finally, out of the corner of my eye, I saw a pair of black boots and police pants. Hold on for a few more seconds, I told myself. I blocked and dodged several more blows, but the boots did not move. Why didn't they get closer? Why was the officer waiting? Couldn't they see I needed help right now? What was wrong?

Then I saw a different pair of boots, the plain black cowboy boots of the smallest woman police officer in the department, Sheila Gardner. In the next split second, her hard, pointed boot connected with Willy's side, raising him. Now I was able to take my right hand off my gun and hit Licks squarely under the chin with a loud smack, snapping his head back.

I rolled him off me and found myself on top while Willy had me by the throat in a death grip. I tried to pull Willy's hand off my throat, but even with Sheila's help, I couldn't free myself. At any moment, Willy would choke me out or crush my windpipe. I didn't pull my gun and try to shoot him, afraid he would take it and shoot me, and unless I shot him in the head, he would continue fighting. His strong hand squeezed tighter and tighter. He was strangling me to death.

I started hitting him with blows to the face, right, left, left, right, trying to force him to let go of my neck. I even stuck my left thumb into his eye but couldn't get it quite deep enough to pull it out. I don't know how many strikes I made before feeling excruciating pain in my right hand. I was dying, when yet another officer showed up and, with great effort, pulled Willy's hand off my throat.

Gasping for breath, I rolled off Willy and crawled until I collapsed onto the sidewalk, holding my throat. By now several other officers arrived and were finally able to cuff Willy, who was still screaming and fighting in his PCP-fueled rage. I caught my breath and watched as the other officers loaded an incredibly violent Willy into the back of a wagon.

I looked around for the cop who had not helped me and saw the officer standing away from everyone else. I stared at the officer, who refused to look at me, and at that moment, I wanted to kill him.

Sergeant Collins came over to check on my condition, interrupting my murderous intentions and bringing me back to reality. I couldn't make a fist, my hand was swelling up fast, and my throat and neck hurt like hell. Sarge sent me to the hospital for my fourth visit to the ER. It wouldn't be my last.

After I arrived at the hospital, everything was checked out, and all I had to do was wait for the X-rays to come back on my hand. I was feeling surprisingly good, having survived the assault with only a sore fist, swelling to my face and left eye, and strangulation marks around my throat and neck. It had been so close.

Soon a doctor came in with an X-ray. He said there was a significant break in my right hand. I would wear a cast on that hand for the next eight weeks, causing me to work limited duty at the station.

The aftermath of the stop of Willy Licks was far-reaching. Several major screw-ups occurred; each almost resulted in my death. The first was record keeping. Somehow Willy was released from jail after shooting a police officer in the handcuff case. Why he was ever released on bond was ridiculous. He should have been interrogated and held without bond. He shot a cop of all things.

Secondly, Licks wasn't listed in the computer as a 10-31 subject, meaning armed and dangerous, known to assault police. Otherwise, any officer encountering Willy through his name, address, or vehicle would be warned, and another car immediately dispatched as a backup.

Then the portable radio was not working correctly. There were blackout areas where the portables did not work, and I was in one of those dead zones and did not know it. It was a matter of putting up another repeater, but the necessary work had not been done for some reason.

The radio system was fixed over the next six months. I was never informed why the records on Willy were so screwed up or why he was even out of jail when I dealt with him. The problem with the county jail wasn't rare, and I had heard of other incidents where prisoners were mistakenly released.

Lastly and the most egregious was the inaction of the first officer at the scene.

A lady watching the fight from her front porch a block away called the dispatcher when it was apparent no help was coming. The dispatcher called an "assist the officer," which mandated any car available go to the officer's aid. This time, the first officer at the scene did nothing to help from the time he arrived until Willy was put in a wagon. It was reported to me later that when the officer was asked why he didn't help but rather stood there and watched me being beaten, he told someone, "I am not paid enough to wrestle on the ground."

I think the officer thought helping a fellow patrolman stay alive was optional, and I believe he should have been summarily fired for cowardice. The officer involved was not fired, but instead, he was rewarded and promoted to sergeant at his first eligibility, and later to captain.

I, on the other hand, was denied promotion to sergeant twice and put under investigation for fighting. I believe the officer was involved with someone high up in the department who valued his deeply personal relationship with the coward more than the life of another officer.

As a result of the fight, Willy almost lost his left eye and required surgery. A year later he was arrested for murder. Willy was high on drugs again when he shot and killed a man, then called the police because the victim refused to get up and leave. This time Willy was not released from jail.

If not for Sheila Gardner and others, I would have been murdered that day, lying on a dirty street while another officer watched it happen.

All because of a stupid traffic stop.

Chapter 61:
The End of Forty Sector

Monday, September 10, 1984, 1730 hours, Forty Sector

I stopped an early seventies four-door Buick for an expired tag in the 3400 block of Tracy. There was nothing notable about Tracy. It was a street with tenement apartment buildings, run-down houses, and vacant lots strewn with bottles, rocks, trash, and overgrown weeds. What did stand out was the yellow two story house where I was parked. The home had "Yahweh Is God" painted in giant, messy letters across the front and sides of the home. It looked like the house had been vandalized.

I had finished writing the driver a ticket when officer Ted Corniel, a friend of mine, pulled up alongside me. "Quick, follow me!"

Ted had come from a long way off to contact me. I thought something was wrong, and he needed my help immediately. He pulled over into a vacant lot several blocks away and stepped out of his car casually. Now I wondered what had been so urgent. I supposed I'd find out.

Ted told me, "A few weeks ago, one of the guys in the support unit was parked in front of the house writing a report when suddenly a host of people came swarming out of the house screaming and yelling at him for no reason and pelted his car with rocks. Luckily the officer wasn't hurt and was able to drive off without any injuries, but his car had broken windows and was covered with dents. Avoid the area around the house, and only go near it if you have a lot of backup. I call it the Yahweh House."

Ted was not one to exaggerate, and I took his information seriously. I could not figure out why the information was not common knowledge. Maybe it would be embarrassing to whoever was in charge of the highly specialized support unit because one of their officers had been chased out of the area, and nothing was done about it. Maybe they thought, as the old saying goes, discretion is the better part of valor. Whatever the reason, the incident was not common knowledge, and that lack of knowledge would have serious repercussions.

Wednesday, September 12, 1984, 1750 hours, Forty Sector

On this day, forty sector had six officers and a sergeant: Relief Sergeant Mary Rollins, radio 240; Officer Sammy DeBliss, radio 241; Officer Tony Debacco, radio 242; myself, radio 243; and Officers Carl Long and Bob Wright, a two-person crew, radio 245.

Officers Carl Long and Bob Wright were hunting for Diamond McDugal, who had an outstanding Jackson County probation warrant for armed robbery. Carl knew where Diamond liked to hang out and had his latest mugshots. Carl was always digging up arrests, but this one was different. They found Diamond standing on the corner of Armour and Tracy.

Carl and Bob got out on a ped check and, naturally, Diamond took off running. Bob grabbed the back of Diamond's hospital scrub pants, but they completely ripped apart and McDougal escaped wearing only his T-shirt and white underwear. Carl and Bob continued to chase McDugal around and between some houses on the east side of Tracy, then last saw him running westbound behind the Yahweh House.

Other forty sector cars would join the search.

I caught up with Carl and Bob in front of the Yahweh House before they headed towards the rear. I told Carl and Bob what Corniel said about the house being full of fanatics who hated the police and to never go around the place unless you had lots of backup. Bob quipped, "Well, Sean, why don't you go over there and watch in case Diamond gets by us?"

Bob pointed across a vacant lot about fifty yards south of the Yahweh House where around twenty men were lounging and drinking out of bottles inside brown paper bags.

It irked me that Bob said that. I felt like he was insinuating I was afraid, and should stay out of the way. I told them, "You should probably be taking along your nightsticks in case something goes wrong."

They kind of smirked, and one of them said, "We're fine since you have one."

That was the second slight at me, but I let it go. I had done my part. I had passed along good information from another officer, and if they chose to ignore it, that was their business. As I walked away, I gave them one final warning: "At least have the dispatcher hold the air until you find out if McDugal is there or not."

Bob had his back to me talking to Carl and waved his hand over his head without turning around. I didn't see anyone around the house and hoped for their sake no one was home.

I walked over to the parking lot, where the men stood around drinking their beers and smoking cigarettes. There were a couple of dirty, broken-down, fabric-torn chairs, and several men relaxed on an old ripped-up sofa that someone had reclaimed from the trash. The furniture had been left out in the elements exposed to rain, heat, and vermin of every sort, and dozens of empty whiskey, wine, and beer bottles littered the ground around the furniture. The area where the men gathered was an old gravel parking lot behind a pair of six-story tenement apartment buildings. The lot was shaded by an enormous old oak tree, relieving some of the late summer's heat.

The parking area was adjacent to a big vacant lot created when a house was torn down. The lot was full of overgrown weeds, trash, broken bottles, and chunks of old concrete. So there was the Yahweh House, a vacant lot, and a parking lot with about twenty men standing around passing the time. As I approached the group I noticed one man run off into the apartment building and made a mental note to return later and do some ped checks.

I asked the men lounging around and asked, "How are you all doing?"

Mostly in their early twenties, the men seemed relaxed, and I did not sense any hostility toward me or threats other than being alone in a group of twenty men who probably did not like the police. I noticed the man that ran off when I approached was back with several other men.

In groups of twos and threes, more men continued to join the group, and I was getting a little anxious because the crowd was getting larger for no apparent reason. The men's voices seemed louder now, somehow busy, more urgent. I had a heightened sense of anticipation; something was about to happen.

I watched the crowd and waited for Carl and Bob to reappear from behind the Yahweh house.

"So, what are you doing here anyway, officer?" asked a man lounging on the filthy couch.

"Oh, you know, looking for some guy who robbed someone, but it's not my call. Those other guys are checking, and they told me to get out of the way. So, I thought I'd come over here and visit with you guys in the shade."

I tried to downplay the whole situation like it was not important, I would be gone shortly and they could go back to their drinking in peace.

Wednesday, September 12, 1984, 1800 hours, Forty Sector

Bob and Carl were now in the backyard by the back porch. Suddenly a massive pit bull sprang up out of some tall overgrown weeds growling and barking loudly enough to wake the dead. I hoped the dog was on a chain, or else those two officers would get mauled if they didn't shoot the dog first. As if on cue, the dog leaped and in midair, was snatched back to the ground by a heavy chain. Both Bob and Carl stumbled, trying to get out of range of the chained dog. I thought about now those two were probably wishing they had listened to me and brought their nightsticks with them.

They had gotten past the pit bull, their eyes fixed on the giant hound and their backs to the house, when all hell broke loose. Out the back door, a dozen men came yelling and screaming at the top of their lungs. Bob and Carl were only half turned around when the first men leaped on top of them, knocking both to the ground.

"Oh f..k!" I said to no one in particular.

I immediately started running toward the officers and notified the dispatcher that two officers were down being attacked by a dozen or so people and called an assist the officer. Out of the corner of my eye, I saw the men from the parking lot now running alongside me toward the downed officers. I hoped they were trying to get a better view of the fight and would not join in against us. The dog was still chained and straining to free himself, his jowls flinging drool with each shake of his massive head.

I got to Carl first, who was on his back with a man on his chest. The man was beating Carl with repeated fists to the face. Another man was kicking Carl in the side while a third man was trying to grab Carl's service revolver. I used my nightstick to hit the man kicking Carl in the side. I struck him across the back, and saw him fall to the ground. I then booted the man sitting on Carl's chest in the ribs, knocking the wind out of him and off Carl. I swung my club again and struck the man trying to pull Carl's gun out of the holster; he howled and fell to the ground holding an injured elbow.

Looking around for attacks to my blind side, I ducked in time to avoid a bottle thrown at my head. I pulled Carl to his feet and held on to him as he was having difficulty standing up. Carl's eyes focused on me, and I yelled at him, "Stay with me, I've got to help Bob!"

The noise was deafening, with the crowd screaming like kids shouting all at once on a playground at recess. Wailing police sirens were approaching from all directions, and the helicopter with its thunderous engine was circling so low overhead I could feel the rotor wash. The sounds all blended to make communication with the dispatcher or other officers on the ground nearly impossible.

I held on to Carl and did a quick look around for Bob. I saw him about ten feet away on the ground, being kicked and beaten by several men. Again, one man sat on Bob's chest, punching him repeatedly about the face, as other men kicked him all over his body.

I let go of Carl and slammed my nightstick into the back of the knee of one of the men kicking Bob. That man dropped to the ground like a sack of potatoes, writhing in agony. Then I backhanded my club into the kneecap of another assailant kicking Bob; that guy also fell to the ground holding his knee and screaming in pain. A third man took off running, leaving the one man on Bob's chest still whaling away.

I raised my stick and brought it down on the top of the assailant's left shoulder. The blow did nothing to stop the attack on Bob. I struck the man again in the same spot, still with no visible results. Bob was moving his head from side to side, avoiding most of the blows, but not all of them. I thought about shooting the assailant but instead raised my stick and brought it down again, this time on the head of the suspect. The man stopped throwing a punch in mid-strike and fell off Bob.

"Are you all right?" I screamed at Bob in order to be heard by the ever-growing crowd.

I heard Sergeant Rollins yelling on the radio, "Radio 140, no more cars are needed."

She had barely got the words out of her mouth when I caught a glimpse of her being knocked off her feet by someone swinging a two-by-four. Amazingly enough, I even heard the helicopter pilot override Sergeant Rollins.

"Ignore that last order! We now have multiple officers down. Repeat, multiple officers down, injured. Send more officers."

Then time did that funny thing of slowing down like when I was fighting Willy Licks. I could see people running all around me, swinging two-by-fours like baseball bats, throwing glass bottles and rocks. I heard moans of agony and lots of cussing. The wail of sirens was one loud emergency warning signal blaring over the crowd. Beside Sergeant Rollins, who was now on the ground, lost in the melee, I could not see any other officers. They would have to fight their way through an angry mob of over a hundred and growing to reach us at the rear of the Yahweh House.

I looked over, and Carl was on the ground again, and Bob was disappearing into the angry mob, being kicked and punched while he tried to defend himself and fight his way back to Carl and me. A blur of faces came in and out of focus as I reached down to pick up Carl again. Carl was hurt; he was not a big man and had already taken a beating, and I didn't know how much more he could take. Carl was slowly moving his head, moaning without saying anything. He would be defenseless unless I could get him to his feet.

All this was happening fast but seemed as if it were all in slow motion. It is simply hard to explain unless you have been in an extremely dangerous incident this violent. The bodies in motion, the screams of pain, the warlike sounds of the attackers shouting at one another, "Get him. Get his gun! Hit him!"

I turned to get to Carl but failed to check my left front... a huge mistake. I did not feel any pain or anything at all and collapsed onto my knees with my butt resting on my heels. There were no sounds, and people were running in all directions, several kicking me. I could not move and didn't know what had happened to me. At this point, I could not turn my head, move my body, or defend myself.

Something drenched my face. I was seriously hurt. It was as if you were watching TV and suddenly the picture went off, then came back on several times a minute. I could see, then everything would go dark, then light again.

A girl came up to me and tried to grab my gun out of the holster. Even though I had no control over my muscles at this point, my right hand held my gun in a death grip, pinning the weapon in the holster. The girl cussed at me and tugged on my hand but could not remove it. A man came up and tried to grab my nightstick out of my other hand, but he was unable to free it from my vise-like grip. He was chased away by the first additional officer I had seen since the fight began. The officer tried to remove my nightstick from my hand, but even he could not pull it away from me. The muscles in my hand were frozen to the club. The officer then left me, going after some other suspect.

Sometime later, the officer who tried to get my club from me reappeared, and now I recognized him as Tom from my crew, and Sergeant Rollins was with him. They were yelling something at me. I was now lying on the ground on my right side and couldn't move. I heard them yelling above the noise, but the words had no meaning. They each grabbed an arm and picked me up off the ground. By now, my nightstick had disappeared.

Tom yelled in my ear, "Walk! Sean, come on, walk!"

I could not move my legs or keep my head up and was in and out of consciousness. With a shoulder under each of my arms, they dragged me across the lot, my boots scraping the ground. I was aware in hazy moments of semi-consciousness of the vicious fight going on all around me; the final outcome was still much in doubt. Police cars, their sirens wailing, were still arriving. Squad cars filled the street for as far as I could see. What started as a residence check for an armed robbery suspect had now escalated into a full-blown riot with hundreds of people, all attacking the police with rocks, bottles, boards, and whatever else they could find and bring to the fight.

Later I learned the apartment buildings I had been standing next to at the beginning had emptied, and people from several blocks around also joined in the fight. The crowd did not even know why we were there in the first place. I think they just hated the police and saw this as their chance to beat up some cops or have some fun throwing bottles on an otherwise dull, late summer afternoon.

I remember being lifted into an ambulance and laid on a gurney. The air conditioner was running full blast, which seemed to revive me somewhat. Dizzy, I wanted to vomit and started gagging. I turned to throw up and saw blood dripping heavily on the floor from my head. A paramedic applied bandages to help stop the bleeding.

I still didn't know what had happened to me and could not talk yet. The words would not form for me, and my brain was a jumble; it was impossible to focus. I tried to speak. My mouth opened, but the words would not come out. My body was numb, but I could turn my head and move my arms again.

I heard a voice I didn't recognize. "Hey, Sean! How are you feeling? You're going to be fine. Hang on there, buddy, you're looking good!"

My head was hurting and the pain was sending blinding white flashes in my brain. The door to the back of the ambulance was still open, and I could see more officers running to the scene between parked police cars. A paramedic told someone they needed to leave and get to the hospital. I started gagging, and with each gag, my head felt like it was going to explode; the pain was so intense it made me pass out. Passing out was my only respite.

I woke up again at the hospital in a large emergency room. I was lying down on a gurney in my filthy uniform, gun belt, and boots. My shirt was soaked with blood. My head was killing me, and the hand that I'd broken months ago was hurting again and bleeding. I found my tongue kept rubbing against my front teeth. Two of my front teeth had been broken off, one on top and one on the bottom, and several of my back teeth felt like there were cracked, pieces missing. I started to assess my situation to find out what else was hurt or broken, but the pain in my head made me pass out again.

When I came to, Bob was standing next to my bed.

"How are you doing, Sean? You are looking good. You have a small cut on your head but nothing serious. You will be fine!"

Something was wrong. Everybody was saying I looked good, I'd be fine. Why did they say that? Nobody else commented to each other, "Hey, you look good; you'll be fine."

For the first time, I noticed everyone from my crew, all five of us including Sergeant Rollins, were in the emergency room. All were hurt to some degree, and nobody was fit to go back to work. The day was over for us. After three hours of work, the whole sector was wiped out and ceased to exist. Other officers had to be called in to fill spots for all the injured officers. Sergeant Rollins made it over to my side and asked, "How are you doing, Sean? You are looking good."

I could see she was concerned, but I couldn't answer.

I passed out again.

This was my fifth trip to the hospital with injuries sustained while on the job. I woke up and heard Sergeant Rollins, who was filling in for the regular sergeant for a day, tell one of the other officers to collect all the gun belts of everyone going to X-ray and from the officers who had a hard time standing up or even walking. I could not remove mine; an officer had to take it off me.

Tom came by the bed and told me what had happened to me during the fight. He said he saw a guy pick up a chunk of concrete, raise it high above him, and smash it down on my head as I bent over to help Carl. CSI later recovered the concrete for evidence in court; it was fourteen inches long. They knew which rock it was because it still had my blood, hair, and skin on it.

I closed my eyes, and when I came to the next time, it was about nine in the evening, and everybody was gone. A nurse told me a plastic surgeon was coming in to sew me up. *A plastic surgeon?* How bad was it?

Someone called my wife, a nurse herself, and she joined me at the hospital. It made me feel good to see her, but I worried she would think I was seriously hurt. Since she was a nurse, she knew what was happening. I believe many wives of officers dread the day when they get notified that their husband is injured and in the hospital. She apparently told me,

"You're slurring your words and have a severe concussion; you probably will have to spend the night here."

She said she talked to me, but I still don't remember it.

The next thing I recall was waking up about eleven that night. The plastic surgeon had arrived and started working on my head. He worked for over an hour. He talked a lot, primarily to my wife, as I still had trouble processing what was being said. I could smell my flesh burning as the surgeon repeatedly used a cauterizing tool to seal the many torn blood vessels on the deep wound. He made over thirty sutures on the outside of the injury and could not count all the stitches on the inside. The doctor also put several stitches on the top of my right hand, which had apparently been cut by a broken bottle.

My head hurt, and I was dizzy, nauseated, and not aware of my surroundings or condition. I was wheeled back to the emergency room where another doctor came in and talked to my wife, then to me. He said, "We would like you to stay overnight for observation."

When he said, "We would like you..." I thought it meant I did not have to stay. So, against the advice of the ER doctor, I had my wife drive us home.

At home, I had to crawl on all fours up the stairs to our bedroom. I was exhausted and wanted to go to sleep, but evidently, you have to be woken up periodically to make sure you haven't developed a bleeder on the brain and were in a coma. I did not know this at the time and resented my wife waking me up each time I fell asleep. This went on all night, and by morning, I did not think I would survive. My wife got a babysitter for our kids and took me down to see my doctor.

I struggled to walk into the doctor's office and was immediately shown to an examination room. Within minutes of seeing the doctor, a nurse moved me by wheelchair to the hospital across the street. I was taken to a room, wheeled to X-ray, then back to my room, where several specialists came in and talked to my wife. She told me I had some possible swelling on the brain they needed to watch and this time I had to stay in the hospital.

It had been over twenty-four hours since I had anything to eat or any sleep, and I was still nauseated and dizzy. Over the next sixteen hours, the nurses let me sleep for a couple of hours at a time, and my condition vastly improved. The next day, I felt a lot better and could talk normally and understand what was being said.

The chief took time out from his schedule for a quick visit. He made my day but I wished it had been under different circumstances.

Several detectives arrived and took pictures of my injuries and a brief statement. I went back to sleep through the rest of the afternoon and night. The staff still woke me regularly but, as tired as I was, I went back to sleep immediately each time. The following day, I was released from the hospital feeling sick and sore all over. And my head still hurt.

I had a month off on injury leave. When I returned to work, my teeth had been fixed, and I sported a long scar on the left side of my forehead back about four inches into my hairline and a small scar on my right hand. When I brought my uniform to the dry cleaner, the front of the shirt was all dark-stained. The worker asked if the stain was blood, and I told her, "Yeah, I had a bad day at the office."

It turns out that fight was the biggest in the city within the last fifteen years. All the officers in Center Zone, including captains, sergeants, and wagon drivers, had responded to the scene. That alone was thirty officers. That was not enough, and all the East Zone and Metro Zone officers responded, and half the cars in South

Zone and North Zone. Officers had been called in from days off to manage vacant districts.

At 1830 hours, two crimes scene detectives were dispatched, only to be ordered back by their sergeant because the area was not secure and had been released to a crowd of about seventy-five hostile citizens.

Six officers were sent to the hospital. Fortunately for the department, I was the most seriously injured officer. It was a miracle that no officers or those attacking the police were killed. Several officers would not return to work for a week, and everybody had cuts and bruises. I was told the concrete that hurt me was a glancing blow and that had it been over by a fraction of an inch, I probably would have died.

Bob and Carl had never asked me to go on the residence check with them. I had gone over there to warn them, but they didn't listen. I do believe if I hadn't been there that day watching Bob and Carl, they probably would have been killed. The way they were suddenly and violently attacked, and by such a large number of assailants, there was no possibility they could have gotten on the radio to call for help on their own. They were too busy fighting for their lives.

Diamond McDugal was not found that day. It turns out he was a close relative of the family that lived in the Yahweh House and was probably hiding in the residence. A month later, Diamond was caught walking down a street by Metro Zone officers.

Wednesday, September 12, 1984, 1830 hours, Forty Sector Center Zone became nonoperational.

Tragedy

Tragedies occur every day, and we have all experienced them in our lives. Police have personal tragedies they endure like everyone else, but they are also loaded down with many more through their work. It all weighs heavily on an officer's emotions.

Chapter 62:
Boo Smith

Steve Smith, everybody called him Boo, like Boo Radley in Harper Lee's book *To Kill a Mockingbird*, was a handsome, tall, athletic kid. He was seventeen years of age, a junior in high school and lived with his mother in a single-parent home. The home was well kept, and the yard had flowers blooming.

The house was only a block south of Thirty-first and Brooklyn, where all the drug activity occurred. It seems Boo was skipping school and liked hanging out with the drug pushers up the street, so his mother called the station and wanted an officer to come and talk to her son. I was the one they sent.

I went to the residence one mild spring evening. Mrs. Smith answered the doorbell with a pleasant, "Good evening, officer, please come in." She was a woman in her early forties, had prematurely gray hair, and was wearing an old faded blue dress.

She led me to the small living room. It had worn furniture and threadbare carpet, but the room itself was immaculate, obviously a point of pride for Mrs. Smith. I complimented her on her home, then focused my attention on Boo.

Boo was known at the station through several minor incidents that included riding in a stolen car, hanging out with the dealers up the street, and constantly being truant from school. I got to the point, "Why are you skipping school, Boo?"

"I don't like it. I want to quit." Boo turned his head away and looked down at the carpet, rubbing his shoe on some nonexistent bug.

"Boo, you're a big strong kid. Why don't you go out for sports? Maybe football? As big as you are, you would likely be a starter, and who knows, you might wind up with a college scholarship!"

He smiled at that but would not look at me.

"Boo," I said, "you have to start going to school, or the truant officer will put you in juvenile hall, and you will not like it there. Your mother loves you. Don't you love her and appreciate the good home she provides for you?" He didn't answer.

"Boo, you can make something of yourself, but hanging around the dealers up the street is a straight path to prison or death. You are too smart to waste your life the way you are acting."

Boo never said a word and continued to stare at the carpet.

I spent an hour with Boo and his mom. Mrs. Smith's eyes began to water, knowing her son was already lost to the street. One last plea: "Boo, you are breaking your mom's heart. You can't do this to her."

Boo did not seem to care about anything I said or his mother's feelings. Boo was going to do what Boo wanted. The success rate of getting through to these kids wasn't good. It was so frustrating to lose one to the street, especially when the kid had a good home with a mother who loved him.

Within a week, Boo stopped going to school altogether and would disappear from home for several days at a time. No one could reach him. Five months after I talked to Boo, he finally crossed the line big time. He shot Jerome Belton over a drug turf war and now was wanted for aggravated assault. He had turned eighteen and would be tried as an adult.

Mrs. Smith turned Boo in. She was trying to keep him alive. He was trapped at home but escaped by going to the attic and cutting a hole in the roof. From the top of the house, Boo jumped into an oak tree sixty feet off the ground and was eventually captured climbing down. I never saw Boo on the street again. Even though you try, sometimes you cannot make a difference.

I saw Mrs. Smith several more times, once walking down the sidewalk carrying what looked like a heavy grocery sack. Three older teens were bullying her, poking at her bag, and yelling at her. I parked and walked up behind the group unseen.

"Well, hello, guys, Mrs. Smith, how is everybody doing? Are you asking how Boo is doing? Oh, where are my manners? One of you boys take those heavy groceries from Mrs. Smith. I appreciate you helping her. It means a lot to her and me!"

The teens hemmed and hawed, tugging on their loose-fitting pants.

I pointed to one of the teens in a white T-shirt and blue jeans, and said, "Now, you take the groceries up to her front door. Then come back down here. I want to have a word with you fine gentlemen."

When the young man handed Mrs. Smith back her groceries at the door, I could hear her say, "Thank you, young man."

"You're welcome, Mrs. Smith." The young man returned to our group.

"Okay, guys, that was a nice act on your part. Mrs. Smith has been through a lot and could use a friend now and then. I like her, she is a friend of mine, and I check in on her regularly. If I ever see one of you guys on the street not helping her by carrying her groceries, I will personally make your life miserable in any way possible."

"I will tell all my buddies on patrol to always stop you as you like to hassle little old ladies. No one will want to talk to you on the street because they know they will be stopped for associating with you. Lastly, I will tell everyone I stop at the Blue Room that you are a snitch. Then see how long you think you can last around here! Now, do you get the picture?"

"Yes, sir, we're sorry. We will do like you say."

I believed them and let them go, and never had problems with those kids again. Maybe I got to them before it was too late. Some of the other people in the neighborhood noticed: A policeman cared.

Mrs. Smith had tried everything from the Big Brothers organization to social workers. She even called me to try to help her son. Finally, Mrs. Smith turned her son into the police to keep him alive, and it broke her heart.

Chapter 63:
Center Zone Mentally Ill

This section is not funny, there are no specific stories I can tell you, but it is a problem I had to deal with constantly with little or no training or resources to do the job. I am not standing on my bully pulpit to chastise the public but merely reflecting on a problem that needs to be addressed.

An often-overlooked portion of police work deals with people suffering from some form of mental health problems. The people I encountered have endured everything from schizophrenia, psychotic episodes, delusional ravings, drug abuse and withdrawals, along with many other mental issues. Severe alcoholism is a major problem on the street, but many times the alcoholism itself is caused by other cognitive problems; alcohol is used to self-medicate. I do not recall ever having any training in dealing with mental health.

There were a couple of homeless shelters where someone could get a shower, something to eat, and a cot to sleep on out of the elements. These homeless shelters required the person wanting a respite from the street to be sober, but all the other mental health issues would surface if the person was straight. The shelter would not accept disruptive, ranting, or hallucinating people. If a drunk did manage to sober up for a few hours, painful DTs would begin, more alcohol was the only cure, and the cycle would start all over.

Dealing with people with mental health problems always seemed hopeless, a never-ending task that I could not correct or alleviate even in some small way. The "mentals," as we referred to them in the early eighties, were always there, some in plain sight and others hidden behind trash dumpsters like discarded waste. These people were also referred to as bums, winos, and about any name you could think of, except what they were: human beings.

These people of the street carried knives for protection from other men needing a few coins for another bottle of wine, or mean individuals who for some reason liked the idea of kicking the shit out of a wino for the thrill of it. I always thought the guys who bragged to their friends they rolled a bum were not robbing him, they were hurting a defenseless person and covering up their own twisted mental issues.

Sometimes I'd get a call, a mental screaming at someone or something only they could see on a busy midtown sidewalk. Most calls were the same: someone was out of place, did not belong, and the police were needed to get that person out of the area or at least out of sight. It was making the caller uncomfortable.

Often the caller would say they were worried about the individual and the police needed to help the poor soul. That same person would not vote for a tax increase for more mental health facilities or rehab centers, but they did something to ameliorate their guilt, if they had any, to begin with: They called the police. The police would help them; the police knew how to handle the situation; the police were trained to handle all problems.

The truth was, there was little I could do. If the complaint was a wino sleeping on a sidewalk,

I would wake him up and send him on his way. There was no need to run his name through the computer. He had no identification on him, and half the time, he did not know his own name or birthday. He had a moniker the other street people called him, but no name he called himself. Sometimes a drunk would not wake up, so I always carried an ammonia capsule, which I broke open under the nose of the sleeping man, pulling him back into his reality of another day on the street.

Occasionally, I would find one of these lost souls hell-bent on killing himself one way or another. Only then would this man have to be admitted to a psych center for evaluation. It was one of the few chances these street people had to get some medical attention. An involuntary committal for twenty-four to forty-eight hours was usually enough time for the subject to return to some outward resemblance of a normal person. Enough, anyway, to be released back on the street.

Enough medication might be given until the patient could see his doctor. The patient never took the medicine, and it was a joke that he would ever see a doctor unless he became the victim of an overdose or assault. Occasionally, a room in a state-run psychiatric hospital might become available, and the man may get longer-term care.

I found several midtown apartment buildings used solely for the housing of somewhat functional mental health patients. Most patients were confined to the building, but some were let out to walk the streets or go to a day job. This was an ideal situation where people with a mental health condition could be looked after and possibly learn to cope with their illness.

Within a year, a patient was found dead in his room, and none of the staff noticed for several days. The state closed the building, and most patients were left to wander the streets.

Next, another tax cut or other priorities led to even more cutbacks in mental health care. However, a new solution was now available to the police. With no room in any local psychiatric centers, the people with mental health conditions were put in protective care and taken to jail to sober up or calm down enough to be released back out on the street.

One of the first things I noticed about Center Zone was the large number of men roaming the streets or sleeping in alleyways and vacant storefronts. The men often had a wine bottle clasped in their hand, hence the name "wino." Irish Rose wine seemed to be the preferred brand, probably because it was the cheapest.

I learned why wine was the perfect drink. It seems a person could get drunk on wine, pass out, then wake up, drink some water, and be drunk again. I do not know the exact reason for this phenomenon, but all the winos I ever talked to swore by it.

Another observation. I never saw a fat or overweight wino. In fact, most winos seemed on the verge of starvation. They didn't eat anything and never had any food on their person, not even a candy bar. My first thought was all of their money went for wine but then realized there was a darker reason.

When you were sleeping outside at night, the rats came out. If you were passed out in a drunken stupor, rats would be inside your coat, nibbling on any crumbs you left behind. The rats would chew on human flesh when the crumbs ran out. I saw many homeless men with open sores and chunks bitten out of their faces and arms from rats.

Now do not confuse the well-fed, clear-eyed man with clean clothes standing by a stop sign with a sign saying "Will Work for Food" or "Lost

My Job" with the real homeless man with filthy clothes and body. I had personally stopped some of the street sign begging people who drove off in newer model cars when I made them leave the area. Once, I stopped a man who rented his begging rights on a corner to another guy. Those beggars are not legit and are scamming people. The people that truly need the help are too sick to ask for it.

So what is the answer? There needs to be more mental health centers and beds for long and short-term treatment. I am not a doctor, but I dealt with the problem all my career and believe more can be done. I know there are not enough available beds so start there and then find the next area that needs improvement. The problems with mental health will never go away, and not everyone can be saved. It is not like polio or smallpox; it can never be wiped out, but it can be helped.

Chapter 64:
Crashes

On a cool fall afternoon, I was dispatched to a crash involving a semi-truck on a highway. An accident investigation unit and paramedics were also en route. Traffic was heavy, and even with my emergency equipment on, it still took me several minutes to travel one mile.

Arriving at the scene, I saw a semi-truck and trailer straddling two lanes with what appeared to be a white two-door car stuck under the trailer. At the rear of the trailer, a stout man wearing bib overalls and a baseball hat was jumping up and down with his hands covering his mouth. Then he turned from the wreck, bent over, and began vomiting.

A few other motorists had exited their vehicles, looked at the wreck, and then quickly turned away from the mangled car. I parked my cruiser with the emergency lights on to block any more vehicles from getting closer to the scene, then ran to the trapped vehicle.

At first glance, the trailer appeared undamaged, and the front of a small white car had minor damage and was tucked neatly under the trailer. However, the windshield and front half of the roof had been ripped from the car's body and folded like an accordion. The mangled top was stuck above the front bucket seats.

A thick steel frame hung from the back of the trailer that kept the truck from backing up too far at delivery docks. The steel frame was still in place and had prevented the top of the car from going under the trailer.

It was eerily silent. I could not hear a sound, people, or opposite lanes of traffic, and the man in the overalls continued to retch even though his stomach was now empty. People moved back as I neared the car, preparing myself for what was likely going to be a fatality with mangled bodies.

I crouched almost to my knees and duckwalked under the steel trailer to the front of the car. The engine hissed as antifreeze boiled out onto the pavement. A thick coppery smell I knew was human blood also permeated the now warm, viscous air. The inside of the car was untouched except for the driver. The driver's head was completely missing.

The seatbelt was still fastened securely around the waist and shoulder, holding the body upright. I could see the spinal column sticking out between two slumped shoulders. Blood had stopped flowing from the severed neck but not before it had completely covered the corpse and the car's interior. I did not see any other passengers.

Blood was dropping steadily from underneath the trailer above the headless body. I looked up, fearing what I would see. Mixed in among the folds of the roof and windshield were clumps of hair hanging down. Then I saw an ear and looked away. I did not want to see anything more. I was about to leave when I heard a frightened little voice cry out, "Mommy! Mommy! I want my mommy!"

I looked past the corpse and saw a little girl, probably not more than three, still strapped in her car seat. Her face, small hands, and clothes were all covered with her mother's blood. Without hesitation, I leaned on the headless corpse and felt the victim's spinal cord press against my chest and blood dripping onto the back of my neck and head.

I reached into the back seat, undid the child restraints, and carefully lifted the girl against my shoulder, blocking the view of her mother's decapitated body. I sat down, holding the girl in one arm and pushing myself out from under the trailer with the other. The paramedics had arrived when I stood up with the little girl. A paramedic took the small child from my arms and spoke gentle, calming words to her.

I took my blood-soaked jacket off, wiped the blood off my hands and neck the best I could, then helped direct traffic until the end of the shift. I do not remember the rest of the day and never told my wife about the crash. The next day at work, it was business as usual. You moved on and kept your feelings and emotions locked away.

∽

Another crash occurred on Christmas Eve. I was dispatched to an accident on the city's east side in another zone because they had no cars available. The dispatcher said there were injuries, and an accident investigation unit, fire, and ambulance would also be en route. I arrived at the scene and turned off my siren but left my red lights on to divert traffic.

The accident was at the bottom of a hill on a dual lane one-way street. At the bottom of the hill was an intersecting road with a stop sign. I could see two cars. One car, a Nissan Z, had been cut in half. There was debris scattered for ninety feet past the initial point of impact. The front half of the car lay on the grass median on the west side of the street, car parts and an engine were in the middle of the road, and the rear of the car rested on the sidewalk on the east side of the street. Farther up the sidewalk were the two front seats.

A tall mature oak tree had a large fresh, deep gouge four feet off the ground where the car must have struck. The driver lay up against the tree, among the wood splinters and broken pieces of car parts. He rested face up, eyes closed, and was unconscious but still breathing. He was dying, and there was nothing I could do to help him. He did not have any visible cuts or obvious broken bones but must have sustained massive internal trauma by the force of the crash.

I knelt next to him, gently held his hand, and told him he was hurt but would make it. I prayed for him and his family. My heart went out to his loved ones, who expected to see him home on this joyous night to celebrate Christmas.

Less than a minute later, the ambulance arrived and transported him to a hospital. By a miracle, he was still breathing.

I retrieved a black wool overcoat that had been covering the young man and handed it back to an elderly gentleman with gray hair and a thin face. He was shivering against the cold December evening. I helped him into his coat, and his wife clutched her husband's arm, resting her head against his shoulder.

He had been out with his wife on the way to a relative's house for a Christmas Eve dinner. He told me, "I had started into the intersection after looking and saw no cars coming. Then two cars crested the hill to my left at what appeared to be over a hundred miles an hour. I hit my brakes, and the lead car, a newer red Mustang, flew by in the far lane, but the other car on the inside lane closest to me swerved to miss me, barely hit my car, then swerved again, losing control, and went over the curb and hit that old oak tree."

He nodded toward the tree, then continued in a shaky voice, "The noise was horrific. If I had entered that intersection one second sooner, my wife and I would be dead now. If I left home a little earlier or later…" He let the words trail off slowly, not finishing his thoughts aloud, and wept softly, lowering his head and putting his gloved hand over his wife's arm.

The man's wife held his arm as she inquired about the driver taken away by the ambulance. I told her that, for now, the young man was still alive. The older man and his wife were crying not for themselves but for the other driver, who they had thought was dead. Their car had only minor damage. I parked it and drove them to a family member's home.

After dropping off the elderly couple, I headed over to the boy's home to tell his parents of the accident. A notification like this requires a personal response. Again, since there were no other cars available, I was sent to notify the parents alone.

I remember going up to the door, and as I rang the doorbell, I heard Christmas songs emanating from inside the house. A tall, thin man wearing a festive red sweater with a big "Ho! Ho!" in white letters emblazoned on the front answered the door. His face was smiling, and I could hear laughter from somewhere in the home. When he saw me, his smile dropped, and his head tilted to one side, looking at me without saying anything.

I asked him as gently as possible, "Are you the father of John Burns?"

"Yes, I am. Why do you ask? Why, what's happened?"

"Your son has been in a terrible accident, and he is in the hospital," I told him where, and as if in a fog, he thanked me, all traces of Christmas cheer drained from his face. He was stunned, in shock. He never asked about his son's condition; I think he knew the instant I told him there had been an accident. As he slowly closed the door, I heard him calling for his wife.

The evidence at the scene confirmed the older couple's story. As expected, the young man died.

That Christmas Eve, I could not quite share my family's joy or speak of the tragedy I had witnessed with my wife. I did not want her saddened on Christmas, as I knew she would have been for the young man's family. The twenty-fifth of December was another day at work, and I kept all the events of Christmas Eve deep within me. A Christmas does not go by that I don't think of that night and pray for the family.

The other driver was never identified.

Chapter 65:
Starving

On a miserably hot August day, in the upper nineties, I was dispatched to a home on the east side of town where a neighbor called for the police to check the children's welfare. Evidently, a young child showed up at the caller's house asking for some food and said she and her brother and sister had not eaten in several days.

I arrived at the house in question, a single-story residence with old, discarded furniture and other trash scattered in a dirt yard. The only things green in the yard were the weeds, and they appeared to be dying. The house last saw a fresh coat of paint probably twenty years ago. The front gutter was mostly hanging off, touching the ground. Windows were broken, and the front door had a hole in the middle where someone had kicked it. The home looked uninhabitable. I already felt sorry for the residents, whoever they were, children or adults.

Standing on the front porch of the house next door, a heavyset woman with a crying baby cradled in one arm pointed to the house while nodding her head up and down. Hans Storch was with me that day when I knocked on the door.

The door vibrated quite a bit. There were no hinges, and it would not even close. It just leaned against the door frame. I looked at Hans. He shrugged his shoulders, took a last drag on his cigarette, then flicked it into the litter-filled yard. The gut-wrenching, awful smell coming out of that house made my eyes water, and I was glad I'd learned my lesson not to eat before or during work.

I knocked again, and a skinny young woman, maybe twenty years old, peeked around the edge of the propped-up door.

"Yes, officers, what can I do for you?"

Her dirty, grimy fingers of one hand gripped the door. There was no doorknob.

Since it was his district, it was Hans' call. He let out a big sigh before answering. "Ah, yeah, ma'am, we were asked by a concerned neighbor to check the welfare of everybody in this house. You need to let us in to make sure everything is okay."

"You'll have to get the door. It's just leaning up. It don't close." The woman released the door and stepped back.

Hans and I lifted the door and set it against the front of the house. The smell was immediate and overpowering. Human excrement combined with urine, left to cook in the sweltering heat of the small home, made the fetid air unbreathable.

What furniture I could see was broken. A couch with more holes than fabric sat in front of an old TV with a broken screen. Trash was everywhere. The floor was crusted with what looked like dried mud but probably wasn't. Parts of the ceiling had fallen in, exposing the roof joists; the plaster was left where it landed. There were no light bulbs in any of the fixtures or lamps visible in the front room of the decrepit house.

The woman was a living skeleton with only thin yellowish skin stretched over bones. Her hair was sparse and falling out, with eyes sunken deep within their sockets. What teeth she had were black set in swollen, bleeding ulcerated gums and open sores covered her arms and legs. A filthy yellowish threadbare house dress covered her emaciated body, and there was a deep sadness in her eyes. She knew the end was coming. A few tears started slowly rolling down her dirty cheeks, leaving streaks of brown in their wake.

Hans broke the silence. "Ma'am, do you live here in this house?"

"Yes, with my three children: a one-year-old boy, a three-year-old girl, and a four-year-old girl." The lady lowered her head while she talked, trying to hide her shame.

"Okay, ma'am, we are going to have to look at the rest of the house and your kids to decide what we need to do to help you. Let us try to help you."

Hans was affected by this scene, and he talked calmly and gently. I called Sergeant O'Brian and told him we would need his assistance.

We followed the woman into the tiny kitchen, where a small table and one chair stood against a greasy wall of unknown color. There was a stove with no oven door and a small refrigerator. The refrigerator was not working, and some sour milk and a half loaf of moldy bread were the only contents. The dirty, colorless linoleum floor was curling up and crackled when you walked on it. I opened a cupboard, and nothing was there but numerous cockroaches scurrying about. Another cabinet held an empty cereal box lying on its side with hundreds more cockroaches running all around. There was no food in the house. I didn't know what the cockroaches were eating.

"Ma'am, when was the last time you or the kids have eaten anything?" Hans asked quietly.

"I'm not sure, but the kids had some cereal and some bread this morning. I feed them, but they've had the diarrhea for some time now, and the food doesn't stick with them much anymore."

She turned her face away from Hans, too ashamed to look at him as she absently scratched at something crawling in her hair.

Hans put his head down and said, "Okay, ma'am, let's go see the kids now."

Hans followed the woman down a short hallway where a bathroom door stood open.

The bathroom was not even remotely functional. The toilet was packed to the brim with human waste; the tub was a quarter full of feces and resembled a swamp. The sink was broken and lying on the floor. Clouds of insects hummed in the area and crawled all over the mess. Some kind of beetles playfully ran in and out of holes in the goo.

The bugs and human waste formed a living ecosystem in the hundred-degree heat. The tub seemed to be percolating and bubbling. The smell was awful and I had to swallow the stomach bile that rose, burning the back of my throat.

"Ma'am, when was the last time there was running water in this house?"

I saw the desperation in the mother's eyes.

"A couple of months, we couldn't pay the water bill or the light bill. See, my husband left to buy some food and never returned. I did not know what to do. We are not from here, and I don't know anybody to call for help." She started sobbing quietly.

"Okay, ma'am, let's go see the kids and where they sleep."

Hans was becoming weary as if each step farther into this putrid nest of human misery was quickly sucking the life out of him. Sweat poured off his face, and he started rubbing his arms, maybe in reaction to the mother's incessant scratching. I thought I was walking on old potato chips until I looked down at the floor and realized what I thought were chips crunching underfoot were many good-sized cockroaches. It got worse.

I felt something on my arm and looked to see a flea making a meal out of my skin. We came to the kids' room only a few feet from the bathroom. There was no door, bed, or lights, and covering the floor was more trash and dirty clothes or rags used as diapers. The light came from a dirty window with no curtain or shade, one of the windowpanes was missing, and the room was stifling hot. Now I slapped at my arms as numerous fleas and other bugs feasted on my exposed skin.

The three children huddled in a corner, holding on to each other, looking like a photo from a German concentration camp. They were dressed in rags that no longer could be identified as any particular piece of clothing. Bug bites covered them; insects and cockroaches were everywhere, even crawling on the kids. They were suffering the worst kind of starvation I had seen in over a year; their eyes were dull, empty of life, and their limbs had no muscle tissue. The children's stomachs were distended and bloated; they were in the last stages of starvation and dying.

At that moment, Sargent O'Brian came into the hallway next to the open bathroom. Putting a big hand over his mouth, he said, "Grab a kid, and let's get outside before someone passes out!"

I was closest to the inside of the room, so I carefully picked up the naked one-year-old boy, and held him to my chest. He felt like he weighed less than ten pounds and he smelled awful. He cried when I picked him up because his bottom was bare, and he had not seen water or a clean cloth for weeks. He had large, festering sores from the back of his knees to his shoulders. It had to be excruciatingly painful for the baby boy to be held, but there was no other way to move him. I did it as gently as possible.

Hans and Sarge each carried a child outside to where it felt like someone had turned on the air conditioner compared to the sickening, sweltering heat inside the house.

We held the children, feeling a sense of deep sadness, knowing what suffering they must have endured. I could see numerous bugs crawling on my shirt and arms and could feel them moving up my neck into my hair. None of us would set a child down to brush the parasites off.

My ward quit crying, and as dehydrated as he was, no tears had come. We held the children until an ambulance arrived with social services to evaluate the children and the mother. They all went to a hospital for severe dehydration, malnutrition, parasite infestation, infected body sores, and probably numerous diseases associated with their living conditions.

I talked to the neighbor who had called in the welfare check that morning. She said, "I didn't know anybody lived in that old house. I thought it was abandoned. Some drunk cracker lived there for a while, but he's gone now for a couple of months.

"This morning a half-starved little White girl came knocking at my door and said she and her brother and sister were hungry and thirsty. The little girl said they lived next door. I gave the girl some milk, a half loaf of bread, and some cereal. It's all I had. Are they going to be okay?"

The mother had deep concern showing in her eyes and held her baby a little bit tighter.

"They are now, thanks to you. Your call might have saved four lives today. You're a good woman, ma'am, with a generous heart." The woman had given the last of her food to help someone she didn't even know.

I reached out and lightly squeezed her hand and gave her a soft smile. She responded with a single tear rolling down her cheek.

I learned from a social worker the mother had been beaten regularly by her common-law husband. He had forbidden her or the kids ever to leave the house or talk to anybody, including the neighbors. Once while he was passed out drunk, she gathered the children to sneak out, but the baby started crying. Her husband woke up and beat her until she could not get up off the floor for two days.

She was terrified ever to leave the house after that last beating. Even when he did not return for two months, she still was afraid to seek help. In constant fear of his return, she only left the house at night to search for the bare essentials of food and water. The mother got their drinking water from the neighbor's water hose and brought it to the children in an old, dirty milk jug. She relied on picking out garbage from nearby trash containers for food.

Slowly, she lost her mind. She never returned to normalcy, and the children became wards of the state. Her onetime paramour was never identified to face justice.

I never told anyone about that call—until now. People wouldn't believe it anyway. They would say that things couldn't be that bad.

Chapter 66:

Last Day in

the Field Complaint

Sometimes people are right. You don't have to get physical with a suspect. You just want to.

On my last day in the field, I was dispatched on a child rape call at a residence in the central part of Kansas City. It was in an exclusive subdivision of beautiful homes with large, manicured lawns shaded by tall oak trees.

I parked in the circle drive of one of those homes and rang the doorbell, not knowing what to expect. The dispatcher said the rape had occurred a week ago. The parents had been to the hospital and only now decided to make a police report.

A middle-aged woman casually dressed in blue jeans, a red sweater, and black penny loafers answered the door and cordially invited me into her home. She had me take a seat on the couch in a tastefully well-appointed living room while she related the story.

"About a week ago, in the middle of the night, my daughter, who is six years old, came into my bedroom and said she was hurt down there and pointed to her vaginal area. There was blood on her legs, in the hallway, and on my daughter's bed. I took her to the hospital, where the doctor who treated my daughter told me my little girl had been raped!"

The mom closed her eyes, bowed her head, and clasped her hands together on her lap, straining to control her emotions.

For unknown reasons, the hospital did not notify the police as mandated by law, and the parents did not call until a week later. All the clothes and sheets had been washed, so no evidence could be recovered from the home.

The mother showed me the girl's bedroom.

"The suspect must have climbed in through the window."

She stood by the door to the little girl's bedroom and pointed to the only window in the room.

"Do you mind if I take a look, ma'am? I want to check for any signs of forced entry."

She nodded her consent.

I pulled the whimsical cartoon-motif curtains back and stared for a moment at the windowsill. It was covered in dust on the outside. I ran my finger along the top of the lower half of the window frame and felt the unbroken seal where the window had been painted shut years ago. The window was latched, and dust around and on the latch had not been disturbed. Obviously, it had not been opened for a long time.

"Ma'am, the suspect did not come in through the window."

I showed her that the accumulated dust had not been disturbed, and the window was painted shut. She had me check each window in the house. The results were the same.

"Ma'am, I have to tell you nobody climbed in through any window and raped your daughter."

I tried to say it softly but noticed something in her reaction. I think she already knew no one had climbed through a window. Her face tightened, and she clenched her teeth.

The mother had me follow her to the kitchen to finish our conversation. Her little girl sat in the kitchen with her uncle, a thin man in his early thirties, eating ice cream cones.

I remember the uncle eating the ice cream sitting on a barstool, and leaning over on the counter. He never looked at me and seemed to not care less about what I was investigating. His sole attention was on the little girl, her face a foot away from his. The way he opened his mouth wide, as if he were trying to fit the whole cone in his mouth at once, while looking at his niece, was repugnant. The act seemed somewhat perverted at the time, almost a lewd, suggestive behavior. Something was not quite right about this situation.

I was three feet from the girl and her uncle. I was on one side of the man, and the mother was on the other while we had this conversation. "Ma'am, who was in the home the night this occurred?"

"My husband was at work, so that left only me, our other two children, under eight years old, and my husband's brother Earl. He is staying with us. Oh, and our alarm was set, so nobody came in through the front or back door."

When she mentioned Earl, she turned her head slightly toward him, raised one eyebrow, and had a noticeable sneer on her face. I didn't know what the family dynamics were but had a feeling I was only there to confirm the mother's suspicions.

I told the mom straight out what she already knew. "Ma'am, no person entered this house through any window and attacked your daughter. Since the alarm was set, nobody came in through the front or back door. It had to be somebody staying in the house that night."

I turned my head away from the mother and looked down directly at Earl.

Earl never looked at me. He continued to eat his ice cream cone with long slow licks of his pink tongue while smiling at his niece. The uncle was making me nauseated watching him lick that cone, and I wanted so badly to grab his head and smash his face into the counter. It was obvious that he was the one that raped the little girl!

"So what are you saying, officer? You think someone in this house did this to my daughter?"

She was mad now.

I looked her directly in the eye. "Yes, ma'am, I do."

She knew what I was saying was the truth, which made her angry, and even with this exchange between the mother and me, the uncle still did not look up from eating his damned ice cream cone.

The mother said, "You can leave, and I will be sure to make a complaint about your total incompetence and insensitivity to imply it was someone in our own family!"

I stepped outside, and she slammed the door behind me.

In the academy, I learned a pedophile would give little gifts, treats, and special attention to the victim to ensure his deviant behavior was not reported to anyone. I called the Sex Crimes Unit and reported my suspicions.

The next day I arrived at the Sex Crimes Unit as a new detective, and the captain of the unit said two things that made me feel welcome.

"Oh, you are Sean? I thought when I selected you for this unit, you were someone else. Oh well. You also have your first complaint. The rape report you took yesterday of the little girl. Well, the mother filed a complaint that you dared to imply someone in their own family had committed the crime!"

I smiled, thinking I might as well let it all out. "Oh, I'm sorry, Captain, she must have heard me wrong. I did not simply imply, I said someone in the family did it, and between you and me, it was the creepy uncle."

The captain, who I liked working for, opened her mouth, started to say something, thought about it, then spun on her heel and walked away.

I felt at the time I wasn't going to be there long, and it turns out I wasn't. But that's another story.

Two days later, the uncle confessed. I think that, after the victim's father learned of my conclusions, he beat the truth out of him.

Chapter 67:
The Price

For many officers, the job severely affects their personal lives. Not all officers have problems, but enough did to be worth mentioning here. Some officers told me bits and pieces of their feelings.

Once you put on that badge, your life changes. You change by degrees week after week by the violent and horrific things you see and physically endure. You become some sort of an amorphous being, not quite yourself anymore. Your wife and children notice you're different, moodier, and less caring. They don't understand. You are not around the house much, and when you are, it's to sleep. Your days off are spent in training or at some off-duty job. You don't communicate with your wife like you used to, and you're not the same man she married. Things have changed.

Soon you lose your identity. You become *that cop*. Your wife becomes *that cop's wife*, and your children are now *that cop's kids*. People look at you differently. You've become the image of the cop on the six o'clock news. Sometimes you are the hero, but more than likely, you're not.

The dispatched calls play over and over in your mind and the what-ifs. You can't talk about it to your wife. You keep it all inside. Horrible accidents and murder scenes wake you up and cause you to moan in the middle of the night. You tell your wife it was a muscle spasm.

Although you try to hide it, she notices your new stitches or bruises. You can't hide the broken bones. Then the dreaded call comes: Your husband is in the emergency room. He has been shot or injured. Could you respond? There's the newspaper story with your name prominently listed and people ask, "What did he do?" Your wife doesn't know. You don't tell her anything. You're not who you once were.

Finally, the pressure gets to be too much. Your wife calls it quits. Your lack of empathy and communication; the emotional distancing;

working weekends, midnights, and holidays; and the constant danger have taken their toll. You put your life on the line for so many others but now your life is in shambles. Congratulations, you've made it… you're now a cop.

It is not only the spouses and children who have a hard time taking the pressure. I once helped disarm an officer. He seemed fine at the beginning of the shift but later suffered a complete mental breakdown on the street. I knew another officer who killed himself in busy afternoon traffic. Then there was a macabre so-called joke that went around the ranks: The leading cause of death among retired officers was from eating their guns.

In social gatherings, different people would ask about catching murderers and robbers, and how you dealt with prostitutes. You would tell them without adding any embellishment. The stories were all real. They weren't secondhand; You were there. You later find out they thought you were making up stories to make yourself look good.

People thought nothing ever happened the way you told the story. Even when you were off work with some visible injury, people could not believe it was that bad on the street. You must have done something wrong to deserve your injuries. You quickly learn not to talk about your job to anyone not connected to the police department. Nobody could understand the violent and dangerous situations you often faced unless you were there.

Sometimes I ask myself... did I make a difference?

I think I made a difference. I know for certain I saved some lives and genuinely helped many others.

Do I think my sacrifice was appreciated?

Rarely.

Was it worth the price my family and I had to pay?

No.

Would I do it again?

No.

Epilogue

I hope this book opened your mind and made you think about what you would have done in these situations. Think of the emotional baggage you would carry for the rest of your life: the grossly brutalized dead bodies, starving children, heartbroken mothers, rape victims, personal physical trauma, and the toll on your marriage. Risking your life so many times you never thought about it until someone said to you, "You don't care about people in the inner city," and you think about the poor girl being raped in the alley or the Jamaican drug dealers. How did you answer?... What have you done?

Someone asks, "Why aren't you out stopping real crime instead of writing me a ticket?" and you think about the little girl in the backseat of her mother's car. Or the statement "People don't attack the police for no reason. You must have done something wrong," and your mind drifts back to Willy Licks. Then there are the people who say, "It's not that bad. You must be making it all up," and you feel the long scar on your forehead from the Yahweh House and remember the starving children.

Some people tell you, "Try talking. You don't need to get physical," and your mind wanders to Louis the Pimp or the PCP knife fight. Or, "Why do you carry a gun all the time?" and you think about cutting your lawn or the beaches on Padre Island. Sometimes you can only sigh and walk away.

Has your opinion of the police changed? I bet it has, one way or another. I promised it would.

Now think. You read the book. How would you feel if you lived it? Then realize this was only the beginning... you have another twenty-four years to go.

Will the nightmares ever go away?

Glossary

ATF: Alcohol, tobacco, and firearms.

Around the world: Straight sex, fellatio, and anal sex.

Assist the officer: A officer is in extreme need of help! All available officers must respond to the scene to help the officer.

Blow job: Slang for fellatio.

Boning knife: Strong, razor-sharp six-inch knife used by butchers to remove meat from bones.

CCW: Carrying a concealed weapon.

CID: Criminal Investigation Division.

Cracker: Poor, redneck, white southerners.

DUI: Driving under the influence. This means you may not be legally drunk, but you are under the influence, and it is affecting your driving.

DWI: Driving while intoxicated, i.e., legally drunk.

FBI: Federal Bureau of Investigation.

Forestock: A section of a gunstock between the receiver and the muzzle usually made of wood or reinforced plastic.

FTO: Field Training Officer. This officer provides the new officer's training before he goes out on his own.

Half-and-Half: Straight intercourse and fellatio.

IRS: Internal Revenue Service.
Jimmie: Slang for a Slim Jim, a thin flat two-foot by two-inch piece of flexible metal used to unlock cars.
Johns: Men who use prostitutes.
Moniker: Made-up names used by criminals i.e., June Bug, Fat Wally, Ches, Boo, etc.
Ped check: Stopping a pedestrian and checking them for guns, drugs, warrants, or any nefarious acts.
Pimps: Men who profit from making women perform sexual acts for money.
Prostitutes' nicknames: Whores, hookers, vampires, streetwalkers.
Racking: Ejecting a shell from a shotgun or loading a shell into the firing mode.
Sex acts: Any number of sexual acts performed by prostitutes in exchange for money.
Slapper: A ten-inch-long thick piece of leather covering a piece of lead.
Slick car: A late-model car without any police equipment used by undercover officers.
Slim Jim: A thin two-foot strip of metal about two inches wide with a cut at the bottom forming a hook used to pull up the door lock, thus unlocking the car.
Stable: A pimp's harem of girls he controls for prostitution.

Support Squad: Another name for SWAT.

SWAT: Special Weapons and Tactics Unit.

Tricks: Another name for men who use prostitutes.

Wagon: Police truck or van used for transporting prisoners. Also known as a paddy wagon.

Author's Notes

After my first three years in the field, I went to the Sex Crimes Unit as a detective and worked on some of the most violent crimes imaginable, including incest and child rape. Then I went to the Special Investigations Division where, as an undercover detective, I specialized in drug-related crimes such as money laundering and bank fraud. I served on several drug task forces with the IRS Criminal Investigations Division, FBI, U.S. Customs, ATF, and U.S. Marshals service. I helped convict high-profile drug dealers, seizing cars, real estate, and cash in the process.

I left the KCMO (Kansas City, Missouri) Police Department to work with OTS, or Office of Thrift Supervision, a bureau under the Department of the Treasury to investigate savings and loan fraud. I filed criminal cases totaling over half a billion dollars. I finished my career working for a small suburban city police department. I have been issued a written commendation for performance under an extremely dangerous situation, a silver award for valor, a bronze award for valor, and a unit citation for excellent performance.

www.ingramcontent.com/pod-product-compliance
Lightning Source LLC
Chambersburg PA
CBHW062110020426
42335CB00013B/910